TOO MUCH TO DREAM

TOO MUCH TO DREAM

a psychedelic american boyhood

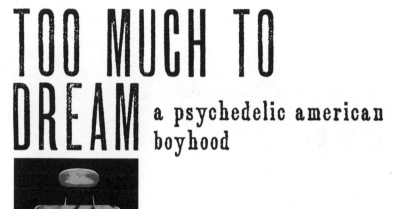

PETER BEBERGAL

SOFT SKULL PRESS | AN IMPRINT OF COUNTERPOINT

Library of Congress Cataloging-in-Publication Data

Bebergal, Peter.
  Too much to dream : a psychedelic boyhood / Peter Bebergal ; foreword by Peter Coyote.
     p. cm.
  Includes bibliographical references and index.
  ISBN 978-1-59376-382-4
  1. Bebergal, Peter. 2. Drug addicts—United States—Biography. 3. Drug addicts—Family relationships. 4. Bebergal, Peter—Religion. I. Title.

  HV5805.B43B34 2011
  362.29'4092—dc23
  [B]
                                    2011025082

Cover design by Domini Dragoone
Interior design by Neuwirth and Associates, Inc.

Soft Skull Press
An imprint of COUNTERPOINT
1919 Fifth Street
Berkeley, CA 94710

www.softskull.com
www.counterpointpress.com

Distributed by Publishers Group West
Printed in the United States of America

10 9 8 7 6 5 4 3 2 1

to Amy, who altered my whole life

foreword

Contrary to popular stereotypes, addicts are among the most sensitive of souls. As one once among them, I still remember the pre-drug shocks and stresses of life that left me flattened, confused, and overwhelmed by anxiety and indecision. Adding to my humiliation was the fact that most of my peers seemed to glide over the waters I floundered in, as effortlessly as swans.

Peter Bebergal's story elegantly elucidates that adolescent murk. Between his dedication to comic books and games of Dungeons & Dragons, an estranged and confusing suburban existence in an unsteady secular Jewish home, and with older siblings slipping beyond his grasp into their tantalizing, initiated, teenhoods, Bebergal describes his personal quest for wholeness and meaning with language that's fresh and new, and yet also timeless:

> ... what I was looking for was spiritual in nature. Mysticism or magic, communion with God, or power over his angels.

His journey, essentially religious, no matter how waylaid and temporarily diverted by youth, drugs, and error it may have been, was as familiar to me as my childhood room. Like Bebergal, I started in early adolescence pursuing an intuition that might bind my world into a cohesive, meaningful entity. Like him, I was also betrayed, waylaid, fooled—by others, and by my own credulity— and too easily satisfied. Though the content of our adventures was different, the dedication to the pursuit was similar. Everything that could be "practiced" in Carlos Castaneda's Don Juan books, I mastered—inventories of everyone I had ever met; walking with eyes slightly crossed; lucid dreaming; finally meeting Castaneda himself and recording two of his books. I pursued these skills for the same reason that Bebergal pursued knowledge, for "power over angels." I was crazed to possess an admission ticket to the integrated, illuminated world I could sense shimmering behind the shabby façade of the one to which I had been sentenced.

Like all good writers, Peter Bebergal has made me see my own experiences in his and made mine fresh and vivid to me again. His alienated world of parents subsumed by work, loss, and disappointment; his knowledge of the Beats, and drugs; and his intuition that there were people on Earth (not him, not I) leading visionary and compelling lives mirrored my own feelings at that age. Through him, I relived my compulsion to acquire authentic experience, to be transformed into something brave and admirable, and revisited too the tortured, dangerous, sullied, sometimes ecstatic paths I was impelled along by those compulsions, groping like a mole in the worm-filled dark of my personal earth.

I envy his innocence; his pattern-seeking in the realms of comic books, Dungeons & Dragons, runes and signs; even his disastrous initiation by a disturbed security guard. I must have once been that innocent, but on the verge of seventy, memories of that age are often no longer as vivid and have acquired the remove of photos in some other family's album.

And yet, concurrences and synchronicities between our lives do exist. If they can join him and me, separated by decades, geography, and experience, I suspect they can resonate in the psyches of many readers. Bebergal's is a compelling voice— honest, tinged with yearning, leavened by the knowledge that acts are irreversible, and seasoned by what twelve-steppers refer to as a "fearless moral inventory." This is not a child's confession. It is the sober (no pun intended) reflection of a man who has earned his scars and wears them lightly. Like the Buddha, he has risen to teach and share his insights. Coincidentally, as I write this, I am sewing my robes for ordination as a Zen priest. And although Bebergal is not a Buddhist, we are bound by a common dedication to wisdom traditions.

Describing getting high for the first time, Bebergal writes:

I looked around at my comic book and games and models and computer and they were inconsequential. I would no longer be distracted by them. I had glimpsed the sun behind the moon in the middle of the night and its rays had filled me with hope.

The wonder and the hope of life is that we can learn to face its vivid terrors, disappointments, and glories without crutches and delusions. We are free to "glimpse the sun behind the moon in the middle of the night." We can remain upright and fearless, as you may well feel after reading this fine book.

PETER COYOTE

BACK IN THROUGH THE OUT DOOR

> She had found a little hole in the wall of appearances; and peeping
> through, had caught a glimpse of that seething pot of spiritual
> forces whence, now and then, a bubble rises to the surface of
> things . . .
>
> —evelyn underhill

Sobriety is its own kind of altered state of consciousness.
For the addict, it is nothing less than a complete rearrangement
of perception, both internal and external. A consciousness that
beforehand was a fraying patchwork quilt of alcohol, THC,
cocaine, LSD, and sundry delusions is unexpectedly pushed
face-to-face with things as they really are. And those things are
not very pretty. The kind of rationalization required to give up
basic dignity in order to maintain being high and drunk is really
a strip of gauze that lets just enough light through to allow you
to get around without bumping into things, but not enough to
really see any detail.

Removing the pall of daily addiction is like flash powder
going off in your face. At first, it's nearly as blinding. There are

the spots of light that keep you squinting. But soon, as reality itself starts again to take shape, you get to see in perfectly illumined clarity the true state of your life.

Garbage is heaped in piles in the kitchen. The cupboards are empty and the refrigerator is filled with nothing but a once-used jar of mayonnaise and some old soy sauce packets. Then there is the lack of anything around of value; everything of worth has been either sold or stolen by someone else. An empty water bowl for cats that have long since disappeared sits dry in a corner. By the phone are the stacks of bills that seem so incongruous, as if they belonged to another dimension. There is nothing here to love, not really much to hate, but there is shame and a sickly-sweet disgust at what stares back from the mirror.

There are other realities as well. Sleeping for the first time sober and waking up clean is a mystery of boundless grace. A cup of coffee in the basement of a church during a twelve-step meeting tastes like the nectar of the gods. A roast beef sandwich on rye with shredded lettuce, tomatoes, and pickles from the local deli is like eating something from Eden. The first time I saw the new buds of spring while clean, I finally understood what Aldous Huxley meant by the "is-ness" of things. Of course, not being afraid after a very long time—my whole life, in fact—made me only that much more afraid I would lose that gift.

It could very well be that all addicts will find themselves entertaining the notion of picking up their drug of choice at some point, if only momentarily, no matter how long one has been clean. Throughout my own sober life these past twenty years I have certainly been confronted with the simple fact that getting high or drunk would take the edge off whatever stress I was undergoing. Thankfully, I have always been able to think it through, to recall immediately what happened to my life as a result of compulsive drug use. I never wanted just one of anything, and there was no evidence to suggest that being clean for any number of years would make me capable of taking a few hits off a joint, kicking back with a bag of pretzels, and letting the tension of the day slip away.

This is the fact: There is a tiny keyhole secreted away in my psyche that can be unlocked with only the slightest alteration of my consciousness. Once ajar, a door is opened that is very, very hard for me to close. What drove my addiction was not merely a desire to get stoned. It was a craving for what I had always hoped was behind that secret door. Only a mystical experience would finally unify all the weird and wonderful ideas that I had gleaned from a youth spent immersed in an often private cavern of fringe and counterculture artifacts; from the cosmic narratives of Silver Surfer comics to Carlos Castaneda's pseudo-nonfiction writings on shamanism and drugs, from Pink Floyd's psychedelic masterpiece *The Piper at the Gates of Dawn* to the baby-boomer spirituality of Ram Dass. I was awash in the ideas and sounds of a cultural tidal wave that for many ended in cynicism, drug addiction, death, and madness. I was also awash in street drugs of an inferior quality compared with the pure LSD of the early sixties, and tainted with other, nonpsychedelic drugs used to cut it. Street acid was also part and parcel of the larger drug trade, which included cocaine and heroin and, by extension, crime and the ever-present but faint threat of violence.

From the aging hippies in my small town of Swampscott, Massachusetts, I was able to get choice marijuana and fairly decent acid, but there was always a shadow of paranoia. Never knowing whom to trust, the dealers trusted no one, and so procuring these drugs was filled with a kind of dread, which we all masked with stoned chatter and excitement as the money and dope changed hands. Unlike those who pursued the sixties' categorical imperative of set and setting when dropping acid—be in a stable state of mind with people you trust in a place where you are comfortable—my friends and I were mostly left to fend for ourselves. Our gurus and elder spiritual teachers were busy hiding from the police.

At twenty-one, I was a full-blown drug addict and alcoholic. I didn't end up that way just because getting high felt good (which it did) or because I was mentally obsessed with getting high (which I was) or because I had lost the ability to do anything else except get high (which I had). The reason for my ultimate degradation was an addiction to something else: a belief that a profound spiritual understanding of God and the meaning of my life could be found in a state of altered consciousness, and that once I had found it, I would be redeemed from the life I had been living. But was I an addict as a result of this search, or was I looking for God because I was an addict? Carl Jung, in a letter to the cofounder of Alcoholics Anonymous, Bill Wilson, remarked that the Latin for "alcohol" is *spiritus*, which is also the word for "soul," and that the abuse of alcohol was fueled by a desire to know God, to transcend daily drudgery for a glimpse of a greater reality.

Yet, after over two decades building out a lasting sober life, why do I still feel the magnetic force of that desire? While I have a religious life and a spiritual predilection, I pride myself on having moved beyond the superstition and magical thinking that characterized my drug use. I believe in God, in a higher power or reality, but I am a rationalist. I am skeptical that there is any quick route to God. As Umberto Eco writes in his novel *Foucault's Pendulum* during the character's argument about whether a computer can invoke all the billion names of God to mystical effect, "But the important thing is not the finding, it is the seeking, it is the devotion with which one spins the wheel of prayer and scripture, discovering the truth little by little. If this machine gave you the truth immediately, you would not recognize it, because your heart would not have been purified by the long quest."

I am also wary of dogma. I see the value in discipline that comes
from participation in a religious community and its prescribed
practices, but I have no patience for literalism or the idea that
any Scripture is infallible. For all of this I have a deep religious
aspiration. I practice a slight yet earnest form of Judaism, keeping
mildly kosher, fasting on Yom Kippur, and holding a Seder dinner
on Passover. But I mostly avoid those parts of Judaism that speak
of the mystical, not because I didn't want to experience it, but
because I have become convinced these practices were only for
the strictly orthodox and observant. Nevertheless, when I go to
synagogue for a Jewish holiday or gather with friends for Friday
night Sabbath dinners, I quietly look for some esoteric meaning,
a word or phrase in the liturgy and the blessings, that would make
something in me, if only tentatively, begin to take flight. How do
you fly, though, when you know your wings are made of wax and
that any decent proximity to the sun will melt the feathers off
your back and you will plummet out of the sky? After all these
years, is it ecstasy or illumination I'm after?

It turns out that somewhere, a long time ago, I lost any ability
to make that distinction. Indeed, maybe I never really had it.
But now, clean and sober all these many years, I am compelled
by that intuition that there is more to my consciousness than my
worries, stratagems, obsessions, and doubts, and that there is
more to my spiritual life than twelve-step meetings, challah on
Friday night, and quick dashes through prayers and entreaties
on the Jewish high holy days. It wasn't as if in getting sober I
made myself completely immune to flashes of altered insight.
Drug use forever changed the function of my brain. I will never
be able to fully undo this psychedelic sixth sense, a slight expansion of perceptual limits, real or imagined, that can come about
at any moment: when listening to music, when making love, or
when being astonished by something particularly ordinary in a
nonordinary way.

One recent bitter winter morning, I was walking the dog. The sun was barely up, I was cold and half-asleep, and while my dog sniffed around the grass of the park, I lifted my head and looked at the sky. For a moment I wasn't sure what I was seeing. I was so tired, I thought I was still asleep and dreaming. I felt a wave of trepidation; I couldn't get my bearings. I was looking at the largest, brightest object I had ever seen in the sky, except for the moon and the sun. It wasn't a plane, and it wasn't a star. I blinked and squinted at it. It was impossible that such a thing could exist. I was seeing something real but not real, I felt I was awake but not awake. I went into a sort of trance, my consciousness pinned against the object. I was rising up toward it with a kind of clarity that something was about to happen, that I was on the verge of some new and profound awakening. I flickered in and out of this state, as another part of me waited for the orb to turn into a plane to explain it all away. Just as I thought I would reach some kind of rapturous moment, I woke up from my reverie and realized that I was looking at Venus, the morning star. No wonder sailors had relied on it so much. It was astonishingly large and bright. In all my years of trying to notice things, I'd never noticed Venus in the morning.

"It's Venus, you idiot," I said out loud to the dog. "It's just Venus."

Slowly, my recognition of what it really was turned into a new kind of wonder. The sight of Venus, so bright and alive, and the knowledge of what it truly was, felt astonishing. I know that Venus is the second planet from the sun, made up of dreaded volcanoes and a carbon dioxide atmosphere, and that it formed with the other planets about four billion years ago. But I had for a moment experienced an altered state of consciousness. My awe and the dread of the unknown seemed like looking into the eye of God. More important, I was not hallucinating—the planet spinning its own orbit around the sun, in fellowship with our own, was real. I had not imagined it. Nevertheless, I was transported by a sense of otherworldliness that this (mis)perception had invoked. I was reminded that I have always believed there is something real that exists beyond human phenomenal experience that we can be apprehended by and wrestle with, and that we can even embrace the numinous. These moments, particularly in their more dramatic forms, have been traced throughout human history. You find them mainly in religious writings and testimonies. They are also what we experience in those so-called nonordinary states of consciousness, including hypnosis, lucid dreaming, and certain out-of-body experiences.

In 1901 the psychiatrist Richard Bucke tried to codify the more dramatic instances of these states and coined the term "cosmic consciousness," an experience he believed was shared by such a motley crew as Jesus, Buddha, William Blake, and Walt Whitman. Cosmic consciousness, according to Bucke, is the final step on the human evolutionary ladder that began with animal consciousness and then self-consciousness, where religion is redundant in the face of our perfect knowing that we are immortal and "God will be permanently replaced by direct unmistakable intercourse" with the divine. This is all a bit speculative, but Bucke's cataloging of people from different backgrounds having similarly transcendental experiences was the first attempt to popularize what the scholarly types were doing in the academy.

In 1882 the psychologist William James (the novelist Henry's older brother) published a number of articles, both anonymously and under his own name, in which he described his use of nitrous oxide. What we know as laughing gas he believed "simulates the mystical consciousness in an extraordinary degree." James expanded this thesis in his definitive classic on religion, *Varieties of Religious Experience*, in which he captures the essence of his beliefs about mystical consciousness: "It is

that our normal waking consciousness . . . is but one special
type of consciousness, whilst all about it, parted from it by the
filmiest of screens, there lie potential forms of consciousness
entirely different . . . No account of the universe in its totality
can be final which leaves these other forms of consciousness
quite disregarded." From a psychological point of view, James
was convinced there was a common underlying phenomenon
related to mystical states: an overwhelming sense of unity with
the sacred dimension of reality. Call it nirvana, *moksha*, satori,
Christ consciousness, or, in Hebrew, *devekut*—for James it was
all the same.

Ah, but why bother? Maybe it's all bullshit. This thinking
has gotten me nothing but rotting teeth, dirty fingernails, a life
of sick compulsive rituals. One night this thinking had me on
my hands and knees, digging through the carpet for a tiny bit of
hash that turned out to be a broken piece of eraser from a pencil
that I shoved into my pipe and smoked just in case. This is the
precarious tightrope I walk, somewhere between heaven and
hell, between the degradation of drug abuse and enlightenment.
Yet some ache continues to throb inside me. It is an echo of
something, not like a seductive siren song forcing me off course,
but that still consumes my whole consciousness with nostalgia
and a deep, unnameable longing, something that I was only ever
aware of on the periphery of every psychedelic trip.

This promise, this offering that has so long been associated
with LSD and other psychedelic drugs, has meant different
things to different people. For some it was the promise of liberation from those social norms that seemed to homogenize and
dilute real experience. For others it was the promise of liberation
from the ego. Some have written about hidden worlds, layers
of dimensions that transcend the science of physics. Others
wanted nothing more than to know God or some aspect of a
divine consciousness. Maybe it was revelation, or prophecy of a

sort, an experience not unlike those had by saints and mystics. It was a promise of universal transformation. In other circles, there was, and still is, the hope that drugs could alter the effects of mental illness. ·

My experiences, and what I hoped they would bring me, were in no way pure. They were in fact molded by an enormous and complex set of phenomena that included rock 'n' roll, sixties drug literature, *The Lord of the Rings*, occultism, American movies, comic books, and the conjecture and experience of my friends, peers, and even the adults who tried to persuade me with their own stories and their own synthesis of culture and religion. By the time I was twenty-one my desire for whatever I imagined knowledge to ultimately be turned into a compulsion and an obsession that almost killed me. Consequently, I lived my life for the next twenty years as if this kind of experience was something that either was not real or, if it was, wasn't for me to know. This desire had become too awash in superstition, addiction, and despair.

As I continued to stay clean I began to wonder if somewhere along the way, I had misunderstood the nature of some of the drugs I took, and that my circumstances—the age in which I lived, the place where I grew up, the people I talked to and hung around with, and, more important, my religious background at the time—had made it impossible for me to ever have experienced anything other than addiction and despair. The literature is clear: People all across the ages have had sublime experiences with psychedelic substances (and other spiritual exercises) to no ill effect.

There is indication that as early as ancient Greece the cult of Eleusis drank a mixture made with ergot, a fungus with certain hallucinogenic properties. For hundreds of years in Central American and Mexican Indian tradition, believers have used mushrooms containing the psychoactive substance psilocybin in their religious rituals, and some scholars have claimed the mushroom amanita was what the Vedas—the 'sacred Hindu texts—referred to as Soma, the method for seeing the gods. Even today the Native American Church uses peyote as a sacrament, what it calls the flesh of God, and believes it is a healing spirit for both mind and body. In Brazil, members of the Santo Daime Church—a syncretism of Catholicism, animism, and other indigenous beliefs—drink the hallucinogenic brew ayahuasca as part of their religious practice. In all these cases the drugs have been and continue to be used within a very particular context. They are gifts from the community, wrapped in deep mythologies, language, and custom. The experiences are always contained within the particularities of that religion.

What I realized was that my experiences were also contained, but within a very different kind of community. For me, and many of my peers who grew up in the seventies and eighties, the context was not religious, but a manifestation of popular culture. At times it took on the facade of religion, using words like "karma" and "nirvana," but it was secular to the core. The context of our drug experiences was infused with rock 'n' roll, comic books, literature, counterculture celebrities, and whatever romanticized notion we somehow managed to glean from television and movies. All of these things, whether we were aware of it or not, were themselves charged like capacitors with occultism and Eastern mysticism, a charge that slowly discharges to the point where only a few electrons remain.

How could an eighteen-year-old in his parents' suburban basement, tripping on acid and listening to Pink Floyd, expect to commune with the gods, when he didn't even know their names? More than twenty-five years later, I have come across a temple hidden in the jungle. I needed to read the stories written on the walls. I needed to go inside and see the carvings, hear the echo of the drumbeats. This is one of the remarkable achievements of culture, when it acts as a transmitter for that peculiar kind of spiritual consciousness, those moments when we are confronted with the unutterable, the ineffable, and yet the only response is to carve out names in wood, to hammer out the shape of gods in stone, to dance, to sing at the top of our lungs. It's incredible, really, that when we have found ourselves slack-jawed before death and birth and thunder and even stampeding bison, the first thing we do (after the hunting, of course) is turn these experiences into art. It's because, I think, these experiences happen in the world, and despite the feeling of transport, we remain exactly where we are, on the ground, sitting in the dirt, climbing a mountain, walking in a park. We might even be sitting at dinner with friends, the fork still in our hand, the napkin in our lap, a cat rubbing up against our leg, when suddenly we experience a rush of holiness.

Alan Watts is best known for introducing Western audiences to Zen Buddhism in the fifties and was someone who embraced both the human and the mystical. As he once wrote, "The animality of the mystic is always richer, more refined, and more subtly sensuous than the animality of the merely animal man." In Watts's essay "The New Alchemy," he agrees that there is something to be wary about when it comes to quick paths to a mystical experience, what can be described as God in a bottle. But he also points out that many mystical experiences are a result of "grace" or, to put it another way, they are unplanned experiences often had by those who believed themselves undeserving. Watts goes on to suggest that psychedelics are not themselves capable of furnishing a full-blown mystical experience, but rather function as what he calls "an aid to perception in the same way as telescope, microscope, or spectroscope." It's only through actual practice and concentration that these substances can produce a classical mystical experience.

The writer and psychedelic researcher Huston Smith, growing disenchanted with the sixties American drug culture, noted that experiencing a religious vision by way of psychedelics does not necessarily compel one to begin to lead a religious life, to act ethically, or to subscribe to a set of spiritual exercises. In fact, Smith complained about a "religion of religious experiences," wherein the vision itself became the end, rather than the means toward a true religious consciousness. How can we today learn from Watts, who recommended, "When you get the message, hang up the phone"?

Sober these many years, I was skeptical this spiritual consciousness could be found in the way I had once sought it, but the idea persisted: It was possible to achieve some kind of religious and mystical consciousness aided by certain kinds of chemicals and plants. I knew I could never do those things again, but I needed to find out what is so beguiling about the possibility they promise. How is it that, now sober twenty years—my life richer and fuller than anything I could have imagined for myself—the desire has descended upon me once more, yet in an entirely unexpected form? I don't crave the feeling of being high, but I crave the spiritual insight that I sought back then. Why would I feel compelled to pursue now the same spiritual insight I was after at fifteen? Partly it's because the compulsion has never gone away. I have simply quieted it with other, more worldly pursuits, education, marriage, a child, a career. All of these are precious, but they can never completely subdue something that Aldous Huxley calls "the urge to transcend self-conscious selfhood . . . a principle appetite of the soul."

What follows is my attempt to square my experience as a pre-adolescent, teenager, and young man with the cultural story that surrounded me, an experience that went from being a promise of liberation to full-blown addiction, from spiritual awareness to spiritual degradation, and finally from paranoia and disease to a new kind of consciousness. Despite this new awareness, I still hold dear to my heart those songs, comics, stories, art, and, yes, even my own desperate, sometimes ugly, often sincere, mangled attempt to have a spiritual experience. In the course of this journey I was fortunate to speak with many fellow travelers, those who came before, and those brave psychonauts who are continuing to journey through the vast unmapped levels of consciousness, what Huxley called the "antipodes of the mind," with music and art. And, yes, sometimes even drugs. For those, I must watch from afar and listen to their stories with fear and trembling.

chapter one

HIGHWAYS TO HEAVEN

> There is a correspondence of all things of heaven with all things of man.
>
> —emmanuel swedenborg

I would hate to start a rumor that there is a link between role-playing games and drug addiction, but my compulsive search for spiritual meaning really did begin in an essential way with some twenty-sided die, a few sheets of graph paper, lead figurines, and the 1977 boxed set of Dungeons & Dragons. Maybe it began there because role-playing a half-elf ranger who could hear and interpret the voices of stone, wind, and rippling water, who could see in the darkness of a forest in the dead of night, who could track deer or orc or hobgoblin with equal acuity, who was schooled in various types of magic but was no slouch with a bow and a short sword, was immeasurably better than what I was: a thirteen-year-old boy with a piece of wire (from his electronics workbench) in place of one of the temples on his glasses, his hair hanging down to his shoulders in greasy strands, his clothes from Bradlees, and his sneakers from Caldor. But it more likely began with D&D because that venerable role-playing game was a perfect storm of the various fantastical narratives that had found their way into every aspect of my consciousness and organized my world in a meaningful way. It was the 1970s, and for a boy filled with nameless, unspoken anxiety and fear, all the weird and unusual pop-culture artifacts—from a resurgent love of J. R. R. Tolkien's *The Lord of the Rings* trilogy to the black hole called Cygnus X-I on the progressive rock band Rush's album *A Farewell to Kings*—reflected and comforted my adolescent existential unease. Uncannily, Dungeons & Dragons distilled it all into a perfect interactive chronicle of my consciousness.

The storefront of the one shop that sold Dungeons & Dragons was completely nondescript, but inside was a gallery of wonders: boxed war games covering every military engagement of every century, games based on every well-known fantasy and science fiction novel, die of every conceivable shape, and glorious miniatures, tiny lead figurines depicting elves, trolls, dragons, and wizards. The owner was a tall, bespectacled, surprisingly friendly misanthrope with hair and glasses not unlike mine. He kept his fingernails sharp and long, the better to pick up die-cut gaming pieces for the massive historic strategy games he kept set up in a back room.

In those days, Avalon Hill and Strategic Simulations were the main companies producing these kinds of games, but in 1974 a small upstart company, Tactical Studies Rules—founded by Gary Gygax and Don Kaye—starting publishing rules for Dungeons & Dragons. D&D had its origins in an even earlier game, Chainmail, which played like a more traditional war game, but eventually Gygax added monsters and a few magic spells. The year 1977 saw the release of Basic Dungeons & Dragons, a boxed edition that made the game immediately playable, the cover showing a dragon staring down a group of adventurers, illustrated by someone, it seemed, not much older than I was.

The essential game play of early D&D was the dungeon crawl. Players discovered the opening to a cave or a tomb or a basement of a castle, then engaged in a sequence of checking rooms, disarming traps, fighting monsters, and looking for treasure. Boiled down to its mythological essence, D&D is a quest story, in which the hero must complete a series of tests and trials through which he is eventually rewarded with power or some other transformation. Into the underworld the players go, like all heroes must, facing their deepest fears in the form of many-eyed beholders, gelatinous cubes, kobolds, the ubiquitous orc, and maybe even a dragon or two. Sometimes they are helped along the way by benevolent creatures (the lammasu, a kind-faced lion with eagle's wings, was always my favorite), but more often than not the quest is one treacherous encounter after another: poison darts, armies of hobgoblins, camouflaged pits, slime, and fungus, and even the treasure—if discovered at all—might contain only a few silver pieces and a cursed sword.

This, of course, was nothing like my actual life. The tedium of junior high school coupled with the even worse monotony of being singled out for minor abuses (spitballs, threatening collar-grabs, unkind laughter) by other kids was easily cast off with an adventure in a moldering and crumbling dungeon.

D&D had its own repetitiveness, to be sure (enter room, check for traps, fight monster, get treasure, repeat), but it was the eternal quest that was so attractive, the never-ending circular campaign in search of that elusive something, some hidden power, some great magic item that would make the users like gods, give them control over demons and fair maidens alike. Beyond the most obvious sorts of desires, there was something else that kept compelling me toward the game. I had fellow players who didn't make me feel like a freak, but there was something else that had me up every night studying the rule books, going over each statistic, creating dungeons and maps, rolling and rolling and rolling forever those many-sided dice. It was that the game understood, at its core, something about the value of hidden treasures and the even greater value of having to fight your way toward uncovering them.

I grew up around hidden things, hidden fears, hidden worries. It was the suburbs, after all, and despite their origins, which were a promise of new beginnings and open possibilities, mine was a familial and social culture built on the barely hidden restlessness of the generation that preceded mine. We had all arrived here the same way: on a highway through history, encouraged by the end of a great war and the spiritual fortitude that was a result of being victorious.

After World War II, thousands of veterans were educated on the GI Bill and the country produced the first postwar generation of engineers, tradesmen, salesmen, and financial executives that would ultimately shape the economy and the culture. One of the perks of a good job was the once unaffordable automobile. Making deals with the car industry and oil companies, the government built highway after highway, making it possible to travel easily from city to city, as well as to flee the city where you did business and reside elsewhere. One of the most important results of the highway was that what had once been rural areas, accessible only by long and winding routes, were now easily tamed by asphalt. The suburbs sprouted up like pastel flowers, and the homogeneity of America began in earnest. All it took was a steady job and a plot of land, and you could have a house of your own away from the cities and their crowded apartment buildings, exposed trash, exposed poverty, crime, and destitution. The suburbs offered protection from all of this.

But the life of the suburbs wasn't all that it appeared to be. Schools offered nothing more than textbook responses to the world's ills that the suburbs promised to be ballast against. The suburban sense of security and prosperity was built on the sacrifices and success of World War II. The defeat of Hitler and the Axis was one of this country's greatest sources of pride, but underneath the glory was something dark and ugly. As images and testimonies of the Holocaust and Hiroshima became more and more disclosed, the veil was pulled away, and on the other side were human folly and human-constructed doom. Even our greatest ally, the Soviet Union, had become not merely a threat but the vessel into which the United States poured all its own fears. Despite the reality *Leave It to Beaver* depicted, the struggle for civil rights was a sad shadow behind a very white window dressing. Many people asked if that great promise of the postwar American suburbs was nothing but an illusion or, worse, a collective self-deceit.

The highway to my home had its main route through Brookline, Massachusetts, circa 1956. My parents were newlyweds with a baby girl on the way, and they had moved into their first apartment (150 bucks a month, no utilities). I have a photo of my father sitting on the floor of this apartment, shirtless, eating Chinese food from a box, around him newly placed Scandinavian-design furniture and African figurines. This was my father's city of modernity, a progression away from the old world into the new. His move from Jewish Roxbury to Jewish Brookline was much like his father's move from Eastern Europe to America, also a kind of immigration, from a cultural identity almost inseparable from its religious identity to a cultural identity with a religious nostalgia, often no more or less.

When he was no older than sixteen, my grandfather Samuel left Zacrocym in Poland to meet his father, who was already living in America, having carved out a little slot in modernity for his son. What was Judaism for my grandfather as he left Poland? He was as close to it as one can imagine: Eastern European orthodoxy, a folk observance of ritual and tradition, all mixed with a heavy dose of superstition. When did he abandon it? Was he giving up his phylacteries *and* God? Which one (or was it both?) did he imagine to be incompatible with the life he wanted for himself and his family in America? How much of that great Jewish tradition of mysticism and religious yearning never made it past the shipyard in Eastern Europe? But so be it. Something beyond convention beckoned him.

A few years later, the rest of the family arrived from Poland—seven siblings—and Sam must have found himself feeling back in the old country, surrounded by relatives. And while there might have been little in the way of religion, there was certainly tradition. Even their trade carried over: clothing and other retail pursuits. Eventually he fled to Boston, another leap into the unknown. I inherited this restlessness, this spirit of proto-rebelliousness, not then so named, but the energy was the same. But eventually, like many with a spiritual wanderlust, Sam found he was settling down anyway. He married and, in his last bit of defiance, had one son instead of continuing the tradition of a large family.

My own father grew up in an urban playground, riding the trolley up and down Commonwealth Avenue, working after school in the clothing shops in downtown Boston, saving his small wages for his own fanciful dreams of flight and adventure. When he was in his early teens, World War II was raging, and on newsreels and radio broadcasts he watched and heard stories of almost superhuman bravery in the face of superhuman evil, all of it taking place in locales with dark and portentous names: Berlin, Stalingrad, Kursk, Leningrad.

After high school, the draft over, my father went off to college in the Midwest, choosing a place merely for its being what it was not: home. During this time, his father, Sam, opened a men's clothing store in Waltham, Massachusetts, and (I was to learn much later) my father dropped out of college to help his father run the shop that was named after him: Byron's. They were very successful in the relative way a small, white-collar business that isn't supposed to go global can be. Here they were together in a retail store, two men who had once both felt that potent urge for something else, some abstract *more*—always undefined, but always there on the periphery and as unattainable as a horizon.

Eventually my parents moved to the suburbs and my dad took the Massachusetts Turnpike, built beginning in 1955, to work. That spiritual thirst had no place on the highway between modern house and modern business. But there was another highway, the symbolic highway, which represents the American spiritual journey that brought the Beats and hippies streaming out of the suburbs back into the cities to create the legacy I would inherit. It was the highway that not only bridged cities but pointed the way beyond the cities, as Jack Kerouac writes in *On the Road*: "What is that feeling when you're driving away from people and they recede on the plain till you see their specks dispersing?—it's the too-huge world vaulting us, and it's good-by. But we lean forward to the next crazy venture beneath the skies."

Young men and women fled the suburbs on those same highways that had made possible what angered them. But they also journeyed down other roads. Be it through jazz, abstract expressionism, marijuana, or myriad other avenues that led away from the confines of middle-American existence, the broad and open plain of consciousness beckoned. Eastern religion stood out as the visionary philosophy that would ultimately underpin much artistic and personal expression. Allan Ginsberg's *Howl* stands as the testament of the Beat generation, but there is another Ginsberg poem that better captures the flight from church and steeple to monastery and mountain. In his 1955 poem "Sunflower Sutra," Ginsberg writes, "A perfect beauty of a sunflower! a perfect excellent lovely sunflower existence! a sweet natural eye to the new hip moon, woke up alive and excited grasping in the sunset shadow sunrise golden monthly breeze!"

It was this emphasis on experience, on being in the world, on recognizing the unassuming holiness that exists in all of existence, that led young people away from what was perceived as static, conformist, and square. While not the food of the gods they would be for the hippies, drugs played no small role for the Beats as a way to elicit the kind of illumination that revealed the truth behind the veil. As early as 1959 Ginsberg was writing poetry about LSD and "the billion-eyed monster, the Nameless, the Answerless, the Hidden-from-me, the endless being . . ."—an image of God that put up a middle finger to the long-bearded daddy in the sky that haunted traditional Judaism and Christianity. Within this tension between the elusive promise of suburban homesteading and the growing agitation that would take flight in the sixties was where I grew up.

Because I was the youngest of four children with five to ten years between us, my parents always thought it best to protect me from the grave circumstances that characterized the life of our family. The first of these came when my grandfather died in 1972, when I was six. I knew something had utterly changed. I learned through some kind of familial osmosis that he had died, not because anyone sat me down to explain it. I wasn't allowed to go to the funeral. His death was a terrible blow to my father. His death made everyone sad and anxious, but I didn't know why.

The death and funeral, the whispered sobbing—these were things for the adults. But no matter what they did to create a world where death existed only for them, the truth of it was like a smoke that wafted directly into my room. I didn't internalize it as death or loss or even an absence in any way. I came to know it, at least in the pit of my belly, as wordless vulnerability, a sense of being untethered, like a balloon being released from the hand of a child. I felt, for the first time, unease.

A year later, the store my father had to suddenly manage on his own burned down. Again, I don't recall anyone ever explaining to me what had happened, only that there was a new suffering in the house and it seemed to center on my father. I think one of my older sisters told me about the fire and the loss, but she didn't have much more information and anything shared came secondhand, as in a game of telephone. The sense of loss in my home became like ambient sound. Loss was something crafted, but not fully disclosed. My parents were producers of private dismay. There was something purposeful about it, the tension between having to bear so much misfortune and yet not letting on for a moment that they were devastated and all of us would be touched by it.

After another year of trying to handle this new disaster went by, as if he needed one more blow to make sure he was getting the picture that his life would not turn out as he had imagined, my father was diagnosed with debilitating rheumatoid arthritis. It felt for a time, at least to that eight-year-old boy, that his dad had disappeared. Even less was said than had been about the other tragedies. My parents and my older siblings, Lisa, Karen, and Eric, seemed wrecked and worried beyond anything they had envisioned for themselves. They rebelled in all the normal ways, but to me at the time, it was like living in a world where everyone did private things. Lisa began dating a boy my parents hated, and her sobbing could be heard through the walls, as if it had nested in there like mice.

Eric began to wear cologne. He listened to strange music, music that felt apocalyptic, as if the end of everything was coming fast. The Beatles' "Helter Skelter" and "I Am the Walrus" crawled under my skin while I watched my brother get dressed to go out. He brushed his hair with great care, just as my sisters did. There was something forbidden about the world he inhabited, the way he dressed. One night I woke suddenly to find my brother sitting with his head out the open window of our bedroom. A back-draft was sending cigarette smoke into the room toward my bed, where I must have breathed it in while sleeping. A panic rose in my chest. I didn't know what else to do, so I ran into my parents' room and told them Eric was "doing something." He never forgave me that.

My other sister, Karen, the closest to my age and once my playmate, was making her discomfort something precious in her own way. We stopped playing together, and she became fixated on boys who were forever unattainable—David Cassidy and Leif Garrett, her room a shrine of pinups and covers of *Tiger Beat* magazine. Certainly every girl her age had built the same temple to these feather-haired Adonises, but the barely hidden sexual subtext of their pouty poses and their tight jeans was just one more alien encounter in a house where I was feeling progressively anxious.

My own escapes were not so furtive as, but were no less compulsive than, those of my siblings. On Sunday mornings I was the first to wake, so as to get the hefty paper waiting on the front stoop. Once inside, I pulled out the funny pages and TV listings, opening the latter first to see what films were being shown on the Creature Double Feature the following Saturday. I then looked up the titles in my encyclopedic monster-movie book and studied the film stills until the strange and disfigured faces of the featured monster were burned into my head.

Over the next few years my fretfulness started to become a sense of impending doom. I wasn't worried about anything specific, but on occasion it seemed as though the world was a haunted place. The comforts of television and Doritos only made this perception more sharp and exaggerated when it came upon me, but it was filtered through *Star Trek* reruns and *Dr. Who* episodes. Over time the abstract strangeness of the world became more specific, such as in the form of kidnappings, illness, and all the things that could go wrong with the body. One could fall from high places, get kicked in the groin by girls or punched in the stomach by boys. Or you could end up in a plastic bubble like John Travolta, without any immunity to the invisible hordes of germs. (Once, for no reason, I thought I couldn't swallow and spent the evening in my bed, forcing myself to gulp air into my throat to make sure I could.) You could end up abducted. You could be run over. You could find yourself in a tall building suddenly on fire, or in an earthquake. You could be possessed by the Devil. Or, worse, you could die from drugs.

In an episode of the TV series *Police Story*, David Cassidy played an undercover narcotics agent in a high school. In one scene someone put angel dust into a boy's hamburger. Later that day, the boy went onto the roof of the school, calling out, "I can fly! I can fly!" before flinging himself to the ground. Drugs somehow had a life of their own. People could trick you into doing them; they could be in something you might drink. (In the film *Food of the Gods*, a strange organic "food" causes rats and worms to grow into terrible giant monsters. At the end of the movie, after the threat has been eradicated, the camera shows a herd of cows grazing in a pasture containing the food. The scene shifts to ominously show a group of schoolchildren drinking from their milk cartons. During dinner the night after watching it, I couldn't eat a bite, worried that our meal was somehow tainted as well.)

In fifth grade I began to read about drugs in encyclopedias and became an expert on all the various categories and subcategories of drugs and their various effects. I was haunted by all the possibilities, and while I vowed never to take them, I couldn't help imagining how drugs might explain something about the various people around me whom I both avoided and was attracted to. There were the girls with their denim jackets and lip gloss who smelled of cigarettes and some other burnt vegetable, whose eyes glazed over in class but who were not shy about their bodies and didn't try to hide their newly budding breasts and ever-curving curves. Then there was the music that came out of my brother's eight-track player, songs that alluded to something I knew could be understood only under the influence of one of the many drugs mentioned in the pamphlets I collected and whose cartoon panels warned about the horrors and the dangers. So I wrote an essay about drugs for a class project—an objective, fair-minded account until the final sentence, which read: "And for your sake and God's, don't do drugs."

My mother, while not religious, had a deep religious sensibility, but it arose in her as superstitions (we were reminded to throw a bit of salt over our shoulder if we spilled the shaker, to not walk out a different door from the one we had entered through) and quiet reflective moments, as when she lit the Friday night candles by herself, the room darkened, her prayer said quietly. My father, a staunch rationalist, loved the historical Judaism, the Talmud, and the traditions but had no use for mystical pitter-patter. I was torn between these two worlds: the emotionalism and romanticism of my mother and the stoic reasonableness of my father. None of the mysteries of the world was contained by religious stories or ideas. There was no hell or sin, heaven or reward. My only tangible experience with religion as a lived phenomenon was my bar mitzvah with ultra-orthodox Jews.

For five years my family lived in Hollywood, Florida, after exiling ourselves from Massachusetts in 1975. All the collective losses were too much to bear, and my parents were looking for a fresh start. By the time I was twelve, the only group that was willing to take me on as a student without making my parents join their synagogue was the local Chabad House. What I knew of Judaism consisted of Passover meals, my mother lighting Friday night candles, and delicatessens. The Hasidic Jews were something else entirely. My rabbi was one part religious fundamentalist, one part Gandalf the Grey. Over the course of our studies I felt repelled and attracted—repelled by the rules and the structure, attracted to the mystical vibe and the seemingly magical quality of the Hebrew alphabet and some of the prayers. But it didn't stick. I went through with the ritual and felt something akin to being a man—hair in the right places and thoughts to go along with it. Ultimately it didn't conform to the burgeoning magical thinking that would begin to characterize my adolescent awareness.

The truth is, for my family, being Jewish didn't have anything to do with God at all. Not at home around Passover dinner, not even studying the Torah with the rabbi. The mystery of existence, if it was talked about at all, was for adults at funerals. Even then, God was left there to finish piling the dirt on the grave while the mourners went home. Somehow, though, the slight rituals of the Judaism I knew penetrated and I thought about God in my own way. It wasn't connected to external religious experience, but rather was part of an internal world I was constructing out of the brick and mortar of my adolescence. Not a sure foundation, but enough to begin to know, to really know in the deepest parts of myself, that a divine reality existed and that somewhere, meaning existed also. How to access it, though?

Even my rabbi, who I thought was closest to the secret source of knowledge, who read the Bible and other Jewish texts as if he was learning the recipe for creation, was in his own way impotent. He was bound by what I then perceived as conformity to rules. He could impart the law and the tradition, but not the experience of unity. He could tell me that God was "one," but I wanted to encounter that directly.

The only thing that resonated as spiritual was magic. The wizards of fantasy novels appeared to have more direct access to some spiritual reality than my rabbi did. They didn't wear prayer shawls, but they did commune with higher powers. The supernatural monsters that populated those Saturday morning B movies, however overtly fake in their rubber masks and makeup, could still induce chills and feelings of dread because they drew from real legends and myths. Vampires, werewolves, and mummies—even when incarnated by Bela Lugosi, Lon Chaney Jr., and Boris Karloff—key directly into old, maybe even ancient, locks in our unconscious. When Colin Clive playing Victor Frankenstein (in the 1931 Universal Pictures movie shown each year on channel 56) imbues his monster with alchemical life and he cries out, "It's alive!" his eyes reflect a mad ecstasy, a revelation that there are powers and realities beyond the known phenomenal world.

There was another 1970s, to be sure. Posters of Steve Martin and Richard Pryor adorned my walls. In the garage was a tricked-out bike with long handlebars and a blue banana seat. My older brother hid copies of *Penthouse* in his collection of Beetle Bailey comics, and across the street my friend had discovered pornography on his parents' Betamax video machine. One afternoon we watched, in terrible awe, bodily wonders we almost wished had remained unknown.

The asexual elves of *The Lord of the Rings* were more my speed. I read the second-edition Ballantine paperbacks, with Tolkien's own illustrations on the cover. There were no knights flashing swords, no dragons circling a castle on fire, just pastoral landscapes where I could imagine heroic myths being played out. Bilbo Baggins's shire in *The Hobbit* felt more like home. In those imaginary worlds, no one bothered me at school, I was not powerless over the hormones coursing through my veins and keeping me and my dick up all night, and I was not consumed by those nameless fears that crowded out my ability to concentrate for very long on any one thing.

The colorful fantasies of comic books lent a heroic dimension to the implausible, and none treaded in the far-fetched more than those cosmic adventures Marvel Comics published. I bypassed Spider-Man and the Hulk for the enormous, galaxy-spanning adventures of the Fantastic Four, in which the team of misfits met anthropomorphized forces of nature, like the world-eater Galactus, Ego the living planet, and the Celestials, ancient giants whose vast technology secretly altered Earth's history by creating the wondrous Eternals. In the other team comic, *The Avengers*, there were characters like the all-powerful alien Korvac, who wrestled with his godlike powers, a time-traveling despot known as Kang the Conqueror, and the Kree, a race of military scientists forever battling the shape-shifting Skrulls.

These stories' majesty and vigor cooled down the anxiety that was becoming a little heated wire under my skin. In these strange environs, I felt cozy. With the Marvel Universe one could create a massive family tree, an elaborate cosmic drama involving gods, mutants, androids, and heroes. Encyclopedias and atlases mapped out every detail of Tolkien's Middle-earth, and even the music of progressive rock bands like Styx, Rush, and ELO that slid down the record player's spindle one after the other seemed crafted out of intricate stories and mythologies. It wasn't just about getting lost in these otherworldly chronicles; my anxiety was soothed by the vastness of worlds beyond my home. Whether or not they were fiction was irrelevant. Their details made them real. And if they could be real, maybe my own imagination had the power to become actualized.

I took to pretending that under my bed was a keypad into which I typed an alphanumeric sequence that only I knew. The result was a control panel descending from the ceiling into my lap. From there I was able to designate how much I did not want to go to school the next day. A variable control allowed me to set a value that would increase, by measure, the likelihood of my getting sick so that I could stay home. After I made the setting, I would reenter the code under my bed and the control panel would return to its invisible hideaway in the ceiling. I couldn't imagine what happened to my consciousness when I fell asleep, and the notion of an oblivion, of a state of consciousness in which I was not aware of myself, terrified me. Every night after my mother came into my room to say goodnight, I would wait until I heard her footsteps fade. Then I would sneak into the bathroom and splash cold water on my face to try and keep awake.

When everything was dark and the only sound was that of a television in another room, it was easy to explore the dungeons and castles of my own mind. I discovered that by chanting simple phrases over and over again I could induce a kind of trance, to see if there were indeed other worlds to be gleaned beyond my senses. These minor attempts at altering my consciousness gave me a rush of exhilaration, a sense that I was pushing up against some mental boundary that with enough discipline I could break through completely. Once, I tried to travel through time in the front yard of my house. I spun in circles until I was almost nauseatingly dizzy and then ran as fast as I could, thinking I would break the time barrier. I smashed my head on an electrical box and had to have stitches. A precursor of things to come, for sure.

By the time I was fourteen, Dungeons & Dragons campaigns began to take on a different quality, a more profound sense that what we were playing had ramifications for our own lives outside the game. If I was the one to defeat the dragon, my luck would change at school. The jock who intimidated me every day and sneered with a face full of fury would recognize something powerful in me and know, without understanding why, to leave me alone. If I found a magic sword, some real magic would bleed out into the real world and I might have access to some strange ancient force that would give me a sense of empowerment.

Then, like a cliché right out of a parents' handbook on the dangers of Dungeons & Dragons, I started to collect books on magic and witchcraft and imagined what it would be like to have real sorcerous powers. I didn't desire the power to make girls love me or know the future so much as I yearned for magical knowledge. I wanted to know if the astral plane was real, if spirits inhabited rocks and trees and could be communicated with, if behind the veil angelic and demonic beings were engaged in a celestial war. I wanted to know if God was real. This search for spiritual awareness by occult methods was not unique. I was a stowaway on a boat that, by the time it made it to the American suburbs, had undergone such a battering from the winds and storms of time and culture that all I had left was a sliver of wood and a paddle. I was bound only for the river Styx.

An ad in a 1967 edition of the *New York Times* for the *Encyclopedia of Occultism* offered a volume of magical treasures: "2500 Entries . . . From Adjuration to Alchemy to Zodiac, Zohar, and Zoroaster," your gift for joining the Mystic Arts Book Society (with your promise, of course, to buy three more books within a year). Other selections included *Introduction to Yoga*, *The Holy Kabbalah*, and *Relaxation Through Self Hypnosis*. With one mailing you could receive a complete spiritual library devoid of anything that smacked of mainstream Christianity or Judaism. By this time, all the possible spiritual paths had become readily accessible. "What's your sign?" became the first line of inquiry upon meeting a stranger. Tarot cards could be purchased at head shops.

This conglomeration of occultism, Eastern philosophy, magic, and ideas about human potential and "mind power" was at the heart of what is now called the New Age movement. An interest in parapsychology (ESP, telepathy) further combined with UFO sightings to create a kind of scientific rationale behind some of the ideas. The transmission of this Junior Jumble puzzle of spirituality for most of the culture came by way of television and popular magazines.

The general public glommed on to the more sensational bits of New Age ideas, such as paranormal phenomena, UFOs, and witchcraft, which many people mistakenly associated with devil worship and Satanism. By the mid- to late seventies an entire generation of kids sat in front of the television, eating Frosted Flakes and Chef Boyardee Beefaroni while their spiritual anxieties, born of rising divorce rates, fear of nuclear war, hostages, and kidnappings, were funneled through images of UFOs, the Bermuda Triangle, Bigfoot, and devil worshippers showing up on episodes of *Quincy*. The list of appearances by the devil in film includes *Rosemary's Baby*, *The Exorcist*, and my personal favorite, *Devil Dog: Hound from Hell*, in which a brother and sister secretly worship Satan in the form of a German shepherd in the attic of their clean homogenous suburban home.

In the summer of 1972, *Time* published an issue with a shock cover: a hooded figure superimposed with an upside-down pentagram with the headline "The Occult Revival: Satan Returns." The article itself doesn't quite live up to its lurid title; there are those who worship Satan, but only as a representation of personal spiritual freedom, more like a big middle finger to American Christianity than a devotion to an abstract representation of evil and destruction. The occult revival that the article details mainly involves a resurgent interest in astrology, Wicca, and prophecy. Nevertheless, despite the lack of any kind of documented demonic possession or rites of human sacrifice, the seventies proved to be a boon for the paranormal.

By the late seventies, TV shows like *In Search Of*, hosted by Leonard Nimoy, presented anecdotes and testimonies on everything from Bigfoot to killer bees to the Bermuda Triangle, an ironic job for the man whose *Star Trek* character a decade earlier had come to epitomize a hopeful and radical future vision and who was defined by his rationalism.

Those days were a gold mine for the weird and the uncanny— science fiction and fantasy, superheroes, monsters. A resurgence of interest in classic horror movies had produced wonderful magazines, like *Famous Monsters of Filmland*, and a revival of horror comics in *Eerie* and *Creepy*—much like the EC horror comics of the fifties, such as *Tales from the Crypt* and *Haunt of Fear*, which were responsible for the introduction of a Comics Code Authority (CCA) that sought to limit graphic violence in comic books. By the time the seventies rolled around, *MAD* magazine had shown a new generation of artists how to avoid censorship by making their comics the size of regular magazines (thus avoiding the CCA, which applied only to comic books), available on the racks of drugstores and supermarkets.

Creepy and *Eerie* took supernatural themes and coated them with a hefty amount of gore and blood. In these stories, all the darkest imaginings about the occult were brought to bear. There was no room for speculation about mystical and hermetic secrets. Magic was a dark art used for personal gain and revenge.

Drawing from a huge swath of readily identifiable cultural tidbits, *Creepy* #66, published in 1974, offers the story "Pinball Wizard," by Doug Moench and Richard Corben. A young boy watches as the beloved owner of the local soda fountain, Pop, is bullied and beaten by gangsters who insist he install a pinball machine and give them the profits. The boy, Walter, begs Pop to let him get revenge, as he has a way to send the bad guys to hell. Pop chides Walter for suggesting it, but the next day when the boy visits the store, he finds Pop dead. The next page shows the small child sitting in the middle of a huge chalk-drawn penta-gram, calling forth demons that torture and kill each mobster one by one, until, finally, the mob boss himself becomes the ball in a giant, fiendish pinball machine played by an enormous demon.

The idea of magical knowledge as connected to infernal, rather than heavenly, influences would pervade even popular music. Led Zeppelin, specifically their 1971 album known as *Led Zeppelin IV* and referred to lovingly, or superstitiously, as *ZoSo* (based on the strange sigils that adorn the inner sleeve), are often thought of as rock 'n' roll's preeminent magicians, whose music contains the pulse of some malevolent power. Indeed, there is something vaguely mystical going on, in the form of their nods to Tolkien and what Erik Davis, in his book on the album, calls "hippie paganism." Davis asks, "Who do Zeppelin swear fealty to? The devil or the sun? Mordor or Middle-earth?" This tension was possible only in the seventies. As the door shut on the sixties and dusk fell over the Aquarian Age, there seemed little to look forward to, less left to fight for.

By the late sixties and early seventies, the commingling of all these various spiritual ideas manifested into an impenetrable mixture of correspondences. Go into any New Age bookstore to see the result. Everything is permitted, nothing is discerned. Zen sits side by side with *The Satanic Bible*; Rosicrucians snuggle up against accounts of UFOs and ancient astronauts; tarot cards, rune stones, astrology, and water divining are just to the left of JFK assassination conspiracy theories and exposés on the truth of the Knights Templar.

This pockmarked, bumpy, and often treacherous spiritual highway wound its way right into the suburbs north of Boston, where I could be found sitting on the floor, rolling dice, and reading the eternal statistics tables in the D&D manual, wishing that the magic within the confines of the game was not merely drawn from fantasy novels and mythology, but a shadow of something genuine. If magic was real, then maybe these suburbs were also a shadow of some greater reality. Might there be fairies living in small woods adjacent to our house? Even though the townhouse we lived in was built in the 1970s, maybe the spirits of Native Americans that could have hunted on the very spot where my parents parked their car were still haunting this once hallowed ground. The pulp horror author H. P. Lovecraft wrote about ancient alien gods worshipped in the small towns of New England. Could a similarly strange cult have performed their arcane rituals where the mall now sat, and might their terrible deities be waiting for a neophyte to unlock their secrets? But beyond even these questions was another greater mystery: What, if anything, did the God my rabbi spoke of have to do with any of this, with any of these feelings, these imaginings?

The number 455 bus picked me up right in front of the townhouse association and went straight into Salem, which, I assumed, was the best place to learn something about magic. It was here, after all, where real witches lived; at least, that was what the whole city wanted you to believe. The fact that the people accused weren't witches at all has never slowed the constant trickle of tourists into the Witch Museum, Dungeon Museum, and Witch House, as well as into the stores where you can have a wand "charged" with whatever kind of magical energy you request. The history of the city, whether real or imagined, has attracted self-identified Wiccans and neopagans for decades, and so there really is no better place for a thirteen-year-old dungeon master to get a book on real arcane knowledge. So I took a bus alone for the first time, in search of a primer on witchcraft.

Gerald Gardner had shaped a generation with his 1950s books *Witchcraft Today* and *The Meaning of Witchcraft*, in which he developed a strange mix of history and myth—as well as his own inventions—into a stew of confluences known popularly as Wicca. Along with tarot cards, books on astrology, and healing crystals, books on witchcraft were readily available, especially in a New Age bookstore in the heart of Salem. Once inside, dizzy from the smell of patchouli and sandalwood, I chanced upon a book called *The Key of Solomon*, a medieval *grimoire* (magical text) made popular in the late nineteenth century during what is called the Occult Revival.

I had never seen another book like it. This was very different from what I had imagined magic was, as described by the fictional worlds I spent so much time inhabiting. In the early editions of Dungeons & Dragons, magic was something you collected in the form of spells and objects. There was no ritual, practice, or discipline. Spells worked immediately and either hit their intended target or missed, depending on the laws of chance generated by the dice. If an angry, tentacled beholder was coming at your party of adventurers, even a low-level magic user could cast a powerful fireball to set the creature aflame. Magic was not mysterious or dangerous. It involved no sacrifice. You simply learned new spells as you went along. In fantasy novels, magic could be deadly to wizards, but it was usually because they were inexperienced or evil and deserving of their fate. But mostly wizards were drawn as if their power were innate, not anything that required much more than studying a few books, maybe cooking up a potion or two.

The Key of Solomon explained how, through an intensely detailed preparation and ritual, one could conjure demons and bend them to the magician's will, as well as perform other magical feats, like invisibility and flight (with the aid of some magic garters, no less). The rituals involved the construction of magic circles and the use of implements, such as seals, swords, and particular clothing, all of which had to be prepared in almost impossible ways. A spell for invisibility involved writing a certain phrase on the skin of a toad and suspending it from a hair in a cave at midnight.

The text was filled with strange sigils, magical seals, and long incantations. While I had read about spells and tarot cards,

Ouija boards, and spirit knockings, I had never before read something so old and, well, religious. All of the spells in *The Key of Solomon* included prayers to God, and much of the text used Hebrew. This was magic that required great preparation of mind and body, a devout belief in God, and the willingness to risk one's soul. There was almost no practical way in which I was capable of attempting any of the spells or conjurations, but just owning the book was like having access to a source of great power. It was the manifestation of what I wanted to be true about the world, while at the same time being too complex for me to really use. I could barely get away with lighting a candle without instantly alerting my mother's sixth sense of anything on fire. My innate skepticism was held at bay by the impossibility of it all. Nevertheless, *The Key* was an actual key, one that could unlock the secrets of the world.

Having no control over my surroundings, I thought magic seemed like the perfect organizing principle, except that for every stone unturned, another, even stranger one appeared in its place. When all I had to soothe my anxiousness were video games and role-playing, the kind of magic found in *The Key of Solomon the King* offered some small hope that there was a secret order and meaning to the universe, that all things on Earth were a mere reflection of some greater divine truth. That hope, however, led to an even greater confusion. I wasn't sure I knew what I would do if I really did turn invisible or fly. Would I sneak into the girls' locker room or take *Fantastic Four* #1 and *Amazing Fantasy* #15 from the wall behind the clerk's counter at the comics shop?

These weren't the things I wanted magic to attain for me. Even when I played D&D, I was loath to use magic as an offensive weapon. It felt like cheating to cast infinite magic missiles at the hopeless horde of orcs. Even the greatest wizard of all, Gandalf in *The Lord of the Rings*, rarely employed spells. But

I studied the book and felt that smoldering around the edges of the words was something not unlike those forbidden experiences I gleaned from the pamphlets on illegal drugs, and very much like the Led Zeppelin and Black Sabbath albums in my brother's stack of records.

While I wanted to understand something about magic, my instincts told me that God and magic were somehow incompatible, or at least that magic might not be the right tool if what I was looking for was spiritual in nature. Mysticism or magic, communion with God, or power over His angels.

Every day after school I went to the tiny mall a few blocks from my house. The mall was located far enough from the center of town that no one from my school actually hung out there. Strange to believe, but even on the weekends, I was the only teenager there. And it was for the best. I had moved here in the middle of eighth grade, wearing glasses and last year's sneakers. I wandered around the bookstore, the Radio Shack, and the department store, thinking my private thoughts, free in the world, away from my parents and the taunts of other kids. Every once in a while Jacob, the lone security guard would say hello, and eventually we got to talking. Over the course of a few months, we became strangely close—a shy, picked-on, allergy-ridden fourteen-year-old who collected horror comics, and a man in his thirties who had recently lost his father and loved Rush and Black Sabbath. He had long hair and a beard, and to me he looked like a sage or a wizard, hiding out in the uniform of a security guard. He spoke in a mystic babble, and for the first time, all the abstract ideas I was privately interested in took shape in a visible and visceral way. Even though I read books on the occult, part of me refused to believe there really was a secret language that was spoken between the trees and the rocks. But for Jacob, everything was a sign, a symbol that obscured some mysterious meaning. We walked back and forth the length of the mall while he told me stories of how rock 'n' roll could be cracked and listened to as a secret code. Jacob explained that there was no coincidence, that every moment was a serendipitous, fateful event that pointed toward the next and the next. There was correspondence, he told me, between everything we could see and its equivalent in a hidden reality. So above, so below.

As we walked around that depressing little mall, past the stink of the pet shop, the T-shirt store, the ice-cream shop, the card shop, and the deli, Jacob explained to me the connections that proved God was in all things and all things were in God. Every suit of the tarot deck had a corresponding planet, as in astrology, and the planets themselves reflected the human body. Our bodies contain chakras, points of energy that also referred to the tarot suits, and on and on, until the world was a crushing mass of meaning. He would be describing the lyrics to a Black Sabbath song, when some word or phrase he overheard from someone walking by us would make his eyes flare. "Did you hear that?" he would ask. "Just like I said. Just as I said." Jacob spoke as if every thought and idea were a new revelation, but they never resolved into anything pragmatic. It was all circular, pointing back to the details of his life, his own fears, hopes, and desires. I could never tell if God was his salvation or his enemy, if the universe and its myriad associations were a unified perfection or a terrible, indecipherable puzzle that tricked him at every turn with a new significance that undid the previous one.

Jacob started giving me poetry, the stream-of-consciousness engravings of a mystic, but it spoke to me of an intimacy with another person I had not felt before. I was entering adolescence, my hormones filling me with guilt and shame and magical thinking. On the way to the mall, I began to incorporate some of the kinds of protective rituals Jacob had spoken of. I took no chances with the hidden powers that controlled the universe. I began to have to step on a certain brick, touch a certain branch, walk across the abandoned lot in a very precise mazelike pattern, all in the hope of having some kind of control over what felt like, and what Jacob had only clarified for me as, a world that was a bewildering yet mesmerizing series of signs and meanings. He talked in code about something else as well: psychedelic substances that were the key to understanding the cipher of the universe. He never advocated their use, but he recalled experiences and told me stories of bizarre encounters with otherworldly entities, like the mysterious "Dr. Neverno," who came to him in visions and, as Jacob liked to say, played pinball with his psyche.

One afternoon, I decided to let Jacob know how much I had come to love him and depend on him, not only for friendship, but for a guiding light that revealed to me the mystery behind all things and illuminated the path by which I might find my way through. Some years earlier my oldest sister had given me a small pewter scarab necklace. It was a cheap museum trinket but was to me a precious little thing. I gave it to Jacob and he accepted it affectionately. I knew I would never have to feel alone again.

A few weeks later, I found Jacob at the mall in a terrible state. He was rambling about his father's grave and how someone else who had recently died had put up a new tombstone next to where his father was buried. He seemed crazed, afraid, even, that something awful was about to happen. He explained that the name on the new stone was Rush, the name of his favorite band, the band that he believed had the most perfect knowledge of him and the world. He took the scarab and pressed it into my hand and told me that because I had given it to him, everything was lost and some evil had descended into his life. Jacob insinuated it had all started the day he took the necklace from me as a gift of my love. He literally turned his back on me and left while I stood in front of Walgreens, trembling.

I was afraid to go to the mall for weeks, but when I got up the nerve, he was gone. He had quit his job as the security guard. I never heard from him or saw him again.

The effect of his leaving didn't reveal the pathology of his belief. What had been his alone became mine. I used to listen to his madness as if on a radio station I couldn't quite tune in to. But the traumatic results of his final revelation cleared away the static and I became, in some core subconscious place, a true believer in an occult arrangement of cosmic forces, gods, and other invisible beings that shaped our lives—though for good or ill, who could know?

Jacob was a product of that terrible moment when the seventies skidded out of the sixties. LSD was illegal, so even getting it created a drama of illicitness and paranoia. Psychedelics were also big business and were no longer passed out freely at concerts and trip festivals. You couldn't even be sure you were getting authentic doses of whatever you bought. Another drug, sold as mescaline but having nothing to do with the psychoactive peyote cactus, would shake up your insides as if a hyena had been let loose in your skull. Often it didn't matter—drugs started to lose their particularity, and getting high, in whatever way was available, became the de facto intent. If you took acid, you probably smoked pot, and if you smoked pot, you even drank a bit and maybe even tried a little coke or snorted a little heroin.

Jacob, I think, tried to parse it all as best he could, but he was still mixing his LSD with another "drug" that did him in more rapidly than any other, and that years later would take me down a similar path: one part occultism, two parts magic, a heavy dose of gnosticism, and a mighty helping of hermetic philosophy, all arranged nicely by those infinite hidden connections—the secret language of the universe.

Horselover Fat, the protagonist of Philip K. Dick's later novel, *VALIS*, and the alter ego of the author, is also the sad

analogue to those who suffered that peculiar sickness of psychedelics mixed poorly with occult metaphysics. In the novel, Fat
believes he was shot in the brain with a pink laser that revealed
to him not only that reality as we understand it is merely information another entity is downloading to us, a kind of gnostic
demiurge, but that the entity might very well be insane. The
novel reads like a grouping of magical correspondences, one
connection after another, involving hermeticists, secret Christians, and aliens. But Dick is clear on one thing: Dope was the
genesis that resulted in the frying of Fat's brain.

In the afterword of the beloved Dick novel *A Scanner Darkly*
(in which a group of drug users might be legitimately paranoid
about sinister conspiratorial forces), the author eulogizes friends
who were destroyed by drugs in the sixties and early seventies.
It must have been difficult for even the most romantic among
the last hangers-on to admit that the promise of some kind of
mystical liberation through the use of drugs was not going to
happen anytime soon.

I wouldn't know of Dick's warning until it was too late. Jacob
might have left me lonelier and more baffled than I'd been
before I met him, but I still believed he had a kind of spiritual
radar, that despite his frail ability to make sense of his gift, Jacob
was a mystic. Even though it ate him alive, I thought I might be
able to turn what had made him mad into wisdom. I had everything I needed to get started, the most important being that
yearning to find meaning beyond the appearance of the phenomenal world, what early twentieth-century scholar and writer
Evelyn Underhill described as "this divine and infinite life, this
mysterious Cosmic activity in which you are immersed, of which
you are born." I was missing only one ingredient.

We went to the abandoned lot behind my house with a six-pack,
two thick joints, and no bottle opener. My companion pulled the

cap off his beer with the edge of a stone. My attempt cracked the neck, and so I poured the beer into my mouth from above my head, hoping that no bits of glass had fallen into the bottle. I swallowed barely a few mouthfuls, the rest spilling onto the ground as I leapt away so none would get on my shirt. After we clumsily drank the beer, we lit up the joints and I was told to hold each lungful of smoke in as long as I could. The air was clean and cool, and each toke tasted like autumn leaves.

I had heard people didn't get high the first time they smoked pot, but whether or not this was true for most, I got massively stoned that night. After we smoked the second joint, we got on our bikes and rode through the suburban streets, yelling and laughing and feeling, at fifteen, for the first moment, free. The stars were out in a multitude, and their light flew off like sparks. Everything was aglow; even the houses winked and smiled at me. Sometime later that night I went quietly into my house, my parents watching television in their room upstairs, and went down into the basement that had been converted into my bedroom. The sound of my coming home was all they needed to hear. I was trusted, the kid who never got into trouble, and my comings and goings rarely had to be accounted for, as long as I kept to a fairly consistent schedule.

The heat in the house made my ears buzz, and I sat on the couch and just grooved without having to reach for anything to keep me satisfied. The moment was my own. I looked around at my comic books and games and models and computer, and they were inconsequential. They would no longer distract me. I had glimpsed the sun behind the moon in the middle of the night and its rays had filled me with hope.

The weed had chipped away those fissures in my inner mind that were ready to crumble. There were hidden passages on the other side that I had already glimpsed briefly in Jacob's ramblings, occult discourses, Tolkien's imagined world, and even

Rush lyrics. Small auditory hallucinations matched perfectly the movement of my hands if I waved them in front of me. New ideas and inspirations burst forth like Roman candles. Everything, everything, was filled to overflowing with significance.

I got into bed and pressed my fingers to my nose, inhaling the sweet smell of resin as I fell asleep for the first time without having to wait for it, my restless mind coming to a dead stop.

chapter two
JUMP INTO THE FIRE

I was sitting on top of a hill overlooking the mall where I bought my Twizzlers and computer magazine, where the ghost of Jacob lingered as a warning or a beacon, my head awash with a Cocoa Puffs bowl full of correspondences, with the idea that every action had a divine reaction, that all my thoughts were interconnected with the hidden workings of a magical universe. I rolled a monster joint with three papers, a technique I had learned from a friend. The burning perfume taste, the deep fire in my throat, the pop of the stray seed, the first sense that something about the world was *different* . . . it was all of a moment that for years and years would exist just outside my peripheral sense of what life could be like. Anxiety replaced by calm, fear replaced by contemplation, and all the indecipherable tiny symbols and signs that dotted the landscape coalesced for one perfect instant.

Later that night, I met up with some friends at my high school for a Halloween party. We had arrived blasted out of our heads. The principal was standing at the door. He caught my eye the moment we walked past the threshold, the chill October air burning off in the overheated gymnasium, the smell of pot vaporizing right under his nose. A little door popped open in my forehead, and he gazed right in and could see the strange chemical combinations that were erupting within. Our warm buzz kicked into overdrive and turned into an electric current of fear.

We went in to where everyone was dancing. A girl I had barely noticed during the day at school was dressed like a witch, her face painted green. She took on a loveliness that consumed me. I babbled as I tried to somehow charm her, but I was slant-eyed and perma-grinning. Bad spirits were in the air. Everyone knew how high I was. I felt sick with the sense of looming disaster. In the bathroom, I flushed the weed, which I'd rolled up in a plastic bag and tucked under my balls. Any minute the principal's hand would come down on my shoulder. Then it was out of the bathroom and into the gymnasium for one last desperate look for the beautiful witch, and we were back into the night, out onto the golf course directly behind the school, running wildly for what we thought were our lives.

There in that sacred grove, that perfect landscape of M&M-green hills, paths forking in every direction, and the surrounding woods, I became sure that one day this would all mean something. A melancholy swept over me as I realized I was literally alone. Somewhere my companions had taken another turn and had either forgotten to look for me or forgotten I had been with them at all. I stood at the peak of a hill, the light from the nearby strip mall illuminating the golf course as if from a distant celestial body. Inexplicably, impossibly, there was a chair in the grass near one of the sand traps. A simple wooden chair. So God was real after all. Everything crystallized, most important that being alone was best, where my thinking could unite with the spheres without distraction. To sit in the chair would be to redeem whatever had gone wrong with this night. I sat down and waited for Jacob's ladder to appear. I was not afraid. I would skip along the rungs all the way to heaven.

The golf course and the adjacent woods became a refuge for me. I was convinced that underneath was an ancient source of power. In some areas were shallow swampy ponds. One night, a fellow I knew only as the kid who sold three joints for $5 took me into his confidence by taking me fishing in what I had thought was only a deep muddy puddle that never dried, but was actually home to enormous eels. We smoked bowlful after bowlful of bright green buds as I watched him catch the eels with a small rod. As the sun rose I saw the outline of the large supermarket on one side and the golf course on the other. It made no sense, even stoned, that this could be happening here, but the eels were flipping on the hook as my companion tried desperately to pull them off and toss them back into the opaque water. They appeared prehistoric, older than the town itself.

We took to having parties here, and sometimes I would wander off by myself to find some gnarled and fallen branch to sit and meditate on. It was all so charmed, so filled with magic and wonder: Here in the suburbs, only minutes from my school, was a place that was nothing like anything else I knew. Here there was nothing paved, nothing for sale, no jocks or cheerleaders. No one else knew about it, except a few friends who could never sit still long enough to feel what I felt. I would lead them to some special copse of trees, but they would find rocks to throw over the fence and would tremble with laughter when, in the distance, we could hear the stone strike a car or the wall of a store. Even among the few other people whom I got high with, I was alone to glean mysteries they had no interest in. I also wanted to get stoned more often, or so it seemed, and had no internal mechanism guarding me against overindulgence.

While my group of stoned cohorts was small, it appeared everyone in town was holding: the kids with their collarless brown leather jackets and Ozzy Osbourne T-shirts; the grill cooks in the deli where I washed dishes; the daughter of a family friend in town for a few days; the parents of a kid I used to babysit for. It was easier to get drugs than it was to find back issues of *The Avengers* and *Dr. Strange*. And much, much easier to get high than to get drunk. Some invisible wall between teen-agers and adults was torn down, and very quickly I found myself spending time at the homes of people much older than I was. Everyone I knew who got high wanted the company of others who would not judge, who could groove in conversations about auras and government conspiracies.

By the time I was sixteen, I found myself privy to the adult anxieties and dramas of the people whom I bought drugs from and who invited me to hang around to party. One fellow, a normal guy by all accounts, except for his immoderate use of alcohol and pot, often had me over to smoke giant red buds out of a huge glass bong. He drank whiskey while we smoked, and over the course of the night he would become increasingly bel-ligerent and angry at unseen forces that were "ruining his life." Another older man, my main weed connection, had a mistress who lived in an apartment building not far from the mall. He often had me meet him at her home to pick up my $30 quarter-ounce bags (three fingers high), and when I arrived I could tell they had been fighting, if not doing other things I could barely imagine. She would hug me too tightly and light up a joint, and then the next thing I knew we would all be getting stoned together while I watched her continue to fume over something going on between them—some comment or some gesture made—that I was only partially aware of.

It was all so thrilling and, in some strange way, natural to be drawn into this world where suburban folks you saw shopping at the mall were also dealing drugs and behaving indecently, all the while treating me like a peer. Sometimes I would be invited to the home of a young married couple who dealt marijuana to "party." There was always some other palpable tension in the air—not unfriendly, but as if we were all waiting for something else to happen, although it never did.

Most of these adults I knew had come of age in the sixties and still talked about those days with a mix of regret and great veneration. Neil Young was always on someone's turntable, and even as they raged at whatever their lives had become, many of these people, all just old enough to be my parents, still spoke in the spiritual grammar of those days. Words like "karma" were woven into every conversation. Astrology was still the best way to understand someone's personality, and all the promise of peace and love had been a dream so real, it was often referred to as a historical fact, as if there really had been a time when everyone was truly equal, everyone was truly in love with everyone else, and the war machine had been crushed by the sheer weight of all those millions of flowers.

The Monday after that fateful weekend on the golf course, I sat in homeroom and waited to be called into the principal's office, but the request never came. This was a pattern. There was an established sense (or scent) of wrongdoing by whoever was in charge, some authority waiting to trip me up, to have me show my hand and its resin-stained fingers, but despite my transgressions, I was never suspected, never had the trouble-maker in me. Regardless of never doing a lick of work in school,

I wasn't a clown, prone to angry outbursts, or generally sowing chaos. I stayed under the radar, despite being constantly aware of being watched.

In class I took to sitting at the back of the classroom, scrawling band logos on the back of my notebook and reading. The teachers left me alone. Perhaps they wished I was looking at my Western Civilization textbook but were mildly bemused to find instead a copy of *Zen Mind, Beginner's Mind*, by Shunryu Suzuki. This was where I lived during the day, in these books that I stole, borrowed, and then studied obsessively: *Siddhartha*, by Hermann Hesse; the poems of William Blake; *Breakfast of Champions*, by Kurt Vonnegut; *Stranger in a Strange Land*, by Robert Heinlein.

It was easy to find connections, as if every one of these authors, all of them nonconformists in their own way, had seized on the same truth. Suzuki writes, "You should not be a smoky fire. You should burn yourself completely"; Hesse's Siddhartha realizes that "his wound blossomed, his sorrow was radiant, his ego had flowed into the oneness"; in *Breakfast of Champions*, Milo tells Kilgore Trout, "I see a man who is terribly wounded—because he has dared to pass through the fires of truth to the other side, which we have never seen"; and Heinlein's alien redeemer, Michael Valentine Smith, realizes the futility of teaching any of this to us at all: "He realized miserably that, time after time, he brought agitation to these creatures when his purpose was to create oneness."

Surely somewhere in all these books was the perfect invocation, the magic seal that would rise like a hot brand from the page and float across my eyes. Even though I was surrounded by hundreds of other teenagers, it was books that revealed that I was not alone, that there were so many others who had come before me. Where most other adults wouldn't admit to it, here it was that all through history and literature were mad adventurers, braver than any D&D character I could roll. I wanted to follow them, but they had passed along this way already. All I could do was try to walk the path they trod. I had to drop some acid.

There were some considerations. Up to this point my experimentation had been limited to marijuana, with the addition of foul-tasting wine coolers on weekends. Even though my fantasy life strayed far from my suburban home, I was still performing as an average student, respectful of my parents, home in time for dinner. To take acid would cut some essential connection with my family that I was not sure I was willing to sever. In the first place, it was illegal, and felt even more illicit than weed. In all my preadolescent research, LSD had always come out on top as one of the "hard" drugs. Was I willing to become that kind of kid, the kind that used to terrify me when I watched those drug-scare after-school specials? Even more important, I could already feel my interest in school starting to lessen, and intuitively I knew going more deeply into drug use would only quicken my pace away from my responsibilities. Nevertheless, acid was something I had to experience. I would have to risk all the possibilities, not the least of which included getting caught and being shamed in my parents' eyes.

My mother loved to regale us with stories of her own young-adult years, spending long nights in jazz clubs and hanging out with musicians after the doors had closed. There were hints that she had sometimes indulged in a little reefer, as she called it, as it was passed around while she and her friends talked and improvised into the early-morning hours. She spoke about those days with great nostalgia, but also with a resignation, a greater understanding that at some point a door had to be closed so that marriage and a family, the comforts of a home, of nice clothes, of steady and consistent days, could be had. That I, her youngest and most promising, would do drugs made her sacrifice meaningless.

For my father, it was a much simpler equation: The mind was a tool for reason, and to subject it intentionally to delusions was both careless and pointless. There was nothing to be gained from such insights. It was a risk with no benefit. It was, in fact, pathetic.

I also saw and heard how my parents responded when an older sibling was suspected of smelling like pot or booze: Drugs were irresponsible and dangerous, and nothing good would come of them. So I learned from my brother's and sisters' mistakes: First and foremost, do not get caught. It was easy to avoid my parents, to sneak in and out of the house. Our family routine was markedly different now that I was a teenager. My oldest sister and older brother had long since moved out on their own. My job after school at the deli kept me out until after dark, so we rarely even ate together. The little I saw of my parents was like roommates moving past each other as they went out the door in the morning.

There is little unique about my own first trip, except for the fact that it took place on a mountain of anticipation, fears, and expectations. I needed some guide, some map, some sense of not only what to look forward to, but also what I should be on the lookout for. Where else could I look, except to those who had come before me? A voice was calling to me through the decades, an echo in the wilderness of the suburbs.

In the 1940s, Aldous Huxley, the writer of *Brave New World*, was developing his notion of the perennial philosophy, the idea that the variety of religious traditions, despite their difference in practice, are all attempts to unite human beings with their true divine nature and reveal the great reality behind the world of appearances. For Huxley, the Hindu tradition known as Vedanta beautifully synthesized the perennial philosophy and also happened to be a perfect antidote to what many intellectuals perceived to be a Western material and spiritual crisis.

Simply, Vedanta is the body of philosophical teachings that underlie Hindu religion. While someone might worship Krishna, and someone else Ganesh, these deities are simply manifestations of Brahman, the supreme reality in all things. For the Vedantist, the aim of life is to realize that human beings are divine and to recognize that all religious traditions are essentially the same. What makes Vedanta unique is that it recognizes all religious traditions as illuminating aspects of the divine, and, more important, that many of these traditions have produced an enlightened being who seeks to show others the way.

The most important of the Vedic literature, *The Upanishads*, reveals that what we call the soul (Atman) and what we call God (Brahman) are in fact not separate at all, but are a single, joyous, bountiful whole. Brahman and Atman are one. For Huxley, this was the supreme truth of human existence—our absolute divine nature.

The East has always held an unusual attraction for intellectuals and artists, and as early as the 1930s, a few brave souls actually attempted encounters with the religious practice of Vedanta when the yogi Swami Prabhavananda was teaching Eastern philosophy at the Vedanta Society of Southern California. Not long after its opening, the center began to attract noted thinkers and writers, among them the novelist Christopher Isherwood, who for a time was the editor of *Vedanta and the West*, the official journal of the society. Huxley also became closely associated with the Vedanta Society and contributed many essays to its journal.

As an imported spiritual philosophy, Vedanta worked wonders for the intellectual class. It offered metaphysical speculation without superstitions, divine contemplation without gods. It also acted as a reaction against a kind of mysticism that over time had become equated with the occult and spiritualism. Vedantists warned that while psychic and supernatural powers

were a normal consequence of traversing from our waking consciousness to the supreme reality, it was easy to believe that these
represented the highest kinds of spiritual truth.

Then, in the spring of 1953, Aldous Huxley took mescaline under the supervision of Humphrey Osmond, a Canadian
psychiatrist who had been doing research related to hallucinogenic drugs and schizophrenia. Huxley was very excited. A
month before Osmond was to arrive, Huxley wrote to arrange
their meeting and seemed worried that it might take some time
before they could actually get their hands on the mescaline—
the psychotropic agent, found in the peyote cactus, that various Native Americans have long used for religious ceremonies,
mostly in Mexico. For them, peyote is a living spirit and the
use of the plant involves complex rituals and mythology. This
reverence must not have been transmitted by the synthesized
version; Huxley just couldn't wait. "Meanwhile," he wrote, "do
you have any of the stuff on hand?"

Huxley's mescaline trip, reported in his 1954 book, *The Doors
of Perception*, is probably the most poetically realized of its kind. It
underscored an idea that shifted the English schoolteacher's son's
entire spiritual outlook. This notion was that the brain and the
central nervous system, rather than being the seat of awareness
and perception, are actually filters that prevent human beings from
being overwhelmed by what Huxley calls Mind at Large. This
inherent omni-consciousness is actually capable of having total
understanding of the whole universe all at once. Being human,
consequently, means having to filter most, if not all, of Mind at
Large so that we can go about the business of making babies, com-
puters, and nation-states. Mescaline, as well as other psychotropic
drugs and other, more rigorous methods, like fasting, can open the
valve and let true reality flow unimpeded.

Huxley's experience was one of both aesthetic and spiritual
revelations, owing to the "excessive, too obvious glory" of

flowers, draperies, and music. Within this hidden holiness of things, he was also, at one moment, overwhelmed by his own corruptibility. In one of the most profound moments of this little book, Huxley becomes aware of the total spiritual significance of the universe and the human incapacity to measure up, to be worthy of such insight.

After his mescaline experience, Huxley no longer believed that true visionary experience was limited to a religiously disciplined life, which was surprising given that during his association with Vedanta, he had written forcefully about the necessity for sacrifice and discipline and warned of the danger of being fooled into believing that a piece of psychic pyrite is spiritual gold: "At present there is a lamentable tendency to confound the psychic with the spiritual, to regard every supernormal phenomenon, every unusual mental state as coming from God." Once Huxley had established for himself the efficacy of mescaline, he thought better of urging a rigorous spiritual preparation before one could attain "a direct apprehension of Reality and Eternity." Why, Huxley asked, would the person seeking this experience waste his or her time with meditation and fasting, when modern chemistry had synthesized Soma, the nectar of the gods?

This turnaround would deeply affect his relationship with the Vedanta Society and set the stage for how many Eastern gurus in the West would deal with the rising tide of psychedelic drug use in their midst. Swami Prabhavananda, Huxley's teacher, was so distressed by his student's new method and ideas about the nature of the religious experience that he was actually concerned for the state of Huxley's soul. According to the nun Pravrajika Vrajaprana, who lives at the Vedanta Society, "Swami Prabhavananda was *virulently* opposed to people taking psychedelic drugs with the idea that it could provide some sort of illumination or spiritual help." In an interview, Prabhavananda echoed

Huxley's earlier belief: "Drugs may induce psychic visions, which, to a man ignorant of mystical visions, may appear as spiritual."

When Vrajaprana was younger, she struggled with similar distinctions but eventually followed the advice of her guru: "Prabhavananda would not even give meditation instruction to anyone until they had stopped taking drugs, even smoking marijuana, for six months. Needless to say, that definitely cramped my teenage style, but I was grateful for his care and concern and I followed his instructions."

To fully understand Huxley's new position, it's important to understand that in some ways he was not merely backpedaling, but evolving. Huxley was deeply influenced by religious mystical traditions and his own practice, but he was also a modern, and wanted to understand how more "secular" kinds of visionary experiences were as legitimate, if not arising from the same impulse, as religiously motivated ones. Saints were not the only ones to experience Mind at Large; Huxley believed that artists possessed a kind of intuitive visionary instinct that required neither fasting nor drugs, exemplified by the visionary artist William Blake.

Huxley's title of his now classic book comes from a quote by Blake from his long poem *The Marriage of Heaven and Hell*: "If the doors of perception were cleansed everything would appear to man as it is: Infinite." Would Blake himself have thought his own visions were in the same category as a mescaline user's? Blake, born in 1757 and prone to visions his whole life, did not subscribe to orthodox religious beliefs but was deeply spiritual, as his art reflected. According to the scholar Laura Quinney, what Blake meant by "cleansing the doors of perception" was that sensual pleasure would reveal that the "whole creation is infinite and holy." As for mescaline, Quinney suggests, "On the one hand, Blake might have been intrigued by the 'vision-inducing' capacity of drugs and on the other he might have thought it a cheat and a fraud to get there by any means other than pure imagination." Huxley, however, did not see a difference between pure imagination and pure spirit, both different names for the same ultimate reality contained in the Mind at Large.

The publication of *The Doors of Perception* was nothing scandalous—just radical enough to elicit the notice of many people and to warrant a review in the *New York Times*. The critic Berton Roueché wrote in 1954 that while he enjoyed Huxley's report, he had wished for "a somewhat fuller account of exactly what happened, both objectively and mechanistically, on that recent bright May morning." The critics mostly humored the beloved author of *Brave New World*. Then, a year after Huxley published *The Doors of Perception*, a religion scholar and recent convert to Catholicism, R. C. Zaehner, took 0.4 milligram of mescaline, the same amount Huxley had taken, except Zaehner complemented his dose with a "1/2 tablet of Dramamine to prevent possible nausea." Zaehner wanted to make sure he was giving a fair assessment in what would ultimately be a series of books criticizing Huxley and the new culture of drug-assisted mysticism. Zaehner, already predisposed to a religious awareness, found nothing mystical about mescaline. In fact, he spent most of his trip giggling. He called his experience a "farce."

Zaehner's trip, which reads like that of a stoned teenager watching Bugs Bunny cartoons, is described in *Mysticism Sacred and Profane*, a thorough takedown of Huxley. Zaehner was scared. He was thinking of the younger generation and those crazy beatniks who were meditating and twisting themselves with yoga, the same generation for whom dogma had usurped whatever had been mystical and socially conscious about Christianity. They called for a religion that was experiential. "Experience," however, was a word that seemed to be at odds with morality.

The older generation saw the cry for experience as just another way to act without conscience, another way to pursue pleasure.

The general exoticism of the East and, more specifically, Huxley's embrace of Vedanta were for Zaehner a "total rejection of everything that modern civilization stands for," and if this was the path that brought Huxley to mescaline, then his rejection of those values would surely deepen and calcify. Zaehner's bigger worry was the raising of an Eastern rafter over the roof of Christianity. If the human soul and the pure being of the universe are one and the same, then there is no relationship between God and human beings that can be meaningful in any real sense. It is an affront to the very core of what it means to be Christian. We are not "one with God," but rather His creatures, cast from His presence in the Garden, and crawling back to Him through the mulch of our sin, and thank God for that. By his second book, *Zen, Drugs and Mysticism*, Zaehner showed his hand of what he was really troubled by: dropouts and their "Eastern mysticism, drugs, pop music, and of course, sex."

Following Zaehner, other theologians warned against throwing traditions into some kind of cosmic soup that tries to reduce them to their common elements, rather than their important cultural and theological differences. Nevertheless, Huxley's attempt to show a common transcendent principle underlying all religions and visionary experience was one of the most important contributions to the spiritual life of the West. Even more profound was the suggestion, the promise, that we were all of us capable of these encounters with what his friend Humphrey Osmond called a "pinch of psychedelic."

I discovered *The Doors of Perception* in the school library, hoping to read Huxley's own mescaline trip as a blueprint for what might be in store for me if I ever got up the nerve. But something was missing. All of Huxley's inner adventures happen in a quaint and cozy sitting room, polite conversation with Osmond guiding the experience. I was hoping for a trip into the aether that might involve a little more than sitting in a comfortable room, looking at the drapes. I still had Tolkien and Rush as guiding principles, and my lost friend Jacob's mania looked nothing like Huxley's lilies that "seemed to be standing on the very brink of utterance." *The Doors of Perception*, despite what I perceived as its significance, was kind of square. More important, Huxley's descriptions didn't plug into the circuitry in my head, which was slowly being rewired. He could see that within even the legs of a chair, some Platonic reality could be gleaned, but something about his experience was inactive, without risk. One more flip through the library's card catalog would change everything, though.

"Seeing is not so simple and only the smoke can give you the speed you need to catch a glimpse of that fleeting world. Otherwise you will only look." Don Juan said this to his stubborn student Carlos Castaneda, and those words sent an unconscious shock wave through the collective mind of spiritual seekers everywhere. The book is *A Separate Reality*, and in it Castaneda describes his return to the Mexican shaman, whom he first described meeting in *The Teachings of Don Juan: A Yaqui Way of Knowledge*. Don Juan had schooled him in what Castaneda calls "nonordinary reality," which can be experienced through the use of peyote and other hallucinogenic plant mixtures. Castaneda begins to understand, through his experiences and encounters with a spiritual being called Mescalito, that the perceptible world is a veil that hides a deeper, magical reality. Castaneda turns into a crow, learns to fly, and eventually takes the great leap of faith by jumping into an abyss in the desert. For the seekers of the sixties, what appeared to be real anthropological data by an objective researcher proved the spiritual power of psychedelics.

The world of Don Juan and his teachings was one where every-thing was divine; plants, animals, stones, and sky all pulsed with holiness. This was not a mysticism that abandoned the world in favor of a cloister or a monastery. It was a mysticism that began with reading the text of the world, a text hidden in the flutter of leaves or the smoke of a fire and spoken in the secret language of hallucinogenic plants. Imagine it. Never mind magic spells; knowledge could literally be eaten. Castaneda went on to write twelve books and developed a strong following, although most agree that what he wrote was largely fiction; the man himself remained reclusive and secretive until his death in 1998.

In the beginning of *A Separate Reality*, Castaneda returns to Don Juan after having made a decision to never again smoke the mixture of mushrooms or eat the peyote buttons that first initi-ated him into the way of the warrior, but after being mesmer-ized by a number of inexplicable circumstances (such as when another sorcerer, Don Genaro, seemingly jumps across a water-fall), he is compelled to start his lessons again. Don Juan teaches Castaneda about allies, powerful supernal beings that can take the form of crows, animals, even people. To meet his personal ally, something like a trickster guardian angel, Castaneda has to smoke Don Juan's fungal tobacco until the time comes when he can call forth his ally at will.

Don Juan's message, transmitted to me through both decades and Castaneda's own wild imaginings, was that anything at any time could be carrying a portent meant only for me. It set the foundation for not only what I hoped to experience with LSD and other hallucinogens, but also the delusions I would later suffer. Of the few books in my high school library on mysticism, drugs, and sixties culture, Castaneda's stood out for a number of reasons, some more superficial than others. In the first place, Castaneda could be read as pure fantasy literature, filled with sorcerers, shape-changers, strange landscapes, and prophetic visions. But the only thing that seemed certain was that to effect the necessary change in the author, Don Juan had to give him peyote and mushrooms.

I knew there was no way I could procure a cactus that is found mainly in the Mexican desert. I felt so far away from all of it. This was not my story. True or false, Don Juan's world was not mine. I was trapped in the suburbs, trapped in the town-house association with my parents, trapped by what I thought were the closed and parochial minds of my peers and my town. I would never be able to take peyote; I would never find a shaman teacher. My only option was street-grade LSD. Five dollars a hit, with nary a coyote in sight.

At first I thought I hadn't gotten a good dose. The tab had an illustration of a phoenix rising out of its own flames, so I was waiting impatiently to be consumed. I didn't know there would be a delay before it got going. When the acid did kick in, I could feel myself beginning on a course of burning up and being reborn over and over again for the rest of the night. Up and down, up and down, doing everything I could to hold on, and then letting the acid take me wherever it would next.

We were sitting between the trailers of eighteen-wheeled trucks somewhere in a parking lot in the North End of Boston. My friend Randy and I, both of us just shy of seventeen, had come into the city to buy fireworks, literally out of the back of someone's van. We each got a bag filled with bottle rockets, Roman candles, firecrackers, M-80s, and bloom flowers. Then Randy suggested we go sit in between the trucks, smoke a few joints, and take the acid. I didn't know where he had gotten it from, but he had four hits arranged in a perforated square. He tore one off carefully and handed it to me. I hoped in the dim light of the lot he couldn't see my hand shaking as I laid it on my tongue.

We smoked one joint after another, and slowly I could feel an extra pulse in my chest, alongside my heart, at slightly different intervals. It was an echo of my hearing, but not quite in sync, until every sight and sound reverberated. My insides and outsides were the same. The pulse was from the world, which often felt as familiar as if it were located in my body, and then the next moment it was something alien, something so unlike me, it almost had the quality of mockery. Of making fun of me. Then the whole thing burst into fireworks, as if the ones we had bought were being accidentally set off in the bags next to us. Fireworks over and over again, the pulse now the popping of a million tiny explosions all around us.

I had to walk. Randy had to also. Sometimes it was like we could read each other's minds, but mostly we were just being set upon by different psychic animals. We would glance at each other for practical purposes—which way to go, what we should do when we arrived wherever we ended up, when to sit down, when to get up again—and somehow we knew that we had to catch the bus back home at a certain time.

We eventually found ourselves in an arcade. It wasn't until I had been pumping quarters into the game Space Castle for forty-five minutes that I realized I was peaking. I could not, would not, stop playing the game. There was something far beyond the mere destruction of pixels taking place. My very soul was at stake, my fate bound up in the quickly moving sprites and the twist of my wrist as it controlled the joystick.

On the way home, I sat in the back of the bus, carefully taking drags of a cigarette I held out an open window. I watched the streetlights and the headlights, waiting for one of them to be a different kind of light, to be a vibration from heaven sent to open something in me. For most of the trip I had been wavering between terror and bliss. Even though I was here in the city, the ancient spirits should have found me, the acid acting as a radio, tuning my psychic frequency into the perfect spiritual beacon. Instead I was speeding along the highway toward my house in the suburbs. I thought we could somehow make it to the golf course before I needed to go home, that maybe I had gone too far from my sacred space. I shouldn't be on this bus at all. I should be running alongside it, traveling through hyperspace, headlong into truth. Somehow this was so different from what I had imagined. Something was not right, or the acid was no good, or something, possibly, was wrong with me. Where were the crows with frightful but beautiful eyes delivering omens to me? Where was the sorcerer who would teach me how to *see*?

Despite my experiments with acid, it was weed sprinkled with pieces of black hash that wound up clarifying my path. Randy's mother was gone for the day, and we sat in his kitchen while I watched him roll joint after stupendous joint. Randy had become a master roller, capable of churning out spliffs that were five or six papers long, two papers wide, with the technique of an expert cigar maker. Most of our days, in some form or another, had come to involve getting baked. This meant looking for, buying, and then rolling and sorting as much as it actually meant taking drugs.

Our preference was marijuana, and because our northern Boston suburb was in a choice location, we had ample options. Situated between Lynn—a working-class town kept afloat by a General Electric factory that built turbine engines—and the very well-to-do coastal town of Marblehead, Swampscott got its pot from every approach. For Marblehead, the whole of the coast from Gloucester to Salem fed a steady supply. Lynn bumped up directly against Revere, where drugs flowed like the Nile from Boston through Chelsea and Everett. We only ever had to go as far as Lynn or sometimes Salem, but usually there was an older

townie who probably scored pounds directly from the boats off
the Swampscott piers.

I watched with trembling expectation as Randy tore tiny
bits of the moist hashish and dropped them along the row of
marijuana that lined the open rolling paper. He twisted the
ends and finished it off. I had smoked hash only once before.
A small chunk had been pierced with a band pin (likely R.E.M.
or Ultravox) from someone's jacket. The whole thing was lit
until it was a small burning mass. A glass was placed over it
until it extinguished. When enough smoke filled the vacuum,
I raised the rim just enough to get my mouth under and inhale
the smoke. It didn't work as well as the aesthetic ritual looked.

This time with Randy, though, I consumed the hash perfectly
along with the pot, and by the end of the joint I was thoroughly
stoned. When we had finished smoking, my throat was burning
and something had shifted in me. My consciousness felt like a
morning glory right before the sun. I could sense what was possible, and my old way of thinking about my life, about girls,
about the world outside—fearful and anxious and unwilling to
take risks of any kind—was burned away with the joint.

I had never been in Randy's kitchen before, and it took on an
alien, almost hostile quality. His mother didn't like me, and this
was her domain. (I was surprised Randy was willing to spark
up in there, but he found his own little defiances wherever he
could.) A vague feeling of hopelessness started to cloud my
buzz. I was staring at the cabinet below the kitchen sink and
noticed one of the doors was slightly off its hinges. It was metal,
with little flecks of chipped enamel. I had never before seen anything so devoid of meaning, so empty of significance. A sickness
stirred. I noticed all the old stains, the crumbs, the tiny cracks
in the paint. But there was no deeper fault line below, no abyss
where I could have easily imagined little devils carving infernal
poems into the sulfuric columns. There was no hell below or

heaven above or the span of a universe around us. Just this: this crummy kitchen and my giggling wasted friend.

Nothing I longed for could be found here in the suburbs— now I was certain. Pulling books off the library shelf, my own resin-stained fingers pressing onto the prints of all the kids who had come before, looking for the same thing—a way out, an experience that would reveal the secret language of the cosmos, or just something more than jocks and cheerleaders and teachers and principals—was getting me nowhere. All these ideas in books and at the end of the joint or on the surface of a hit of blotter were just more of the same. Kitchens, bedrooms, golf courses, drugstores, malls, and Chinese restaurants. God wasn't here. Dungeons & Dragons would never get me to the real secret treasure, and even Tolkien's elven language was not the true grammar of a lost civilization.

A little bit of acid, lots of weed, too much Castaneda, and I was ready to move from the magical realm of Middle-earth into a world that was much stranger than any fiction involving stout hairy dwarves and tall white wizards. I sought a world where people took risks with their bodies and their minds, where music fed ideas and action, where sex was not a mysterious ideal but a tangible thing involving jeans and bra straps and saliva. I wanted to find Bifröst, the rainbow bridge that connects mortals to the gods, in the world I inhabited, not a fantasy that ultimately had gotten me little more than picked on and isolated. I didn't quite know it yet, but what I wanted was rock 'n' roll.

chapter three

MUSIC OF THE SPHERES

It's 1982 and I am so fucking high. I'm floating on air. For a split second I look down and below me are dozens of strangers, dozens of kids with shaved heads and Mohawks, T-shirts and leather jackets. I come down into their arms, safe, and they toss me up again, smiling, laughing, shouting. I have never met them before, have been in this room with them for less than an hour, yet they are jostling me as if I am their own little brother. I look up and six or seven more kids are coming down after me.

I am tossed around, and at ninety pounds I float easily along a sea of upstretched and supporting hands. The place is the Channel, a stinking sweaty nightclub on Boston's wharf. It's packed. People of all ages and persuasions are here to see the show. Skinheads, metalheads, straight-edge kids, skate punks, even a few old-school hippie-punks. Mostly people are on the outer edges, surrounding a swirling mass of skinny teenage bodies in the center: the pit.

I look around at all my friends. Never before have I had so many friends. Flea (no relation to the bassist for the Red Hot Chili Peppers), a tall, ominous skinhead in suspenders and combat boots, is in a reverie. He is skanking—arms pumping, legs kicking around the pit—without being aware of anyone else. Yet his own dancing depends upon the rhythm and energy of those about him. There are so many of us, all skinny punks with our leather jackets, our good-hearted sneers, our little fists rarely making contact. But our bodies do as we jostle and push, bounce and flail. I am smaller than most of the kids here, but I feel safe. I know when to duck. I have mistimed it before, however, and know the jarring sting of an elbow grazing across my temple.

I look for an opening onto the stage, find it, cut through the churning circle, and hop up next to the lead singer. He sees me and pushes the mic into my face. I sing into it and then I leap again, and oh my God, I am higher than I have ever been before. When I land on the upturned hands, I crawl along the heads and shoulders in the crowd until I am standing again in the middle of the pit, realizing I have no choice but to dance or get crushed. Flea is still there, dancing with his eyes closed.

I had met Flea a year before, at the now defunct Storyville in Kenmore Square. The Violent Femmes were playing a sold-out Boston gig, and the club was filled to capacity. I wanted to dance, to get on the stage, but it was so crowded there was no way to move from my spot. I kept trying to climb up on people's shoulders, something that at a hardcore show was considered a polite invitation to be lifted up over the crowd. While there were certainly a number of punks at the show, it seemed the majority of kids were in from the suburbs, as I was. But they were all new to this scene and not quite up on the etiquette.

I kept bouncing, trying to get a leg up, when suddenly someone tapped me on the shoulder. I turned around to see a towering skinhead with a freshly gleaming skull. His hands were cupped together, offering a step, and I put my boot into his intertwined fingers. He lifted me up with one try and I was off, sailing over the crowd, until I came down onto their heads. They had no choice but to keep me up. I flew along the rafters and the lights, finally coming back down where I had started, in front of Flea, his hand outstretched for a handshake.

My best friend at the time, a greasy third-generation Beatles fanatic, would take me to his dealer's house to score a dime bag. She was an aging hippie, forever stoned beyond measure, but a suave businesswoman. She was nice enough and she had the choicest herb, but she was always impatient with me, irritated and on edge the minute I walked in the door with my army-official combat boots, Dead Kennedys T-shirt, and leather bracelets. She saw my punk weltanschauung as an affront to everything she had been in the sixties. She could not accept that there were new names for the things we both idealized. I may as well have been a young Republican in her eyes.

Hardcore, the bastard child of punk rock, came into its own during the early eighties after the punk rock of the seventies started getting a little old and shaggy. Punk was a direct attack against the large-scale world of commercial rock at the time—big arenas, big hair, big clothes, and lots of sex and drugs. Simpler song structures, smaller venues, and a guitar, bass, and drum kit were all you needed to start a revolution. But soon, the once exciting and daring seventies punk started to look like the hippies: not much more than aging dropouts having sex, taking drugs, and drinking to excess. To the younger generation of would-be freaks, punk looked a lot like everything else adults had gotten their hands on and ruined. There was nothing here for the next generation, which was hoping for music to signal the start of its own adolescent rebellion. The energy was right, but the track marks were all wrong.

Around the turn of the decade, bands from the West Coast were providing the soundtrack to the burgeoning youth culture raised on skateboards and surfboards. Dead Kennedys, Circle Jerks, and Black Flag were putting on energized all-ages shows in halls and church basements. Around the same time, a bunch of kids from Washington, D.C., started a record label and infamous squat called Dischord House, home to bands like Minor Threat, Faith, Void, and Government Issue. Soon, all around the country, small all-ages venues opened and bands rose up out of the suburbs.

A scene emerged with new values: unity, anti-authority, a kind of disgust for the excess of the late seventies. For many of these kids, a new submovement called straight-edge was a middle finger to their ex-hippie parents and older siblings. No drugs, no alcohol, no promiscuous sex—just music, dancing, skateboarding, making flyers and fanzines, and roaming the streets in packs.

While my new friends and I were far from straight-edge, being with them was a salve to my fretfulness. We got stoned together. And there was sex. My early teen fumblings didn't make me a very good lover, but I finally discovered the energy behind what so much rock 'n' roll was about. Every day I took the bus to Boston, and then the Red Line to Harvard Square. By five o'clock there were a dozen or so kids gathered, all of us in flannel, spiked hair, flattops, and some Mohawks, leather jackets and wristbands, everything covered in stickers, buttons, and pieces of cloth attached with safety pins. The first thing we did was get stoned and share a bottle. Panhandling for change in the Square, we pooled our money and bought cheap schnapps and lousy, seed-ridden pot. We had sex wherever we could, wrestled, made fun of tourists, smoked clove cigarettes, and most of the time did almost nothing at all but sit on the short brick wall in front of Au Bon Pain, which we called the Pit.

For a while, my friends satiated the part of me that was afraid and anxious about God and hidden meaning. The unease that throbbed constantly under my skin was quieted by a good buzz, by the energy of dancing, yelling, and laughing. We walked along the streets as if we owned the city, all of us under eighteen, made invulnerable by apple wine and each other.

The long-haired heavy-metal kids, with their collarless brown leather jackets and tan work boots, always stood outside the Store 24 across the street from the Pit. Heavy metal and its fans represented all the excess in music and pop culture we were against: long hair, noodling guitar solos, and ten-piece drum kits. We all, in our own way, imagined one day we would rumble, like the Jets and the Sharks, dancing our way down Massachusetts Avenue, flashing our spiked leather bracelets, stomping heads with our combat boots. Everything we did and imagined had rhythm and beat, even though it was only three chords deep.

Every day we walked our way from the river to the Pit and back again, then over to Tommy's Pizza for a few games of Spy Hunter and a slice of thin pizza that you pinched in half, raised at an angle, and let the grease spill out of before taking a bite. That rhythm was in everything, even the way we talked and how we imagined our fights would be—just like when we slam-danced and skanked around the wide floor of the Channel, except that on the day we came upon the heavy-metal kids, our little fists would connect.

The aging hippies who asked us for weed and the baby boomer tourists who snapped pictures of us saw us as some kind of alien species, not their children, but the kids of some irradiated misfits who spent too much time in front of their microwave ovens. We felt the same. Theirs was a failed revolution that brought nothing to the world but tie-dye, guitar jams that went on far too long, and patchouli-scented incense. We would never admit how much we had in common, how much the punks owed the hippies for carving out a whole system on which every counter-cultural movement thereafter would subsist. We had no idea that our all-ages flyers were just DIY versions of psychedelic rock show posters, that our shows were in halls rented decades earlier for experimental theater and acid-rock concerts. We couldn't fathom how even our LSD had found its way across the years because a square Harvard professor named Timothy Leary had urged all young people to turn on. For all our color and energy and inverted fashion, we would always be indebted to the spin of dynamism that characterized the Beats, the proto-hippies, and the hippies themselves, from the East Village to Haight-Ashbury and beyond.

The early sixties started to reshape ideas about the inner and the outer, the personal and the political. People started to imagine that maybe the shape of our consciousness was the same as the shape of the universe. Why were we so bent on creating these dichotomies? people began to ask. Huxley had already explained that what had once been thought of as a special kind of experience to be had only by prophets and saints was available to everyone. All we had to do was turn off that filter, that part of our brain that kept us tethered to a stale and mostly unworkable reality, one replete with war, racism, sexual hang-ups, and morality built on an authority of without, rather than an ethic from within.

In California, Ken Kesey was experiencing a different kind of trip, that of being a best-selling author and rebel darling of the media. But there was something else that was energizing him. A few years before he published *One Flew Over the Cuckoo's Nest* in 1962, Kesey was invited by a friend to participate in a CIA-sponsored research project at Stanford, studying the effects of hallucinogenic drugs. LSD was legal, and no one had even yet considered it as a tool for social and political liberation. But Kesey knew there was something special about these drugs, LSD in particular. He got a job at a veterans' hospital where some of the drug experiments were being done and was able to smuggle some acid out for his friends.

Eventually Kesey set up shop in La Honda, where he developed the idea for what would come to be known as acid tests. In the spring of 1964, Kesey and a group of people including Neal Cassady—Jack Kerouac's muse for the semifictional character Dean Moriarty in *On the Road*—and Kesey's friend Ken Babbs, an ex-marine and helicopter pilot, painted a 1939 school bus in Day-Glo colors and became known as the Merry Pranksters. From La Honda to New York, they were a massive living organism, one part surreal theater collective, one part pharmaceutical company. Tom Wolfe, in *The Electric Kool-Aid Acid Test* (a book that reads like an authorized account, but which many of the Pranksters looked upon with a bit of disdain), describes it as a mad experiment, both spiritual and psychological: "The trip, in fact, the whole deal, was a risk-all balls-out plunge into the unknown, and it was assumed merely that more and more of what was already inside a person would come out and expand, gloriously or otherwise."

But was it a quest for enlightenment, as future generations would come to see it? As Ken Babbs would tell it, "[Being on the bus] probably had spiritual ramifications, but we were too busy to talk about it." Once they arrived back in San Francisco, the Pranksters put on what are the now infamous Acid Tests.

As Tom Wolfe describes them, the Acid Tests of the midsixties were simply an enlarged version of the parties that Kesey had in La Honda. The Pranksters rented huge spaces and put up flyers that asked, "Can you pass the acid test?" The halls were wired with sound systems, film projectors, microphones, and strobe lights. Add the long LSD-fueled jams by the Grateful Dead and hundreds of dancing, tripping bodies, and the look and feel and sound of the counterculture were set for the rest of the decade. Wolfe explains that everything from acid rock to psychedelic poster art was formed out of the swirling flashing organic mass of the Acid Tests.

In 1966, the Acid Tests gave way to the three-day-long Trips Festival at Longshoreman's Hall in San Francisco, spearheaded by Stewart Brand, better known as a utopian futurist and the author of the *Whole Earth Catalog*. The Trips Festival combined the Acid Tests with experimental theater, drum-and-bugle corps, performance art, and copious amounts of LSD provided by the in-house chemist Owsley Stanley III. The program for the festival describes the events of January 21 as

America needs indians, sensorium 9-slides, movies, sound-tracks, flowers, food, rock 'n' roll, eagle lone whistle, indians (senecasm, chippewas, hopi, Sioux, blackfeet, etc.) & anthro-pologists, open theater, "revelations"—nude projections, "the god box" by ben jacopetti, the endless explosion, the congress of wonders, liquid projections, the jazz mice, the loading zone rock 'n' roll, steve fowler, amanda foulger, rain jacopetti, & the unexpectable.

What was the larger hope of events like the Trips Festival and, later, the Human Be-In, which took place in the January before the Summer of Love of 1967? To change the world? To get as many people high as possible while listening to the best music in the country? The underground newspaper *The Oracle* said of the Human Be-In that out of the event, "A new concept of human relations . . . must emerge, become conscious, and be shared so that a revolution of form can be filled with a Renaissance of compassion, awareness and love in the Revelation of the unity of mankind." High hopes, indeed.

Gary Duncan of Quicksilver Messenger Service, one of the bands on the bill, never wanted to change the world. "Nor do I think anything we or anyone else did or could change the world," he recounts. "What would be the point? If creation is perfect, who are we to think we should even consider changing what creation labored so hard to construct in the first place?" Duncan and many others considered themselves artists first and foremost, not revolutionaries and certainly not spiritual leaders—just a bunch of kids who were pretty good with a musical instrument and who loved to get high.

The clown prince of the counterculture, Wavy Gravy, would beg to differ. One of the early peace activists, Wavy thought for a time that by expanding people's consciousness, they would come to see the futility and idiocy of war. If they looked at the world through a spiritual lens, they would perceive all people as part of a greater unity. He often said, "We're all the same person trying to shake hands with ourselves." Wavy and many others believed that psychedelics were a window into the possibility of leading meaningful lives without war and materialism.

But this was not how both history and the media would spin it. It's true that by this time Haight-Ashbury had become the premier point of departure for some of the most seminal psychedelic bands of the sixties, including the Grateful Dead, Jefferson Airplane, Country Joe and the Fish, and the aforementioned Quicksilver Messenger Service. It also drew together every kind of young person looking for the focal point of counterculture. The newspapers might have missed the point, but they loved the color. According to Charles Perry writing for *Rolling Stone*, the whole country was gawking at Haight-Ashbury: "Between March and September 1967, virtually every major publication and certainly every TV network did at least one story on the 'Hashbury.'" One *New York Times* editorial defined the Haight-Ashbury aesthetic as the "cop-out": "wearing guru suits and hair, attending 'be-ins,' making a to-do about Oriental philosophy, not paying the rent, using marijuana gaspers, talking about universal love, saying 'to hell with the government,' and so forth."

In an article on the Haight for the *New York Times Magazine*, Hunter S. Thompson recounted the essential problem with trying to write about the hippies in "Hashbury." The only way to really get the full story was to be part of the culture, but because of the strict drug laws, "to write from experience would be an admission of felonious guilt." No one who wasn't part of the scene could really be trusted. "'Love' is the password in the Haight-Ashbury but paranoia is the style," Thompson lamented.

The hippies and the squares couldn't always agree as to what was actually going on, but sometimes one can locate an honest and unsparing look at the daily life of a kid in Haight-Ashbury. Joan Didion's unflinching piece of New Journalism "Slouching Towards Bethlehem" recounts her days spent amongst the misspent youth: the runaways, the good-natured activists who gave their young children acid, and the paranoid radicals who didn't trust anyone. Didion's essay has moments of humor, and sometimes a sense that these young people were motivated by more than just the next high, but there is an undercurrent of darkness and sadness. No one really knows what's next, and getting enough to eat, with some money left over for a joint or two, lies heavy, like thick hashish smoke. Didion meets meth and dope users; even the acid is cut with methadrine.

As much as things seemed right for the people in Haight-Ashbury, it is apparent that the experiment in squatting and staying high could quickly go wrong. "Slouching Towards Bethlehem" is prescient, not only because of the way hard drugs would take over, but because the coming disillusionment is in the air, even as one character Didion meets, Max, is still finding his glory: "You can get high on a mantra," he says, "but I'm holy on acid."

What I knew intuitively about the suburbs became abundantly clear in the form of the way I was treated just because I wore an earring and listened to unheard-of music by a bunch of unknown bands. I had never felt like I belonged, but being singled out as different, as a freak, felt in many ways like being branded a saint. It wasn't that I felt better than everyone in town; it was more a feeling of pity, that they were missing out on something greater than any of us could even realize. Music was just a beacon, a light showing the way to real experience. Drugs only amplified how vacant I thought the town really was.

It was all there for me in the city, from Harvard Square to the corner of Massachusetts Avenue and Newbury Street, where the drunks and punks hung out together outside the Trident Bookstore and Café. There was more than I had ever imagined to being in the company of all the misfits and the fringe dwellers, going to all the live shows, and taking all the drugs. But there was something else I hadn't been aware of before. It was a life unlike anything I had known, one where old men propositioned me on the street corner, where panhandlers shared their change to go in on a bottle of wine if you shared some weed. It was a world where girls knew more about sex than boys and would *kiss you in front of everyone*. It was a place where all things were equalized. I still felt like an outsider, but at some point this gave me a certain amount of credibility. I was willing to risk something to be here—the safety of a home and food that I knew not everyone had. Nevertheless, I still needed some of the comforts of home, and there was nothing more reassuring than comic books.

In the basement of a mixed-retail building in Harvard Square nests the venerable Million Year Picnic (MYP). MYP opened in 1974, when there wasn't quite such a thing as a comic-book store proper. The original owners also hoped to cater to the science fiction/fantasy crowd. MYP found that there was still an audience for underground comic books (or comix). For me, at seventeen, it was like finding a hidden layer, a world within a world that I thought I knew absolutely everything about already from reading Marvel Comics—sometimes violent, often sexual, mostly strange and dreamlike. I quickly understood that along with music, this psychedelic thing I was after could be found in every corner of the popular culture. You just had to dig one level deeper from wherever you were, and there it was.

Even so, the characters that were intimately familiar to me had taken on a new importance. The Silver Surfer, who had originally appeared as a regular foe/ally in the *Fantastic Four* comic book, had been given his own titular comic in the late sixties; reprints of these were easy to come by in a later series called *Fantasy Masterpieces*, often found in the twenty-five-cent bin in comic-book stores. The introspective Norrin Radd discovers that his planet is about to be eaten by the cosmic force of nature Galactus, the Devourer of Worlds. Willing to sacrifice himself to save his beloved Shalla-Bal, Norrin offers to become a herald to Galactus, whereby he will seek out other worlds to slake his new master's interstellar hunger. He eventually finds Earth and prepares the people for their coming doom, but of course the planet's protectors, the Fantastic Four, fight back. The Silver Surfer, recognizing the same sacrificial spirit in them that he once had, falls in love with humanity and vows to help stop Galactus. Galactus, angered at this betrayal, strips the Surfer of his space-faring powers, leaving him forever trapped on Earth.

As Stan Lee would write him in the later series, the Silver Surfer is a melancholy mystic, with knowledge and power greater than those of anyone on Earth. Page after page, the Surfer sits on his gleaming surfboard and broods. Every panel can be read as a desire to escape the bonds of mediocrity, to experience the vastness of the true cosmos. I strongly identified with all gloomy and strange Marvel characters: the Vision, a conflicted android who longs to be human but recognizes his superiority; Dr. Strange, master of the mystic arts, whose status is constantly threatened; and Adam Warlock, a genetic messiah even more depressive than the Silver Surfer.

But there in the corner of MYP, a shelf of comics glowed with titles like *Zap*, *Dope*, and *Rip Off Comix*. The covers alone reflected perfectly what was going on in my head: flying eyeballs with wings, twisted and profane figures surrounded by thought bubbles containing holy writ. On one cover, a giant penis cracked through the sidewalk as the people ran in terror. On another, a naked man was raised off the ground by rapturous electric currents through a wire with one end plugged into a wall socket, the other hooked up to his tenders. They were images somewhat familiar, reminiscent of old *MAD* magazines and Wacky Packages, but amped up on speed and acid. A shared sense of what the world begins to look like stoned made underground comix a kind of Esperanto among the counterculture. Most readers at the time would likely identify with something like Robert Crumb's strip where, panel by panel, a small suburban home and its surrounding landscape were slowly transformed into a yin-yang symbol and then, finally, into nothingness.

Other magazines and comics shared the same sensibility about bucking the Comics Code but felt more familiar to me, more like the images from Dungeons & Dragons, which had been engraved like primitive cave paintings on the inside of my head but were illuminated by a drug-fueled fire. *Heavy Metal* magazine had sex and violence alongside wizards and robots.

Epic Illustrated, Marvel Comics' own version of an adult illustrated magazine, had lots of naked women with swords, but it
also ran stories involving traditional superheroes cast in a more
mature, and oftentimes more surreal, light.

One issue even offered a story about Elric of Melniboné, the
great antihero developed by Michael Moorcock in the early sixties. Initially introduced to the public in a series of novellas, the
character fully took hold of the popular imagination with its
1972 self-titled novel. Elric was in many ways the anti-Tolkien
character, a brooding theocrat who used magic given to him by
demons. His people were a society of debauched elves, stoned
on strange hallucinogens and bored by their power and wealth.
Elric had to take copious amounts of drugs to keep his frail
body alive, but he eschewed those that caused hallucinations.
Elric, along with other works of science fiction and fantasy
found in comics, influenced psychedelic thought by grounding
it in an imaginary but tangible world.

Underground comix brought two worlds together for me:
images of fantastical, spiritual, and cosmic figures and forms,
and a method for social rebellion. When I wasn't in Harvard
Square, I was working hard to carve out an identity of radical
values and a punk rock ethos that could be sustained in the suburbs. Ironically, the only other nonconformists in high school
were the computer lab kids. The lab itself acted as a kind of hermetic chamber where esoteric lore was calculated on terminals
and printed out on noisy daisy-wheel teletypes. You could cut
class if you could get permission to be in the lab. I kept close
to those guys even as the world of the city and drugs pulled me
away like a new friend tugging on my sleeve. The computer lab
was a security blanket against the leering, pushing, threatening
jocks. In the lab, no one bothered you. No one came in who
didn't belong. It was the perfect antidote to the gym and locker
room. We listened to college radio while we tapped out BASIC

programs, and sometimes when I found myself in there alone, I would sneak a few hits from a small wooden pipe.

It was also in there that I began to groom myself as a young political activist, at least as far as high school was concerned. An older girlfriend would bring me to her library at the local state college, where they kept archival copies of all the underground student-run newspapers from the sixties and seventies. With a pocketful of dimes, I photocopied page after page. Back home, in the great tradition of the underground rags themselves, I cut and pasted my own fanzine, complete with the poetry and drawings of my friends, and even the musings of the aging grill cooks where I washed dishes every day after school. In the morning, I stood outside the school and pushed them into the hands of students and teachers alike. Later, I was to find out I had my school's equivalent of an FBI file, a dossier of whatever they could collect on me, which I assumed would be used against me if the opportunity presented itself.

My little fanzine was my last attempt to carve something out in my hometown, something that I hoped would gain me some respect while at the same time allowing me to raise my middle finger to the lot of it. It wasn't easy being a punk in my hometown. Even my stoner friend Randy began to resent my cropped hair as his grew longer. He thought the music I listened to was "noise"; coming from another kid my age, this was the worst kind of betrayal. If he didn't get it, then all of us were doomed. Soon our interactions were limited to an exchange of drugs and money.

Chris, a big, good-natured kid who loved to skateboard and loved music even more than I did, was my only real companion. We spent all afternoon in the abandoned lot behind my house or in the mall, getting stoned, smoking cigarettes, and listening to bands like Seven Seconds and Government Issue on a boom box whose handle was broken. We lugged the cumbersome thing all over town, through the golf course and outside school. That crappy tape player was a symbol of our steadfastness, our way to make some noise, to feel that righteous sense that can come only from being on the bottom of the social barrel. We were picked on regularly in school; our only recourse was to show up the next day having changed nothing about ourselves. It was the best "fuck you" in the world. No matter how much we were pressured to change, we stayed true to the one thing that gave us a sense of belonging to something great: punk rock.

For a while in the mid-eighties, mild blue blotter acid was the Harvard Square LSD of choice. My friend Colin, a slightly malevolent fellow, was all charisma and leather jacket, with short-cropped hair, wide daring eyes, and a kind of ironic rage, and spent his free time kicking side-view mirrors off cars in the business district. One early afternoon we dropped two hits apiece and met up with the rest of the kids in front of the subway. While we figured out what to do next, my leg transformed into a three-dimensional grid of cubes. Eventually it dissolved completely into a million tiny particles.

Allen, the quietest of us, had short, striking, spiked red hair that leapt from his head like little flames. He had taken to playing with a butterfly knife, a double-sided blade housed in a handle that can split in two. It could be, with practice, juggled around the fingers on one hand, rapidly opened and closed. While the blue blotter acid was fairly weak, it could suddenly pounce just when you were starting to think it wasn't going anywhere at all. I felt the acid surge, like a bare wire stuck into an electrical outlet, and became suddenly convinced that Allen's technique with the knife was all off. He had to keep starting over, and it was annoying me. I grabbed the knife from him, having never held it before, and started to spin it around my fingers. In a second or two, my hand whipping this way and that, blood was flying all over us. I had sliced into my thumb and was bleeding fast and strong.

One of us, Ruth probably, or Sue—the small, tough skinhead girls who always seemed to know what time it was, where we were supposed to be, and what time everyone needed to go home—swept me up and started walking me to the hospital with the rest of the group in tow. It was a mad, wonderful night. The acid had bonded all of us, maybe even more than the music ever had, and we walked like a pack down the street toward the clinic, all leather and boots and swagger. We were hysterical because of the bloody finger, and when we crashed through the doors of the emergency room, I could see us all as if from above, bug-eyed and laughing, the light of the hospital shining on our wasted faces, as if to illuminate for everyone that we were not of this world. We had touched the secret central heart of the universe and we would live forever.

The nurse who admitted me shooed away all my friends, except for Ruth, who stayed with me until I was stitched up. I had to hurry to Haymarket to catch the last bus, or I would have no way to get home. The walk back to the subway felt empty and disjointed. The acid was wearing off fast. There was something discomforting about my bandaged and throbbing finger. I felt homesick, at seventeen maybe too young to be out here on my own, taking too many drugs. But I also didn't want to be back there, where I would never unlock anything meaningful, where the only magic treasures were the imaginary ones in a Dungeons & Dragons module.

Nevertheless, I was fastened to my parents like a kite on a string; I felt I was flying, but one tug from them and I remained always within their reach. They still represented a kind of reprieve, in that if this adventure I was undertaking got out of control, there was the constant comfort of their familiar rhythms. As much as I tried to avoid them, a part of me ached to be near them, to just sit on the floor at their feet with a stack of comics while they did the crossword puzzle on a Sunday afternoon. I could sense they were trying to give me as much freedom as common sense allowed; only a few years earlier, I had been the shy, isolated kid with barely any friends who spent all his time preoccupied with maps drawn on graph paper and the names of the Avengers' constantly rotating membership. That I would take the bus by myself into the city to meet up with kids my age who were happy to see me must have given them a deep sense of relief. They saw I could be independent, take a few risks, get to know a world outside of endless dungeon passages. But once I pulled away a little, it was easy to keep going, knowing all the while that the heat and light of our home would be a beacon if I ever lost my way.

As I passed the Pit in the Square to get on the subway, Flea was sitting by himself, smoking a cigarette like he was stabbing it into his mouth with every drag. He told me he had no place to go and asked if I had any weed. I offered for him to come home with me, where I had a pin-bar joint in a locked metal box, along with some seeds and stems and a pipe that could possibly be scraped for resin. I had never seen this before. As much as getting high had become a daily habit for me, I had never before seen anyone look desperate for it. Flea was an enigma. I never knew where he lived or how; he was just always there, always in the Square, always at the shows, always ready to dance, always ready to fight.

During the ride home he was quiet and antsy, tapping his boot on the floor, which seemed to be timed to the throbbing of my bandaged finger. The bus let us off in front of the cemetery, across from the townhouse association where I lived. As we walked up the hill toward my unit, I saw it as if for the first time. I was ashamed and embarrassed. Now Flea knew I was a phony. I existed in the city as if I had escaped all this—the deadening manicured lawns and stout trees, the sliding glass doors that opened onto a small flat slab of concrete with the attendant gas grill and plastic lawn chairs. But it wasn't true. I came back here every night, never forgot to call if I was going to be late, went quietly into the house with the key I kept tucked into my back pocket, so I could grab a bagel and leftover lox from the refrigerator before I went into my room to sneak a few one-hitters before going to bed. I was a poseur. My mother had even sewn the Minor Threat patch on my jacket.

We snuck inside quietly, so as not to wake my parents. I took Flea to my room. At least the walls were covered in show flyers: Misfits and FUS at the Channel, GBH at the Rat, Dead Kennedys and DOA at the Waltham VFW. I rolled a towel up and put it across the seam between the closed bedroom door and the floor. We furtively smoked the thin and bitter joint, and the next thing I knew, Flea fell onto the couch and went to sleep.

The next morning, I hurriedly walked Flea out the door with nary a glance at my father as we passed. I'm not sure what embarrassed me more: my father's seeing me with a tall, vaguely malevolent skinhead or Flea's seeing my dad in his suburban habitat. It was not a big deal to have a friend sleep over, but Flea was obviously of another world entirely—the world of the street and of danger—and if we lingered at all, I worried the shock of the two of them being eye to eye would create a kind of atomic fission and something might explode.

As we took the bus back to the city, Flea talked about socialism and rebellion. We were not the same—he had come from a place of real struggle; he might even have lived on the streets. You could see the difference in our drug use and drinking: His had a desperation born of circumstance, whereas mine seemed more a result of neuroses and anxiety.

Nevertheless, I could identify with Flea's quiet rage. My days at school were getting worse, as the glares at me turned into threats of violence. One morning in gym, a particularly meat-headed football player took me by the throat and put me up against a locker, enraged that I would wear a chain fastened with a small lock around my neck. I took to skipping gym and spent the period hiding in a stall in the boys' bathroom, where I smoked cigarettes and drew band logos on the wall. Outside school, it wasn't much better. The town police started to harass me no matter what I was doing, merely because of my spiked hair, leather jacket, and earring. The mall where Chris and I spent so much of our time started to take on a sense of menace. Nothing there changed, and its perpetual ugliness and banality were oppressive: the greeting-card shop with its pewter figurines and smell of vanilla incense, the urine-coated-wood-chip stink and sadness of the pet shop, and the brown, wilted, untended plants in their standing pots.

Even at home, among the things I had once loved, boredom and irritation set in. The computer started to collect dust while I sat on the floor and pored over the complex, violent collages on my Crass records. Sometimes it felt a little weird and guilty to be stoned while listening to the straight-edge band Minor Threat, but a little reggae interlude on Bad Brains' *Rock for Light* record took care of that in a jiffy. The music beat down my anxiety and turned it into a kind of mild fury. I began to externalize the angst with every three-chord wallop and pummeling drum.

It was too late, though. A quicksand of spiritual yearning and bizarre mental habits was dragging down my meek anger. Punks didn't talk about God, and when they did it was to call out religion as another attempt to keep people defeated and make them conform. It was just another part of the system that contained parents and principals and Top 40 hits. This anti-authoritarian refrain translated into a generalized anti-religious sentiment. Anything with a top-down structure was to be distrusted, to be met with ridicule and sneers. At the time it felt impossible to be both punk and "spiritual,"[1] so I kept that side of myself out of the all-ages shows and most definitely out of the Pit in Harvard Square.

I suddenly had a secret among the only people I ever felt truly part of: I wasn't like them, either. I didn't really want to fight. I just wanted to groove on my slowly calcifying stoned perception that a secret spiritual meaning is contained in the caw of crows, the whisper of wind, a poem by William Blake, a glance from a girl from across a room. Part of the problem was that, Bad Brains reggae moments notwithstanding, there was little in hardcore that felt aligned with my burgeoning psychedelic insight. The focus of the music was too external, too much about finger pointing at parents and club bouncers and teachers. I needed something that better expressed an inner awareness while still telling the adult world to fuck off.

Then, in the autumn of 1984, I bought my first psychedelic record.

At a flea market in a parking lot, some guy had set up a table with boxes of records. I pulled one from the bin that had the same kind of homemade quality hardcore records had. The cover was a checkerboard pattern familiar to me from ska, but swirled into a kaleidoscopic pattern. It was a collection of what are called "nuggets," little psychedelic gems by mostly unknown bands from the sixties. When I handed my $5 over to the seller, he started chuckling and called out to his biker friends standing

---

1 Punks and spirituality seem like vinegar and baking powder, but as it turns out, while early hardcore kids saw the Christianity and Judaism of our parents as something to be distrusted, by the late eighties a few bands, notably the Cro-Mags and Youth of Today, turned to Hare Krishna. That movement's vegetarianism and contempt for materialism, and even their shaved heads, wild dancing, and straight-edge values, were the perfect outlet for a deepening sense of spiritual emptiness among many in the hardcore scene.

off to the side, smoking and drinking beers. They looked at me and also started laughing when he held up the record in the air for them to see. I turned red—a hardcore punk hugging a psyche record—and fled with my album.

When I sat down to listen, something inside me stirred. The music hinted at another possible reality, one that for a time punk rock had made irrelevant, when dancing and sex were plenty to keep me distracted. It reminded me of something else, something that had permeated the whole of my childhood: the songs of my older brother and sisters. By this time, my brother had moved out, but in the storage room was a box that held the key to his own restless understanding of the world. I took my Dead Kennedys record off the turntable and plopped on The Beatles' *Magical Mystery Tour*. Part of me intuited it was all one big joke, like Monty Python on acid. But the songs were edged with something I had gleaned when stoned, a certain melancholy touched with a heightened awareness of the way things really are. The fool on the hill was really a prophet, Strawberry Fields was Eden, and there was no more perfect account of being stoned and feeling vaguely lost and confused than the George Harrison–penned "Blue Jay Way."

My awareness of the world began to shift even more rapidly. Now I was certain rock contained some kind of Edenic language, that internal to its function was gnosis. This was the soundtrack to my flowering into addiction and eventual psychosis. Punk was going to take me only so far; psychedelic rock contained a perfect spiritual system at the ready, the greatest justification of excess a budding addict could ask for.

Sixties psychedelic rock was a combination of spaced-out jams and Eastern sitar–soaked instrumentation, due largely to the influence of the Grateful Dead in San Francisco. On the one hand, musicians such as Pink Floyd and the *Pepper*-era Beatles played with every manner of instrument and electronic effect available at the time. On the other, the sixties also saw a strain of neo-Luddite-ism, where many musicians wanted nothing more than to strip away all the conventions of modern society and return to a simpler approach. Think of The Band, Creedence Clearwater Revival, and, for that matter, the later Beatles of *Let It Be* (originally titled *Get Back*). The Rolling Stones provide a striking example of this contrast. Their 1967 release, *Their Satanic Majesties Request*, is a sprawling psychedelic overload, replete with backward guitars and organs. Their next album, the 1968 *Beggars Banquet*, could almost have come from a different band, if not for Mick Jagger's drawl. It's a stripped-down roots record, more blues than rock 'n' roll, and functioned as an internal and external reaction to the direction rock was ultimately moving in.

Lesser-known bands like Marc Bolan's Tyrannosaurus Rex (later known for his glam-rock persona T-Rex) and the Incredible String Band certainly drew from the same well as the more typical American psychedelic pioneers, but along with rock 'n' roll and Eastern music, these bands called upon their non-American, but absolutely Western, roots in British and Scottish folk. Yet what also made the music "psychedelic" was that it played with convention and pushed the boundaries of what was considered rock 'n' roll at the time, just as the underground did with comics, and as an interest in Eastern mysticism challenged normative and pervasive Judeo-Christian doctrine.

Whether or not LSD was the fuel or the style became a little hard to discern. The Beatles' *Sgt. Pepper's Lonely Hearts Club Band* made psychedelic music something that could be produced and constructed out of the right studio equipment and clothing. At least at first, psychedelic music disregarded what was commercially viable in favor of something that better reflected internal revolutions that were paving the way for external change. But by 1967, everyone wanted in on the game. Sometimes it ended up being as saccharine as anything mainstream, like Strawberry Alarm Clock's "Incense and Peppermints," but other bands found both commercial and spiritual possibilities with LSD-inflected sounds and charisma. One of the best and, I would argue, most timeless records of this era is The Zombies' *Odyssey and Oracle*, a failure when it was first released but rediscovered a year later when the band's now iconic song "The Time of the Season" became a Top 40 hit.

But there was only one song that by the 1980s came to epitomize the psychedelic sixties for a teenager growing up in the suburbs. The opening strains of the Electric Prunes' "I Had Too Much to Dream Last Night" distilled for me the entirety of what was possible when you mixed a drug aesthetic with garage-rock sensibilities. Despite the tintinnabulation of a little Eastern-inflected bell, "I Had Too Much to Dream Last Night" was just the right method of travel from punk back to the sixties, my own private TARDIS. Except for a few strange failed attempts at whimsy, the Electric Prunes' titular album was kind of a psych-pop masterpiece.

For the bass player, Mark Tulin, there was no such psychedelic intention, though. "We were just doing stuff the best we knew how to do it, to be a tweak different. We were never a cover band, but we didn't try to fit into anything and consequently fit in between everything." For the band, their sound was just an organic response to how music was being made at the time. The Beatles' *Sgt. Pepper*, Tulin explains, "set the gold standard for what you should be doing in the studio and took an edge off garage rock. The Beatles upped everyone's sophistication level and revolutionized how people made music." Some bands were made and marketed to be psychedelic, like Strawberry Alarm Clock and the Chocolate Watchband, but Tulin had much more modest dreams than to be in the Top 40. "I just wanted to play music, and the only way to do that was to be in a band. I didn't have a grand statement; mine would have been, 'Can I get a date?'"[2]

Nevertheless, the Electric Prunes' third album, *Mass in F Minor*, did seem decidedly more psychedelic and even took up the fascination with religious experiences. The song "Kyrie Eleison" was featured in the film *Easy Rider*, during that movie's infamous LSD cemetery scene in which Peter Fonda whispers desperately to a Madonna statue. Nevertheless, the fellows who actually recorded the song were straight. "The drug experience didn't drive our music," Tulin says. "It enhanced my listening experience, but if I got too high when I was playing, I internalized it. It might have been grand, but it didn't sit with what anyone else [was] playing. The extended jams [of *Mass in F Minor*] were in their own right a drug, and so we didn't need the motivation from without. It came from within." Still, some kind of drug experience was transmitted across the decades; I listened to the Electric Prunes as a Renaissance alchemist studied emblems, teasing out a secret history of the world in which drugs were the method by which not only God was revealed, but great music was crafted.

In the city I had discovered record stores. I could ask questions, get recommendations. The music was part of something else, though, a whole cultural (and pharmaceutical) movement that had broken through the veil of the conventional. Music, and the literature that supported it, revealed that the true path to enlightenment was a kind of spiritual revolution. I liked that I was staying underground. Punk rock showed me the value of

---

2 In a short documentary about how the album cover for the first and titular Crosby, Stills and Nash record came about, David Crosby remembers the group standing in the snow in fur parkas, getting their picture taken for the album's interior gatefold. The final image looks like a group of modern-day mystics, starry-eyed and wise. Crosby breaks the spell by admitting they were thinking about one thing and one thing only at that moment: "pussy."

rebellion, of staying out of the mainstream. Spiritual truth, like good nuggets of psychedelic music, was at the margins, hidden in used bookstores and record shops.

I had already had my head rewired a hundred times listening to *The Piper at the Gates of Dawn*, the Syd Barrett–era Pink Floyd masterpiece, without a doubt the greatest piece of full-blown LSD-inspired psychedelia to come out of the sixties. From the opening track, "Astronomy Domine," featuring what John Cavanagh refers to as the "name-checked planets" in his book on the album, to the final track, "Bike," with its playful menace devolving into a cacophony of noise, *Piper* is an incantation of the spiritual innocence, confusion, and madness of the sixties. I thought I could tease everything I needed out of the secret meanings I would surely discover through repeated listenings of this album alone. Then, like countless teenagers before me and countless long after, one afternoon I got massively, colossally stoned and listened to Pink Floyd's *Dark Side of the Moon*.

Dark Side docsn't contain the rural and sylvan whimsy of *Piper*, but it still conjures bits of madness that come from knocking around the farthest corners of the cosmos. Likc Bowie's "Major Tom" (released four years earlier), *Dark Side of the Moon* is a narrative of psychic extremes cast in the language of astronauts. The screaming opening that comes after the incessant ticking and alarms going off is much scarier and crazier than any of Barrett's cranky gnomes and scarecrows. I had glommed tightly on to *Piper*'s fanciful and dark excursions, but *Dark Side* matured my thinking from cats and bicycles toward the way in which the drug experience could place you at the center of existence. The trouble, also seductive, was how miserable and desperate it all seemed. "Us and Them" is one of the saddest songs in rock history, but its sadness comes from the recognition of how utterly

alone we all are. Only drugs could reveal this so perfectly, so inci-
sively, and in a way that made me seek it out over and over again.
To pursue loneliness seems absurd, but this was where I came to
believe perfect spiritual meaning was to be found, and it wasn't
here on Earth at all; it was in the scariest and most isolated parts
of the galaxy and of my mind.

My next series of trips were exercises in disassociation. I
loved my friends, but they were kind of getting in the way. They
didn't want to plant and watch these kinds of flowers grow. I
wanted to sit and dwell on the silence and the way the train
tracks we walked along stretched out into the blackness and the
void, and where it felt like I could walk forever. They wanted
to throw rocks at abandoned buildings and break windows.
I could smash stuff as well as any person, but I was over all
that. Acid was too precious to waste on petty crimes. What was
needed was constant vigilance in all the corners of the psyche,
on the way light cut across every movement of our hands and
fingers, how voices rang inside the mind and it was then you
realized you could read others' thoughts.

One night we sat on a roof overlooking an open field where
some construction project had been abandoned. The acid had
smoothed everything out. Even the litter and the trash looked
like reflections of some other, Platonic realm, but I kept missing
the significance. My companions were making too much noise,
grooving on their own incessant chatter, which never seemed to
go anywhere except to turn on itself and repeat, like a needle
catching the lock groove at the end of any album. Robert
Crumb's irreverent and horny long-bearded guru, Mr. Natural,
and the gleaming, cosmically sad Silver Surfer peeked out of
little holes in my thinking, and "Brain Damage" from *Dark Side*
vibrated inside my ears. I was losing my shit up here on the roof
because no one understood and they were getting in the way of
my mapping out this perfect geography of hell below and the

firmament above. The margins of music and art were not far enough. I needed to find the people who lived there, just near enough outside the mainstream for me to reach them from the safety of the suburbs, but far enough that I could choose to stay with them and never be found again. Somewhere they were there, the people who knew they were alone but kept to each other for warmth, waiting for a sun that would never rise on that eternal night on the dark side of the moon.

chapter four
SUMMER IN THE CITY

I was trying to get to the bus terminal, but the ten-minute walk from Tremont Street to Haymarket station was taking an eternity. I took this same walk every night and then back again in the morning, but this simple journey had suddenly taken on massive import. A startling clarity arose in me; the veil had been lifted. The world was on fire, but it wasn't being consumed. It was a shimmering furnace being stoked by angels. I walked through it like water, though, and my hands made fiery trails in the air when I raised them. Or my arm was a violin, and each minute movement plucked a string that sent small vibrations out into the aether. Sometimes the fire was so bright I had to close my eyes, but the heat pushed against my eyelids and transformed into multicolored sparks that penetrated my skull.

Because God was so close, little demons ran up and down my spine, sending secret messages about my death. They were no bigger than the head of a pin, but there were thousands of them. My back stiffened and I ground my teeth. I couldn't swallow. I couldn't breathe. A tree with the body of a man had been turned upside down and buried headfirst, the long cracked limbs of his legs reaching up toward forever. Here was God again, in the form of the world tree Yggdrasil, his lower limbs reaching down into the bottom of the world, and out again on the other side. His trunk kept the ground standing. The demons clattered away, taking some of my skin with them. The sky blazed and rained down embers of holiness onto my face.

Then time slowed down. My eyes adjusted to the fading light of the flames, until slowly nothing was as it had been. I was alone, staring at my hands, my filthy fingernails. My back shuddered off the last of the wiry currents that had been coursing through it for hours. The emptiness of coming down was exacerbated by the fact that I could feel nothing of the divine fire that only an hour or so ago had surrounded everything. I had almost reached it, but I had fallen just short, like so many times before. I had almost seen the face of God, and had I seen it, I would have been transformed.

As the acid wore off, the night expanded and contracted until it was one with my breathing, and then it was my breath alone. My spine loosened, my teeth relaxed, but my arms and hands still drew slight trails as they moved. I didn't know what had happened to my friends; I just knew I had to get going so I could catch the bus. No matter where I was, no matter how wasted, I always knew to go home. As much as I wanted to give myself over to this visionary life completely, to live on the street and do nothing but get high, I was terribly afraid of giving up that part of me that wanted the comfort of familiar and safe surroundings, that wanted much more to live than to risk my life on something

I was only vaguely certain had any real meaning. Nonetheless, I would be back the next day to start the cycle again.

The walk the following morning from the bus terminal to the Boston Common took me down Tremont Street and past the Tremont Temple, a massive stone structure that almost fades into the city block, past the glorious little Orpheum Theater, past the pawn shops and the now defunct hobby store, past the cigar shop and the giant Park Street Church. Once there, I would begin my summer day, with all its attendant spiritual exercises: taking drugs, stemming for change, and sitting in the grass with my compatriots, waiting for enlightenment, though any minor illumination would have sufficed. It was the summer between my senior year of high school and the autumn when I was going to have to decide, once and for all, what I wanted to do with my life.

In eleventh grade, on the advice of my principal and with the promise to my parents that I would take classes at the local community college, I dropped out of high school. Everyone could see that I was flailing, that between getting picked on and bullied and my own hardening rebellion, high school was proving to be more damaging than edifying. During that fateful meeting, I watched the stark, expressionless faces of my parents as the principal explained in no uncertain terms that something about the structure of high school and my unique way of doing things was making a public education untenable. What he was really saying, and what no one could admit, was that the system had given up on me.

Amid the assenting and seemingly powerless nods of my parents' heads, the principal convinced us all that my mercurial temperament was better suited to a more free-form junior-college experience. I saw it as a passport to liberation, an official and signed declaration of a kind of deliverance, but instead of blasting off into some imagined better-than-them stratosphere,

I was reduced to bagging groceries at Stop & Shop to make the extra money I needed to get on the bus and keep a few joints in my pocket at all times. This couldn't last. I spent most afternoons waiting outside the school to meet up with the few friends I had in town. With my tail between my legs, I went back and finished eleventh grade, but by the end of the year I had missed so much gym that I spent the summer before twelfth grade mowing the lawn of the school to make up for the physical-education requirement. I just squeaked through my senior year but was so absent, they wouldn't let me graduate. So I made all the right promises about getting a GED and going to community college the following September, except I had my sights set on another promise that the Beats and the hippies and the punks kept transmitting through time, and always from the same place: the city. A job selling flowers from a cart gave me good reason to go into Boston every day that summer.

The Common's footpaths radiated in all directions, some heading toward the small hill where a statue of a star-crowned woman named "America" stood watch over the city. One path led to the large fountain, frozen in the winter for ice-skating. All year, the park was teeming with people. But no matter how crowded, there was a sole gazebo that was often deserted, save for a few men who sipped their whiskey out of bags. The path that led toward this small wooden platform was called Cadillac Avenue, named not by the city council but by the people who needed to know: drug addicts, their dealers, the homeless. Unless you belonged to this class of meek and destitute, you somehow knew to avoid this path and the gazebo at the end of it. But one man, Carl, lived among the faded few who walked any path they chose.

Carl's hair was a tangled nest of short, stubby dreadlocks. He was extremely tall, dauntingly so, with fierce eyes, but he was shy, almost timid. But his real power was his raincoat, a filthy gray affair of which every inch was covered in signs, symbols, sigils, mathematical formulas, quotes from scripture, and all the dense and thickly woven meanderings of his mind, which formed a perfectly whole cosmology. He slept on the grass and on benches. He was invisible to most, but everyone who passed him left a mark on his coat. He recorded it all. He recorded all our beliefs, our dreams, our doubts, our prayers. All the hopes and fears we couldn't speak aloud, he bore witness to in the folds of his coat, which formed an ever-expanding universe where God was both the creator and the constantly receding edges.

For Gilgamesh, the story was written on the very bricks of the wall of the city of Ur. The story for my friends was written on the fraying raincoat of a man no one would even speak to. Gilgamesh, the story goes, was two-thirds human, one-third divine, and he had to leave the city to find the story of creation, to learn about the great flood and the gods. He walked the deep forests and the long plains, searching. We walked up and down the paths of the Common, battling the bull of heaven that was our all-too-human conscience and our fears.

I kept a small gas-mask bag procured at the local Army/Navy over my shoulder, filled with beads; crystals; various little Buddhist, Vedanta, and Hare Krishna tracts; tiny satchels filled with herbs I hoped would protect me from evil; and a Bible. The Bible came from the aforementioned Tremont Temple. One afternoon, stoned beyond measure, I had knocked on the minister's office door, desperately needing to look up a passage that seemed perfectly relevant and cosmically important to some fleeting thought that was going to *change my life*. The kind but thoroughly baffled minister pushed a softcover Bible into my hand and told me to go, keep it, God bless you. I left behind the sickly sweet smell of pot, cigarettes, and whatever stink had been on the clothes I wore, which I had not changed for nearly a week.

We made our way to the Common every day and gathered under an umbrella of drugs and cheap bottles of white

wine—young Hare Krishnas, homeless veterans, hippie hold-
outs, all of us marginal in some way, misfits the lot of us, but
sharing a single common desire: enlightenment by way of excess.

I had found my way to them through a homeless man named
Richard, piano player and panhandler extraordinaire, the winter
before. The pond that in the spring and summer was filled with
swan-shaped paddleboats and ducks had been drained, and the
muddy bottom had frozen. If you were careful, you could walk
over to the island—a mound of dirt, really—in the center. It was
the perfect place to get high alone, hidden in the brush and the
small trees that grew there.

One afternoon, as I stuffed a small, moist red bud into
my wooden pipe, someone else emerged from the weeds—a
bearded Aqualung of a man, worn wool coat, warm smile, and
old wretched eyes. He asked if I would share, and in turn he
would open his bottle of wine.

Every day that summer that I went looking for Richard, and
every day I found him on the same bench, politely asking pas-
sersby for change. We sat and he taught me how to panhandle,
to look people in the eye and not down at the ground like a dog,
to have dignity, no matter how undignified, and to treat everyone with respect. He must have known I wasn't homeless, that
at any time I could retreat to the safety of my suburban home,
which I left every morning with a quick nod to my mother and
father, who saw my comings and goings as normal summertime
frivolity. Their cozy and warm consistency was always there, but
it seemed sterile and without spiritual nourishment—as did the
mezuzah on our front door, which didn't glow with any significance when I walked by. I felt more at home with Richard, on
the margins, where his daily desperation was like poetry to me.
No one before had seemed so real, so alive. Like Jacob at the
mall, Richard was my teacher of the outside world, however con-
fined to the Common, and wise to something that seemed just

beyond my reach. Richard's age and cleverness, however, made him even more of a saint—Saint Francis of the filthy pigeons.

Richard introduced me to others who were drawn to the park, a Jerusalem in the center of a world. There was Bill, a pill-popping Vietnam vet who spoke in mystical gibberish; the pot-dealing mother, whom we called Mom, who claimed Native American heritage and made sure to bail anyone out of jail who was caught holding, but who had a streak of calm viciousness that made you know never to cross her; Michael, the Coast Guard officer on shore leave who preached forgiveness from an altar of LSD and performed public exorcisms on the darker souls among us; and finally Linda, the goddess of the street, whose private past demons glittered in her eyes but whom I loved and trusted the most, and who introduced me to the album that became the soundtrack of that summer, Joni Mitchell's *Blue*, a most decidedly nonpsychedelic record that still could somehow calm all the unfathomable feelings storming inside me.

All of us were pilgrims, finding our way here, to where God sat on his holy throne; or, forgoing that, the one place where the cops left us alone. We were never hassled, even when we sparked up joint after joint and took pull after pull of wine. There was something fantastic, wondrous, even, about the way we were allowed to do as we pleased in a public place. The days passed mostly without incident: digging up just enough change to get two hamburgers, a small fry, and a Coke at the Burger King across the street; using the bathrooms in the Parker House Hotel for all they offered by way of running water and towels; wandering from one side of the park to the other in packs of two, three, or more; and figuring out who was holding, what they had, and how much they were willing to front, share, or sell.

But this was all just the pedaling motion toward the much grander and isolated intention. God was all around us, but hidden behind the opaque lens of normal perceptions. The illusion was maintained by the city itself, and only the right kind of drugs in their proper dosage, or whatever we could afford, would turn off what Huxley called the "reducing-valve" of the mind so that true reality could reveal itself.

I called it mysticism, but I was undermined by a stingy morality that instinctually knew the kind of union I was ultimately seeking could not include the body and the thick-knotted tie to the ego and the self. I wanted to know God, but I thought only drugs would provide that insight. I wanted to feel the pleasure of being high while denouncing the world as illusion and all my attachments as keeping me from salvation. I didn't know it, but I was locked in a cycle of chasing a feeling of bliss, not understanding how this made a final climactic vision of the celestial chariot impossible. Ram Dass, in *Be Here Now*, warns of such a phenomenon when he writes: "The intensity with which psychedelics show you 'more' makes you greedy to be done [with spiritual practices] before you are ready. This attaches you to the experience of 'getting high' which after a period of time becomes a *cul-de-sac*." This was not a conflict unique to me by any means. It was a struggle that had driven a wedge into American spirituality in the sixties, beginning with Vedanta, and would continue to be woven into the very fabric of American spiritual consciousness.

What I inherited from this secularized cosmic drama was a new definition of ecstasy. It was not the one originally used to describe a particular kind of tremendous religious experience, which the religion writer Evelyn Underhill's 1911 book, *Mysticism*, defined as the moment when the "concentration of interest on the Transcendent is so complete, the gathering up and pouring out of life on this one point so intense, that the subject is more or less entranced, and becomes, for the time of the ecstasy, unconscious of the external world." No other pleasure or love is desired. In this way your soul is enraptured, captured. It's what Europa felt as she rode the bull Zeus across the raging sea.

This new definition of ecstasy was not even the one used in the early days of psychedelic research by Gordon Wasson (the person attributed with hipping the West to the magic mushroom used by Mazatecs in Mexico), when he explained why he didn't take the mushrooms that often: "Ecstasy! . . . Your very soul is seized and shaken until it tingles." The definition of ecstasy that was to enrapture my generation had already entranced the baby boomers before me. It was Timothy Leary's designation of ecstasy as "Individual Freedom."

In his 1968 book *The Politics of Ecstasy*, Leary writes, "The great kick of mystic experience, the exultant ecstatic hit, is the sudden relief from emotional pressure." His vision for a society born anew out of ecstatic experiences via psychedelics was to "support, nurture, teach, protect individual freedom and personal growth." This also meant relief from guilt, shame, fear, and, for some, that nagging moral conscience. The method, according to Leary, was LSD, for no other substance had the power to transform the sexual, social, psychological, and spiritual bummer the whole country was afflicted with.

At the most basic level, LSD is an odorless and colorless compound that, biologically speaking, acts on a number of receptors in the brain, including dopamine and serotonin. Researchers are still mostly baffled by how a drug that is so powerful has been proven to have no lasting physiological effects. No six- to ten-hour LSD trip is likely to be the same for two people or really for any one person, but there are some commonalities. After about thirty minutes, there are subtle perceptual changes. Trails seem to ripple off of every moving thing, and objects take on a shimmering edge. A most profound realization can come when visual distortions are also "felt." There begins to be less and less separation between body and mind. When two or more people are together during an acid trip, they may have feelings of psychic excitation, as if they can read each other's minds. Simple gestures begin to take on immense significance. As the trip begins to accelerate, normal perceptions of time shift. It becomes impossible to tell how much time has passed. At this peak point, LSD reveals quite elegantly that our normal, or at least familiar, waking consciousness is only one way of being. This is also the moment when things can go terribly wrong. Being in a strange place, anxious or worried, or in an environment that feels hostile can often produce the classic bad trip.

LSD is nothing like being drunk, or even splendidly stoned on marijuana. Unlike most other drugs, except for other psychedelics, LSD can bring forth what has been called non-dual consciousness or awareness, where the ego dissolves and, as Huxley describes, turns off that pesky filter that keeps total awareness at bay. But this often proves to be an elusive promise.

It's at the precise moment of the ego slipping that one often feels a desire to hold on. Giving up control can feel like the worst possible decision when the other side is replete with unknowns. It is the void that can be terrifying, what Huxley calls "the horror of infinitude." The most likely experience is one of vacillating between holding on and letting go, being and nonbeing, self and no self.

Albert Hofmann, a chemist with Sandoz Laboratories, synthesized the compound lysergic acid diethylamide (or LSD) from ergot fungus in 1938 during his investigations into the medical properties of plants. The substance seemed inert, at least in its initial testing on animals. But on April 16, 1943, working with LSD again, Hofmann accidentally absorbed the compound through his fingertips and began experiencing "an uninterrupted stream of fantastic pictures, extraordinary shapes with intense, kaleidoscopic play of colors."

A few days later, in a moment that has taken on the quality of a cosmic creation myth, Hofmann dissolved some of the compound in water and deliberately swallowed a dose. Somewhat incongruously, he got on his bicycle and rode home. It was the most consequential bike ride in history. It wasn't starting out as a very good first trip, as hellish forms menaced him. Once home, he experienced almost complete ego dissolution, vacillating between bliss and panic. Once the peak part of the trip was over, Hofmann relaxed into a visionary wonderland: "Kaleidoscopic, fantastic images surged in on me, alternating, variegated, opening and then closing themselves in circles and spirals, exploding in colored fountains, rearranging and hybridizing themselves in constant flux." When it was all over and he realized he had suffered no ill effects, Hofmann knew he had discovered something unlike any other synthetic compound. But no matter his vision for its possibilities in medicine and psychiatry, he could not foresee that his "problem child" would change the world.

It was the summer of 1960, and Timothy Leary was on vacation in Mexico after his first semester at Harvard in the Center for Research in Personality, where he had just begun a research position. In Cuernavaca he met an acquaintance, Gerhardt Braun, who was studying the religious history of psilocybin mushrooms. Leary decided to try them for himself. He wrote later that they completely transformed his understanding of consciousness and sent him on a path from which, except for a few stints in prison, he would never stray: "In four hours by the swimming pool in Cuernavaca I learned more about the mind, the brain, and its structures than I did in the preceding fifteen years as a diligent psychologist."

Back at Harvard, along with his colleague Richard Alpert, Leary was able to begin a legitimate study of psilocybin, sanctioned by the university with the promise that Leary and Alpert would keep it aboveboard and the drugs out of the hands of undergraduates.

Soon, Leary was approached by Walter Pahnke, a minister and at that time a doctoral student at Harvard, who was eager to study the relationship between hallucinogens and mysticism. Pahnke wanted to put into practice a theory that began when William James established what he called the four categories, or characteristics, of mystical experience: ineffability (the experience defies expression), noetic quality (the experience offers a new form of knowledge or insight), transiency (the experiences are short-lived and often difficult to recollect in full), and passivity (despite possible preparation, the actual experience is something that happens to a person). In 1960, the philosopher Walter Stace built on James's initial categories and described two types of mysticism, introverted and extroverted, which contained a number of similar features, including a vision of unity, a sense of divinity, and feelings of joy.

Pahnke would add to and amplify these categories into a slightly different set: unity, the most ubiquitous aspect of all mystical experiences, in which one no longer feels separate from the external world; objectivity and reality, in which one feels a sense of profound understanding of the true nature of the universe; transcendence of space and time; sense of sacredness, in which everything is imbued with holiness; deeply felt positive mood; paradoxicality, often experienced as an awareness that one has died and yet can reflect on the phenomenon; ineffability; transiency; and positive changes in attitude or behavior as a result of the experience.

These categories set up a kind of litmus test that revealed the possibility of a universal mystical core that any human being can access and that is independent of the way these mystical states are described using particular religious language. More important, this mystical consciousness might be available through the use of psychedelics.

So on April 20, 1962, in the basement of the Marsh Chapel at Boston University, twenty theology students were divided into two groups, one of which was given psilocybin and the other a placebo. The students then watched a live feed of a Good Friday liturgy. It could have been a den of medieval mystics, yet just outside traffic on Commonwealth Avenue whizzed by and pedestrians walked on unaware. Had a beatific vision descended upon a modern university, or were a bunch of stoned theology students rising up to meet it?

The results included dramatic experiences not unlike those documented by medieval and other mystics. One of the more common occurrences reported, a sense of being pulled out of finitude into infinity, typifies the mystical experience, what Pahnke calls transcending space and time. The seventeenth-century German mystic Jacob Boehme describes a vision in which he gains "the true understanding, which, according to the nature of the eternal wisdom, is immeasurable and abyssal, being of the One which is All. Therefore one only will, if it has divine light in it, may draw from this fountain and behold infinity." In an interview with one of the participants in Pahnke's experiment, one divinity student echoes Boehme: "All of a sudden I felt sort of drawn out into infinity, and all of a sudden I had lost touch with my mind. I felt that I was caught up in the vastness of Creation . . . Sometimes you would look up and see the light on the altar and it would just be a blinding sort of light and radiations. The main thing about it was a sense of timelessness."

In *The Varieties of Religious Experience*, William James notes that some cases of mystical experience are without religious imagery of any kind. The sixteenth-century Spanish mystic St.

John of the Cross describes such a moment in his classic on Christian mysticism, *Dark Night of the Soul*: "We receive this mystical knowledge of God clothed in none of the kinds of images, in none of the sensible representations, which our mind makes use of in other circumstances." Similarly, one participant in the Good Friday experiment also describes a lack of specifics: "There was one universal man, personhood, whatever you want to call it . . . a lot of connectedness with everybody and everything. I don't think Christ or other religious images that I can remember came into it."

This notion that there are elements common to all mystical experience was to have enormous influence on the nascent psychedelic research of the late 1950s and early 1960s. It offered legitimate and philosophical support to an idea already circulating in some groups, particularly occult- and Eastern-influenced religious movements: that all religions are ultimately the same, but simply offer a different—albeit winding—path to the top of the mountain. The deeper implication—that people from dissimilar religious traditions and backgrounds would recall similar characteristics of mystical experiences—was enormous, particularly for a young generation that was becoming disenchanted with traditional Judeo-Christian institutions. What it meant was that one could explore varying dimensions of religious ideas and practice without having to commit to any single tradition. Eastern religions in particular appealed to young Westerners looking for something that appealed to their desire for the exotic and the esoteric.

Despite this apparent success involving psychedelics, drug research at Harvard was already pushing up against the red brick of the institution. The center could not hold. Leary recalls one occasion when a student accidentally found himself with a friend at Leary's home on the very night that the Beat poet Allen Ginsberg was to have his first psilocybin trip. The student had no idea what was going on, or what any of it had to do with science.

The next day on campus, there was an explosion of talk about naked gay men and all-night drug parties at Leary's house, and in 1963, Alpert and Leary were fired from Harvard. A number of accounts regarding what exactly happened exist, but they all seem to pivot around the fact that despite the researchers' promise to keep the drugs within the confines of the programs, many a hallucinogen was finding its way into the hands of undergraduates and friends.

That same year, Leary, Alpert, and a number of their friends set up shop in Millbrook, New York, in a huge, crumbling mansion given to them by Peggy Hitchcock, an heir to the Mellon family fortune. There, they attempted to form a kind of altered collective consciousness. Hitchcock recalls, "We hoped that by living . . . via LSD with different kinds of people we could develop a hive consciousness, each person contributing a specific function, playing a definite role in the created family." No longer bound by Harvard administration, they had no boundaries, and stories of excess at Millbrook abound. Alpert recounted a group of people going into a separate, smaller house on the grounds and taking massive doses of acid for three weeks, until they walked out hating each other.

Everyone, it seemed, wanted to visit Millbrook; even Ken Kesey and his Pranksters made it up at one point, although claims about what happened when they did differ, depending on who tells the story. In Tom Wolfe's *The Electric Kool-Aid Acid Test*, the noisy and gregarious Pranksters spoiled Millbrook's calm, meditative vibe and Leary refused to come out and talk to them. But Leary recalls a meeting of the minds where he and Kesey essentially agreed to work on various sides of the same goal: turning on America.

Richard Alpert would find God in a slightly more traditional venue: In 1967, he went off to India in search of the kind of spiritual experience he had encountered on acid. There he met Neem Karoli Baba, who became his guru. It was under the teachings of Maharajji that Alpert, who was then given the name Ram Dass, started to change his spiritual outlook. He began to believe that psychedelics, while certainly a powerful way to bring about spiritual experience, if only for a moment, were only one "method" by which to reach some kind of religious consciousness. But, more important, he began to see his true religious purpose as one of service. Returning home, he quickly became a leader of new spirituality for the soon-to-be baby boomers. Many of the hippies were growing up, and they were afraid that when they left their youth behind, their newfound liberating spirituality would have to go, too. But Ram Dass offered them something else: a spiritual life that could be incorporated into a traditional middle-class existence.

The book *Be Here Now*, first published in 1971 (and in print ever since), is a triptych of memoir, religious graffiti, and spiritual instruction. Ram Dass acknowledges the role that psychedelics played in helping him recognize the spiritual dimension within him and the world, but in a section of the book that describes possible spiritual methods, he warns that the experience of psychedelics might make other spiritual disciplines less attractive as one gets attached to "getting high." Furthermore, he warns, psychedelic experiences often keep one bound to the astral planes where the ego is still mucking about.

Ram Dass admits he assumed that LSD had held the key, but during his meeting with the Maharajji, when he asks the true meaning of his life, the guru responds, "Serve people, feed people." Dramatic psychics and mystical experiences might compel you to travel thousands of miles from home in search of

more answers, but a more practical, and lasting, spiritual experience is to be had by simply being of service to others. There
can be no greater disparity than this between Ram Dass and
Timothy Leary, despite their being tied forever by their work at
Harvard. While Ram Dass would continue to emphasize service
and humility, Timothy Leary had already decided that any teachings he was looking for could be found in the drug itself, and
dubbed himself the "High Priest" of LSD.

Many of the original researchers, including Hofmann, the
father of LSD, were unhappy with where Leary had taken the
public understanding. Hofmann always believed his vision-
inducing synthesis should be respected. He once compared it
to morphine, in that what can be one of the most useful tools in
medicine can also destroy. While he insisted that LSD had deep
psychiatric and medical value, he thought its use on the street
was an unfortunate occurrence. In a 1996 interview, Hofmann
(who died in 2008) said, "[A]s long as people fail to truly understand psychedelics and continue to use them as pleasure drugs
and fail to appreciate the very deep, deep, psychic experiences
they may induce, then their medical use will be held back . . . On
the streets the drugs are misunderstood, and accidents occur."
Nevertheless, the street is where the drugs are found most,
but Hofmann was a scientist and understood consciousness as
something to be investigated, like any other science. Amateurs
might once in a while discover something worthwhile, but they
had neither the discipline nor the peer-review safeguards to
keep it safe and legitimate.

This notion of a suprapersonal mystical reality, of a spiritual
characteristic of human psychology that transcends the unique
qualities of religious traditions, would eventually become the
core idea in a discipline known as transpersonal psychology, the
redheaded stepchild of academic psychology, which also had its
roots in the psychedelic experience. While the counterculture

had taken hold of psychedelic spirituality and called it its own, and the taint of the Harvard scandals had made any other attempt at legitimate research impossible, a quiet few still believed that psychedelic drugs had opened up a portal by which to understand an essential part of the human, an idea that found its amplification in the Human Potential Movement and in the mountains of Big Sur at the Esalen Institute, created and founded in 1962 by Richard Price and Michael Murphy.

When Michael Murphy was a boy, he thought he would one day be an Episcopalian priest. But a Comparative Religions class with the eminent professor Frederic Spiegelberg at Stanford during Murphy's sophomore year changed his life course. Through Spiegelberg, he encountered the teachings of Sri Aurobindo, the Indian independence leader turned mystic who saw the entire cosmos as the unfolding of God. Aurobindo's evolutionary pantheism provided Murphy with the foundational vision that would guide his life. In this worldview, the divine is both transcendent and immanent in the world at large and manifests its glories, however haphazardly, in the course of time. Humans, Murphy believes, can incarnate their latent divinity through transformative practices such as yoga, meditation, and prayer.

Murphy started meditating six to eight hours a day, and when he was twenty-five traveled to India to join the Sri Aurobindo Ashram. Then, in 1962, at the age of thirty-one, he founded the Esalen Institute in Big Sur, California, with his Stanford classmate Richard Price. Murphy and Price aimed to explore their vision of a greater life opening for humankind; by 1970, they were presenting several hundred seminars and conferences a year on a wide range of practices to promote personal and social transformation.

Eventually psychedelics came to Esalen, but Murphy's own experiences left much to be desired. He had eight trips between

1962 and 1966 (his first time was with Aldous Huxley) and each time was worse than the preceding one. He recalls, "I thought, *If I keep this up I am going to damage myself.* By that time I had been meditating for twelve years, and this experience could not remotely match the illuminations I had in meditation."

Some people told him he simply had to keep taking the drugs because eventually he would push through. But he was already convinced that neither he nor others could effectively "advance in consciousness with drugs." Like Ram Dass, he accepted their usefulness as an initiatory experience but believed that without the inner work, they would take you nowhere worth going. "When psychedelics came in, people had no transformative practice, nothing to hold it, and it just became very destructive." In his book on the most thorough and far-reaching study on Esalen, Jeffrey Kripal explains that there were other considerations: The work at Esalen was too important, and drugs not central enough to it, to risk being shut down over them.

At Esalen, transformation came not just to the spirit, but to the body as well, and not because of the grace of gods but through the human agent, who was capable of supernormal feats—great agility, the ability to withstand pain—"resulting in an era of boundless potential." This ultra-enabled human could become the catalyst for the New Age movement, which offered an entire tool kit at one's fingertips capable of effecting change: yoga, astrology, channeling, ESP, tarot cards, and meditation. These things were all in the service of empowerment, or, as Harold Bloom mockingly calls it, "the contemporary debasement of Gnosticism." The human and the divine were intimately connected through these practices, so, as Catherine Albanese writes, "there was energy and there was healing; there was the power of the mind and the correspondence between body-self, Higher Self, nature, universe, and God."

James Fadiman, a psychedelic psychotherapist and one of the founders of the Institute of Transpersonal Psychology, has long believed that conventional psychology will one day have to reconcile the mental and the spiritual, an idea that first saw fruit in his own experiences with altered consciousness. With a BA in social relations from Harvard University, the young Fadiman decided on a year in Europe to figure out his next move. It was 1961, and he was surprised to meet up in Paris with one of his professors, Richard Alpert, who, along with Leary and Aldous Huxley, was on his way to Copenhagen for the very first conference on psychedelics. Alpert told Fadiman that something extraordinary had happened to him and that he wanted Fadiman to experience it as well. As Fadiman describes it, "He then reached in his breast pocket in his sports coat and took out a little bottle of pills and I thought, *What the devil is that?*"

Not long after, they were in Fadiman's fifth-floor walk-up and the young Harvard graduate did not have a mystical experience, but rather made a deep human connection that the Jewish philosopher Martin Buber calls an "I-Thou" relationship, in which the person is seen not merely as external object, but as part and parcel of the divine.

Fadiman followed Alpert to Copenhagen, where he had another psilocybin experience and what he describes as a feeling that the world was not something to struggle against. He also realized for the first time something astonishing for a Harvard man: "I actually could live without my books."

Back in the United States, however, it was safer to choose books when the only options were either graduate school or the Vietnam War. Fadiman entered the psychology department at Stanford University, but nothing was being taught there that could speak to his psilocybin experiences. Curiously,

Fadiman stumbled upon a course in the electrical engineering department, called The Human Potential. The professor, Willis Harman, explained that there was no more room in the course. As Fadiman recounts, he shut the door to Harman's office and admitted to taking psychedelic drugs. As a result, he wound up coteaching the course with Harman because, as he put it, "I wasn't afraid to discuss my psychedelic experiences and he, very appropriately, was."

At about the same time, Harman and another researcher, Myron Stoloroff, started doing research with LSD and its use in psychotherapy as a catalyzing agent for profound psychological insight within a therapeutic environment. It was then that Fadiman took acid for the first time. His only spiritual life had come from his polite Unitarian services in college; this was something else. "Suddenly I was aware that Atman was Brahman and that I was part of all things." It was the beginning of an understanding that a transpersonal identity exists beyond the ego; he describes walking around the hills above the Stanford campus later that same day and feeling something akin to godlike, "very proud of creation because I clearly had done it."

How could the current thinking in psychology speak to this? Well, Fadiman understood immediately that it couldn't. Psychology, as a discipline, was at that time decidedly anti-religious and anti-spiritual. But turning to theology wasn't an option: It lacked the appropriate tools to get at the question of human consciousness. Fadiman wrote his PhD thesis on psychedelics and was grudgingly awarded his degree by the department.

There was now no way that traditional psychology was going to be able to provide Fadiman with the tools he needed to do the work he wanted, although "I don't blame psychology for missing the boat," he says—there was no reason why psychologists needed to be interested in mystical ideas. So, in 1975, Fadiman, along with another Harvard-trained psychologist,

Dr. Robert Frager, founded the Institute of Transpersonal Psychology, a place where others could be trained to understand whatever human consciousness is capable of.

The timing was just about perfect. Mainstream culture was simply not going to accept a new spiritual message from a bunch of hippies. But a new generation of therapists trained in spiritual psychology could actually minister to the needs of a growing baby boomer audience who wanted to leave their acid behind but continue to explore varying ideas about consciousness as it related to more banal aspects of life: kids, jobs, and spouses. The New Age movement, by way of Esalen and transpersonal psychology, was exactly what they needed—something they could take with them to the suburbs and that could fit into a life that no longer involved "dropping out."

For those who had experienced the expansion of both social and religious consciousness, spirituality became an open system of possibility. Head shops and mercantiles gave way to New Age bookstores that sold magazines like *Yoga Journal* and *New Age Journal*. *Psychology Today* gave way to *Omni*. Black-light posters were replaced by charts outlining chakras, the kabbalistic tree of the *Sefirot*, and acupressure points. Bongs gave way to crystals, incense, and meditation beads. Certainly, many people continued their search for enlightenment with drugs, but discussion of the physical benefits of practices like yoga increased.

The New Age popularization of Eastern religion helped to teach naive Westerners that there was more to Hinduism than kids chanting "Hare Krishna" in the park, but it also diluted some of the more rigorous disciplines associated with these traditions. Yoga, for example, was not originally intended to be merely a novel way to stretch. It involved a commitment to an entire ethical and contemplative way of life. On the other hand, serious practitioners of Buddhism and Hinduism opened ashrams and Zen centers in major cities, and psychologists and clinicians slowly began to accept that nontraditional forms of medicine, such as acupuncture and meditation, actually enhanced patients' overall care.

Nixon was president; holding a dime bag could land you in jail. By the mid-seventies, getting high and turning on was the stuff of discotheques, rather than be-ins. In a 1976 *New York* magazine article, Tom Wolfe decried the trend from activism to self-obsession as the "Me-Decade." Esalen had preached human potential, but what had been an echo of an ancient cry to bring forth what Michael Murphy called our latent divinity became a narcissistic obsession. Wolfe writes, "The old alchemical dream was changing base metals into gold. The new alchemical dream is: changing one's personality—remaking, remodeling, elevating, and polishing one's very *self* . . . and observing, studying, and doting on it. (Me!)"

This cultural shift was prophesised most poignantly on The Beatles' *White Album*. Released in 1968, it anticipated not only The Beatles' own ultimate disintegration, but the implosion of the counterculture into aspects of violence and pessimism. The Beatles' music was a constant thrum in my house growing up, and many of their songs had embedded themselves in the origins of my anxiety. But listening to it years later, by myself, older and *stoned*, I felt as if there were two levels: one for the average pop-music consumer, and another, deeper stage for those willing to really *listen*. There were messages here not unlike what had already been oscillating around my psychic detector.

The album I had was inherited from my brother, who had covered both sides of the all-white sleeve with graffiti. There were little Kilroys peeking over a single horizontal line, "thinking" the lyrics to the songs. There was the smoke of swollen joints floating around hastily drawn naked girls. Eric's fairly competent renderings of Robert Crumb's "Keep on Truckin'" figures long-limbed their way across white fields of mushrooms and abstract spirals. I tried and failed to tease out a world of meaning from my older brother's stream-of-consciousness doodles.

Inserted within every recognizable moment of Beatles playfulness ("Ob-La-Di, Ob-La-Da") and narcissistic name checking ("Glass Onion") were things more sinister: "Happiness Is a Warm Gun," "Piggies," "Revolution 1," and, of course, "Helter Skelter." By the time I really listened to it, it was impossible not to feel the weight of history and the darkness that bled between the decades.

That implosion was rendered acutely the following year in two incidents that for many historians and those who lived through them pointed to both the calendric and symbolic closing of the sixties. The Rolling Stones concert at Altamont Speedway in California on December 6, 1969, was one. Woodstock was thought to be the Platonic form of all musical festivals, a perfect representation of many stoned, filthy, peace-loving, horny people dancing and grooving to the best music their age had to offer, with nary a hitch. Altamont, on the other hand, was a violent spectacle, with Hells Angels serving as security and a fatal stabbing taking place.

The second incident was the news, in March of that same year, of the LSD-fueled murders the Manson Family had committed under the tutelage of their leader, Charles Manson. For my generation, Manson loomed. There was no better stand-in for the Devil himself in the imagination of a generation that knew of World War II and the Holocaust only from movies and school. In the popular consciousness of the generation coming of age post-sixties, even the Vietnam War paled before the visage of the smiling, bearded man with a swastika carved into his forehead. As the scholar and writer Nick Bromell recalls, "Manson was insane, but he was also representative. When everything connects, the vision can only be one of joy or terror . . . bummers and bliss. Madness and ecstasy. Evil and love."

Manson, via the *White Album*, revealed the dual nature of seeking gnosis, or knowledge of the self. God might very well be within, but what if paradise is really nothing but a fool's game, designed by a dangerous and insane demiurge to keep us from the truth? Psychedelic drugs, if they really were opening those doors of perception, were also revealing, as Bromell writes, "a horror that comes and goes, nodding and winking, just there behind the lattice of the primal elements into which the social construction of reality has temporarily dissolved." As Joan Didion writes in her essay on her own personal and cultural encounter with those fateful final days of the sixties and the news of the Manson Family's murder of Sharon Tate, "I remember that no one was surprised."

My companions in the Boston park and I felt the litter of the intervening decade bump up against our heels. The Vietnam War and the criminalization of drugs made for a much more paranoid and slightly edgy time of it. The Boston Common was nothing like the sprawling mansion in Millbrook, which Leary described as a "space colony" where they were "attempting to create a new paganism and a new dedication to life as art." Our own assembly was, however, also an experiment in the furthest reaches of consciousness, an exploration of Huxley's antipodes where saints and madmen alike have traveled. We were, sadly, bound by certain restrictions that Leary and his companions could not foresee or warn us about; they could not send us psychic messages through the void to prepare us for the state we would find ourselves in, even as we began. Our acid was weak, there was no counterculture to mediate our schizophrenic muddle of spirituality and rebellion, and paranoia and mistrust passed among us like joints.

Even then I knew not to cross certain people. At any moment, any one of us could turn; while we talked about taking care of each other, self-preservation came at any cost. A lesbian couple who sold magic mushrooms and listened to Suzanne Vega and Kitaro would invite me into their home to sell me some 'shrooms, but they wouldn't ask me to stay and trip with them and they would watch me with suspicious eyes, worried about some abstract betrayal I might be capable of. One afternoon I asked someone I had known fairly well for a match to light a cigarette. He handed me a lighter, and at that moment someone called my name and I turned away from him. Suddenly he was on me, a knife to my throat, rabidly mad and accusing me of trying to steal his seventy-five-cent Bic.

On another occasion, I bought some hash in the Boston Common from a fellow with darting eyes and quick hands. It turned out to be a piece of stale Entenmann's cake. When I tried to hand it back to him, he got aggressive, saying, "Hey, man, you made me take it out. You have to buy it now, man! You have to buy it now!" I tried to smoke it anyway.

Despite these short, sharp explosions of personality, every day during that summer, some small group of us sat in a circle in the shade and laid blotter on our tongues or chewed bitter mushrooms and grooved on each other, reading each other's minds and, in those moments, trusting each other beyond measure. Enlightenment was an idea always on the threshold, and God made an appearance every now and then, but it was fleeting and quickly lost amid the leftover detritus of America's spiritual ache.

Tea-leaf readers set up shop right above the pawn shops on Tremont Street, Evangelicals put up revival tents and handed out Jack Chick Bible tracts in which we learned that even Buddhism would send us straight to hell. We knew to stay away from both kinds of false prophets (fortune-tellers and Christians), so every night we smoked some hash and then went to the Hare Krishna temple on Commonwealth Avenue for dinner and chanting. I was fascinated by the song and dance, the rapturous and almost violent clapping and stomping, not so different from a hardcore punk show. The words, however—*Hare Krishna Hare Krishna / Krishna Krishna Hare Hare / Hare Rama Hare Rama / Rama Rama Hare Hare*—failed to lift me; they went in and out of my consciousness like any religious hymn or song. I always balked at these moments, kept myself stiff and tight so as not to be carried away.

All of us in the Boston Common, it seemed, in one way or another, were desperate to know God in the way that prophets and mythmakers had always warned against. In the story that relates the birth of the Greek god Dionysus, Zeus is having an affair with the mortal girl Semele. Zeus insists he is indeed Zeus, but when Semele tells her friends that her lover is the king of the gods, they tease her. Semele finally confronts Zeus and says that she will no longer sleep with him if he doesn't prove he is Zeus. So he reveals himself in his full glory and she is immediately incinerated. Even Moses is told by God, "No one shall look upon me and live." We had thought the only way to truly know if God was real was to see Him face-to-face—the frenzied dancing of neither the Hasidic Jews nor the Hare Krishnas was sufficient.

I was not opposed to seeing Krishna, or Christ, or any one of a number of deities that might inhabit the divine landscape. But I was waiting for the right one to come to me. I would never go to any of them willingly, could never imagine "choosing" in that way. If God was going to reveal the true nature of His incarnation, I would be ready. I watched the young bald Krishna kids in their orange robes dance and I was envious of their belief. Talking to them was a different story. After the chanting, during the meal, they had very little to say that was original or revelatory. I knew we would be back the next night for the wonderful curried potatoes and bread, but there was no spiritual sustenance here, no pure path to the spirit. It was all too much of itself, and nothing else.

Autumn was coming on fast, and before I knew it, my companions were drifting back to their own private realms to get ready for the long winter. I had met almost all of them in May, and by early September there was no one around. Some were heading back to college, others simply stayed warm in the bars, and still others left town completely. As summer wound down, another door was closing, the portal that we all walked in and out of to access those visions that we believed told greater truths about ourselves and the world. The only problem was that they were mostly indecipherable. I was starting to see that drugs and some Hare Krishna chants were not getting me to where the deeper wells of spiritual knowledge could be found, but I had convinced myself that by summer's end we would all be transformed. I was changing, all right, but I just seemed to be getting dirtier and more afraid. Why was I not being illuminated like those brave adventurers who had come before me? What had I gotten wrong: set or setting?

While Hofmann and Huxley, and James before them, were taking a decidedly intellectual approach to the exploration of psychedelics, their access to these experiences was privileged. At least Leary wanted to equalize everything, take LSD and psilocybin out of the lab and put them into the hands of people who might really know what to do with them. He understood that these drugs had been used outside of the world of research for thousands of years. Only so much religion could go on in a lab; eventually you needed the *people* to have at it.

But Leary was also coming at this situation from a privileged position. From the outset, he prescribed what he called "set and setting." In *The Psychedelic Experience: A Manual Based on the Tibetan Book of the Dead*, Leary (writing with Alpert and Ralph Metzner) describes how LSD is dependent on context:

The nature of the experience depends almost entirely on set and setting. Set denotes the preparation of the individual, including his personality structure and his mood at the time. Setting is physical—the weather, the room's atmosphere; social—feelings of persons present towards one another; and cultural—prevailing views as to what is real.

A few years later, in a *Playboy* interview, Leary again stressed context, urging inexperienced LSD adventurers to find a guide.[3] He also insisted that those under age twenty-five were the "holiest" generation (at least in 1966), and that a fifteen-year-old was likely to have a much more insightful experience with acid than a fifty-year-old: "Because a fifteen-year-old is going to use a new form of energy to have fun, to intensify sensation, to make love, for curiosity, for personal growth." The trouble—as many a fifteen-year-old, including me, would experience—was that spiritual LSD guides were hard to come by. Leary and his colleagues, educated, moneyed, and safe in their upstate New York mansions, had the luxury of sitting for an interview with *Playboy* magazine, talking about set and setting and the future of youth, but the youth were just trying to get by.

While many young people of that generation and the next wanted a religious experience, they were distrustful of religion in any form, even one that looked and smelled and sounded like what they imagined an authentic faith might look like. Leary's message was one the youth wanted to hear. In all religious traditions, it has been the mystic that has challenged the status quo, that has sought to reveal the hidden and invisible reality that the hierarchical and moral have buried. In many cases, the mystic has been accused of being a heretic. But the mystic is also the

---

3 In the same interview, Leary talks about how sex on LSD can produce multiple orgasms and is also a "cure" for homosexuality.

prophet, the one who has the direct experience with God and then delivers a radical and often counterauthority message.

As the beatniks handed the torch to the hippies, they passed along a kind of mystical prophecy. It was a message that the religion found in the churches and synagogues was a trap, a trick to keep us from our true destiny, and that the word of God was not at the pulpit, nor was He looking down with a threat of hell in one hand and a promise of heaven in the other. God could be found within, and once He was discovered, liberation from every kind of war, heartache, and injustice could be found.

Leary taught that religion is a matter of *experience*. Music and drugs, dancing and sex—this is where God is revealed. LSD and psilocybin had become illegal in 1968 and 1970, respectively, and Leary had taken psychedelics out of the purview of science and into the hands of freaks waving flowers and singing "Hare Krishna."

Timothy Leary would go so far as to say that he was continuing the work of Aleister Crowley and putting into practice the magician's most quoted maxim, "Do what thou wilt shall be the whole of the law." Most of the baby boomers would find the teachings of Ram Dass less problematic for the suburbs; their children, however, would hear only the echo of Leary, but with neither acid potent enough nor a counterculture cohesive enough to help them do little more than use it as an excuse to get immaculately stoned.

Without guidance, without some formula, my friends and I were going in circles, having the same trip over and over again, getting close to some realization that would be our salvation and then coming down, baffled and exhausted. I wasn't even sure what I wanted to be saved from. All I knew was that I was becoming afraid again, my anxiety starting to surface. The promise of freedom built on drugs and music and art was fizzling out. Our own Aquarian Age had not arrived, and much as

the hippies before us had had to accept eventually, it was getting to be time to look for jobs, go back to school, and become
responsible, to grow up. I was left alone there in the Common,
refusing to go. Each day was getting colder, rainier, and still I
took the bus to Boston and walked those city blocks, past the
church and the hotel, to where only a few weeks earlier I had
still been greeted with hugs and smiles and little tabs of blotter
acid being pressed gently onto my tongue. Now it was getting
so I could barely score a few joints, and no one, at least no one I
knew or trusted, was there to welcome me.

I was going to have to give my folks a plan for my life, but the
only thing I wanted to do was continue on as I had been doing.
At the least, I needed to get a steady job washing dishes or flip-
ping burgers. I had made a promise to start taking classes at the
community college, so that looked like where I was headed. But
the idea of giving up on the city, resigning myself to the suburbs,
felt like a small death. For the most part, I had been able to keep
my head down while living with my parents. Even when I had
dropped out of school, a couple of passionate speeches about
finding my own way, needing more time to figure things out, had
sufficed. I tried to convince them that dropping out of almost
everything but the most basic kinds of jobs (bag boy, dishwasher,
grill cook) was not mere laziness or stoned lethargy, but a way
of being in the world free from convention, free from what I
perceived as the middle-class suburban grind, in the search for
greater meaning. I had dropped out of school, sure, but I was
an autodidact, a voracious reader. I wrote poetry, thought about
politics and music and how to change the spiritual condition
of the world. On some level, my parents must have identified
this as a legitimate path for a nineteen-year-old. As long as they
never got a call from the police, even when I seemed particularly crazy in my short, sharp pronouncements about "fields of
energy" and "cosmic awareness," they somehow continued to

believe I would be okay, that this was all just a phase, no worse than that of any other kid who took longer than usual to find his way.

But eventually I knew I couldn't go much longer until they confronted me. I was no longer a kid; my rebellious gestures were not just harmless teenage growing pains. My parents had afforded me all the freedom they could, teaching me in their quiet way how to be independent from them, but learning how to fly and actually being able to survive on my own were two different things. I signed up for classes at the community college, and for a while, despite the phantoms haunting all its crevices and corners, my day-to-day life took on the quality of normalcy. I got up in the morning and went to class, from there to work, and then home after my parents were asleep. Much of the time I never made it to school at all, but when we saw each other for brief moments, I had some exciting thing to say about a book being read or an idea being formed in one of my classes. *Everything is going to be okay* was the refrain, albeit mostly unspoken, between us.

I told myself the same thing, and so there was a secret hope between my parents and me that everything was as it should be, at least for now. Maybe we assumed we would all deal with the next thing when it presented itself. But for now we would all agree to carry on until some abstract moment in the future when I would know myself perfectly, know exactly what my destiny was, and pursue that with all my might. Their trust and my keeping out of larger trouble kept them at bay. What they didn't know was that it wasn't community college that was preparing me, but rather taking acid and smoking pot were the methods by which I expanded my consciousness to better prepare myself for this abstract, impossible future. None of us knew the next thing was right around the corner, and it wasn't anything my parents could have foreseen for their odd but good-natured son.

Getting stoned and tripping had started off as adventures in spelunking the caverns of my consciousness. It was a game to see how far I could go, how wasted I could get, and what I could learn about the malleability of reality. The deeper I went, the more treasures there were to be found, a veritable hollow earth of hidden temples and ancient echoes. I had discovered Agartha, the lost city in the center of the earth. It was the greatest dungeon I had ever explored; it made my old D&D maps seem the stuff of a more feeble imagination. Getting high was the key to unlocking something beyond my own petty imaginings.

By the end of my summer in the city, I was starting to be a little lost within this underground labyrinth. Getting stoned with other people was becoming increasingly uncomfortable. There was always something sinister in the hidden meaning behind every gesture and every mannerism. My awareness became more and more internalized; I was self-centered to the point of paranoia. These feelings were particularly acute when I was on acid. I felt I was nothing more than an amplifier and a receiver for everyone else's moods and desires. One fall day, my friends and I had the bright idea to see the film *Legend*, starring Tom Cruise as a young hero who battles a massive horned devil, played by Tim Curry. How could I have known the film would reveal the great cosmic battle between good and evil, with me at the center, tripping my balls off, feeling the entire audience's collective fear and wonderment? Throughout the whole movie, I absorbed and released tiny microdots of spiritual confusion. When I sighed, the audience sighed. When I caught a glimpse of some secret message in the dialogue, I transmitted it and everyone nodded in agreement.

When I wasn't high, the feelings lingered, and spending time alone was the best antidote. When I had to be around other people, for work or the occasional dinner with my parents, I was distracted and hyper, but I always managed to get through. My

mind was still elastic enough that I could snap back to a kind of
stoner good-naturedness. But once alone, I would quickly get
high and start the cycle over again.

More and more when stoned, I felt like I was absorbing cosmic
rays, like I was the focal point of a vast, intergalactic message
system. The energy that all this sound and movement generated
and sent hurtling out into the astral planes rained down around
me like cherry blossoms. This wasn't God, but something else,
some other divine being—archangel, principality, power—
sorting through the astral planes for what I needed, transmitting back to me. I dug up my old copy of *The Key of Solomon
the King* and, with acid-glazed eyes, finally understood where
it explains that individual spirits govern every aspect of the
hidden and truer reality and correspond to the most basic elements of life: air, water, earth, and fire. Moreover, learning their
names can provide "service to that man who shall have the good
fortune to understand their nature, and to know how to attract
them." It was becoming clear that each spirit was a reflection of
every thought I had, but somewhere within the whole realm was
my personal guardian, my daemon that plugged me directly into
the heart of the celestial reality.

chapter five

SIGNS AND PORTENTS

Hexagram 24 of *The I Ching*, known as *fu*, or return, was where the secret must lie: "All movements are accomplished in six stages, and the seventh brings return." It was powerful enough that even Syd Barrett channeled it on Pink Floyd's debut album, *The Piper at the Gates of Dawn*, in the song "Chapter 24," which was spinning on my turntable. I sat with my legs crossed while incense smoldered in a brass holder on an altar, a joint burning slowly in an ashtray next to me. I kept rolling the coins in the hopes of manifesting *fu*, but I was getting pushed further away from, not toward, change, the great transformation the hexagram promised.

After a time, I began to roll the I Ching to get a reading on the previous hexagram, in an attempt for a more definitive answer,

and then again with the new one, ad infinitum, until it seemed
to circle back on itself and I was left with only a deepening abyss
of confusion and fear. I was falling into an awareness of another
kind of change—my death—as reflected in Hexagram 23, *po*, or
splitting apart: "Those who persevere are destroyed . . ." over
and over again.

The *I Ching*, or *Book of Changes*, is an ancient Chinese text
that serves as both an oracle and a book of wisdom. The oracle,
easily recognized by the six-lined hexagram, was made popular
by a translator of Chinese, the German Richard Wilhelm, in
1950. Originally conceived around four thousand years ago as
eight trigrams corresponding to certain types of natural phenomena (heaven, earth, thunder, water, mountain, wind/wood,
fire, lake), the six were organized again into sixty-four possible
hexagrams. Unlike traditional forms of divination or fortune-
telling, the hexagrams reveal not what will happen, but what
the potential courses of action are, depending on the question
posed. For example, one might ask, "Will I find love?" and roll
the hexagram *heng*, or duration, whose judgment reads: "Perseverance furthers. It furthers one to have somewhere to go."
The *I Ching* does not answer yes or no, but rather suggests the
following strategy: Persevere, keep your ideal ahead of you, and
keep moving forward. Like most systems of correspondence,
The *I Ching* also explains Earth and heaven as reflections of each
other, and so a deeper spiritual meaning can be found in even
the most mundane of circumstances. All things must persevere
in their cycles: the seasons and the very movement of the stars.

The traditional means of posing inquiries to the oracle
involves a complex manipulation of yarrow stalks, but a simpli-
fied method—and more practical for suburban basements—is
to roll three coins six times and, depending on the roll, mark
either a broken or unbroken line one below the other. This
practice has a powerful and subtle psychological effect that

is markedly different from, say, going to a fortune-teller. The agency involved in rolling three coins is, admittedly, not much, but it reveals both the randomness and the coincidence involved in even the simplest of acts. The oracle does not reveal what is probable, only what is possible. But for someone incapable of making any decision whose outcome was not absolutely clear, any kind of ambiguity or doubt only paralyzed me.

The I Ching was not just capable of illuminating the secrets of the ancient mysteries that had become codified at various points throughout history; it was even the inspiration for song lyrics. One possibly apocryphal story explains that George Harrison's beloved song "While My Guitar Gently Weeps" was inspired by opening *The I Ching* at random and coming upon the phrase "gently weeps."

Sitting as close to me as my bag of sticky-sweet sinsemilla was my deck of tarot cards. I took them out of the box and began to shuffle them, the oversize cards a bit awkward when one is used to regular playing cards. I took a deep breath and snapped them down in the proper alignment.

All the occult texts I read regarded the tarot as a most powerful tool for explaining the celestial counterpart to our own earthbound and fleshy business, although the history of the tarot is mired in speculation; as with many details related to the occult, believers want to ascribe ancient provenance to it. What we do know is that there is really no evidence to suggest tarot cards were used for anything more than card games until the late 1700s, when the occultist and Freemason Antoine Court de Gébelin, following a burgeoning interest in all things Egyptian, stated that the cards had hidden, ancient meaning drawn from Egyptian religion.

It is surprising, to be sure, that this didn't happen earlier. Playing cards are inherently mysterious and, like *The I Ching,* seemingly prone to both chance and fate when dealt. During

the occult revival of the nineteenth century, magical fraterni-
ties made tarot cards part of their ever-widening sphere of esoteric teachings. It wasn't until the occult scholar Edward Waite
developed his take on the deck that the public took notice. The
Rider-Waite deck, as it came to be known, was illustrated by
Pamela Colman Smith in the typical turn-of-the-century style
and was immediately recognizable as something both modern
and yet containing the richness of the past. The Rider-Waite
deck was the standard deck until Aleister Crowley's own version, which he worked on for years before his death, was published in 1969.

In 1947, an American who was one part stage magician, one
part teacher of the ancient mysteries, Paul Foster Case, wrote
what would be his legacy, *The Tarot: A Key to the Wisdom of
the Ages.* Case, like many before him, believed magical societies placed far too much emphasis on secrecy and on requiring
intense and complex initiatory rites to learn basic occult teachings. He started an organization, the Builders of the Adytum,
and taught magic and the occult through the mail. *The Tarot*
was his most concise work and examined his belief that the
cards corresponded to the Jewish kabbalistic structure of the
universe, a structure that was already a foundation of all occult
teachings.

While traditional Judaism prohibited the use of magic, there
is clear evidence that Jews not only practiced it as early as the
sixth century, but have been responsible for influencing many
magical systems. In all times, Jews hammered out amulets, practiced divination, crushed herbs, and called out God's name
and those of his angels to smite enemies and to gain affections.
Even the more mundane chicken soup has long been thought to
draw its healing properties from arcane sources. For occultists
through the ages, Judaism represented the authoritative ancient
tradition, with enough of its own mystical and legendary magical

practice to perfectly complement an already complex configura-
tion of ideas and practices.

In particular, it was the *Sefirot*, the ten aspects of the divine
that spring forth from the unknowable godhead, or Eyn Sof,
that were central to Western occultists. Kabbalah presented a
cosmology that could be laid out like geography. The *Sefirot* are
a beautifully realized and, in some sense, materialistic view of
the universe. Each aspect of creation is delineated by a temperament, and not only was it easy to show how each individual
Sefirah has a corresponding numerological and astrological
meaning, but images of the *Sefirot* harken back to the Renaissance alchemical emblems. Along with the *Sefirot, gematria*,
the art of finding hidden meaning by assigning numerical value
to Hebrew letters, became the holy grail of magical practice.
Even more significant, Hebrew letters became a kind of occult
wallpaper. Adorn something as simple as a pentagram with the
tetragrammaton (the name of God rendered in the Torah as the
Hebrew letters *yod, heh, vav, heh*), and you suddenly have a
symbol of immense power.

Case's book is a crash course in how numerology, astrology,
tarot, kabbalah, and magic can be understood to belong to a
single, universal system of correspondences. Tarot functions
much as the emblems Renaissance magicians used in their study
of alchemy: The magus would contemplate a picture that contained a number of symbolic elements. In one sixteenth-
century emblem, four creatures—a bird, a lion, a mermaid,
and a dragon—sit in four corners, connected by chains. Each
creature is surrounded by fire. The magus would meditate on
each figure, their relationship to each other both free and yet
bound, and the corresponding number four as it relates to the
elements, the cardinal points, the four archangels, and the four
letters that make up the tetragrammaton. True adepts could
arrange their own mind to function as a storehouse of these

ideas and symbols, once referred to as the "art of memory," which the Renaissance mage/astronomer Giordano Bruno perfected in the fashion of a true magician. The great occult scholar Francis Yates describes this role as "one who both knows the reality beyond the multiplicity of appearances through having conformed his imagination to archetypal images, and also has powers through this insight."

Through a conflation of psychedelic spirituality via Leary and Castaneda and an occult cosmology via tarot cards and *The Key of Solomon the King*, I believed drugs were the means by which to stitch these arcane symbols and signs onto my brain. It wasn't enough to roll the I Ching or consult the tarot. Only when I was stoned was I receptive enough to understand their deeper messages. Because the constant repetition and compulsion continued to leave me mentally confused and spiritually bereft, I contrived a cosmic drama wherein all this occult knowledge was a path to a more pure mystical experience and evil forces were keeping me from true revelatory secrets.

Once in a while, often moments before I turned over the first tarot card for a new reading, I would be struck with another idea: I was the manic, burnt-out idiot who had created this dilemma in the first place. God didn't need me to trick the cosmos into revealing the divine will. In fact, if I put down the cards and the coins and the candles and the books and simply *prayed*, everything I needed to know would be revealed. This tension between manipulating divine forces through personal will and being a vessel for divine will was at the heart of the history of the occult and had found me, here in my parents' basement.

The Renaissance is a time most of us perceive as a reaction against the dark Middle Ages and the superstitious and often violent thread that ran through Christianity. It's true that there was a growing interest in empiricism and Greek philosophy, but the Renaissance was also a hotbed of interest in astrology, magic, and alchemy. The truth is, people still held fast to Christian theology, but it was said by some brave souls that the internal mysteries of the tradition had become bogged down by fevered dogma and politics. It was thought that one way of accessing the more romantic and sublime truth of Christianity was to go back to Greco-Roman and Egyptian philosophy and mystery cults.

The *Corpus Hermeticum*, compiled from a series of other works in the fifteenth century, some possibly dating back to third-century Egypt, was once believed to be a collection of ancient Egyptian writing. Its author was said to be Hermes Trismegestus, a synthesis of the Greek god Hermes and the Egyptian deity Thoth, both of whom were messenger gods. Renaissance scholars revived the texts, a move that influenced occult and esoteric thought even today.

The *Corpus* explains that human beings are not distinct from God, but are in fact perfect reflections of the divine, as epitomized in one of its most lasting pronouncements: "As above, so below." Only our ignorance and our material senses keep us from this understanding. As the protagonist in the text eventually comes to understand, "In Heaven am I, in earth, in water, air; I am in animals, in plants; I'm in the womb, before the womb, after the womb; I'm everywhere!" Erik Davis, in his book *Techgnosis*, describes it in such a way as to show how the *Corpus* prefigures psychedelic thought: "The Hermetica pictures the cosmos as a living soul, a magnetic network of correspondences that linked the earth, the body, the stars, and the remote spiritual realms of the godhead." These correspondences created a cosmology in which everything was seen as connected to everything else. The Renaissance hermeticists saw the hieroglyphics of Egypt as a magical and sacred language that taught this truth of correspondence through pictorial representation. They also believed the natural world was essentially a system of symbols that referenced the divine. Many hermetic teachings were accomplished through the use of emblems, those drawings that contained myriad symbols and signs that required meditation and contemplation for their meaning to be released.

For the most part, the Church and the Enlightenment, in their own ways, were both able to bury hermetic teachings. The Church deemed them heretical, and the burgeoning scientific impulse turned alchemy into chemistry and astrology into astronomy. Nevertheless, a time would come when people were finding both normative religious teachings and an ever-growing positivist scientific spirit to be lacking. Neither could account for that perpetual human instinct that there is more to God's creation than the Bible can explain, more to the cosmos than a telescope can reveal.

People wanted to feel their lives were governed by a spiritual reality, but many had become wary of Christian dogma. Science was proving the fallibility of scripture, but it didn't have all the answers. By the nineteenth century alternative means of igniting spiritual fires were nothing to be ashamed of, and people had long stopped being afraid of being branded witches or warlocks when their religious proclivities did not fall in line with those of the Church. Writers, businessmen, artists, and entertainers were all interested in both ancient esotericism and what were perceived as new discoveries in the psychic sciences. Sir Arthur Conan Doyle, the man behind Sherlock Holmes, collected stories of faerie photography and after the death of many family members turned to spiritualism. Harry Houdini so believed he might be able to communicate with his deceased mother that he spent his time trying to discern whether mediums were indeed frauds, hoping to discover one that might make contact with the spirit world.

One way of making contact, called skrying in the spirit vision, was a technique for talking to angelic beings, and one of Samuel

Liddell MacGregor Mathers's favorite pastimes. Mathers, a veg-
etarian, amateur war historian, and Freemason, was a personality
of some force and, in the later part of the nineteenth century, the
founding member of an occult fraternity known then and now
as the Hermetic Order of the Golden Dawn, formed around
1888, a time when in both England and America psychic and
spiritual phenomena were all the rage and a polite séance in the
home of a society maven was common.

Taking his cue from the more highly regarded magician
John Dee, Mathers perfected skrying as a system of clairvoy-
ance. Dee, an astrologer and mathematician who gave advice
to Queen Elizabeth I, used a shew stone (showing stone) for
speaking to angels and recording their secret language. Proper
skrying, as Mathers practiced it in the 1890s, requires a knowledge of divine names—those particular names of the angels and
other celestial creatures that actually impart celestial secrets.
These names (Hosen, Saraph, Proxosos, Habhi, Acuar, Tirana,
Alluph, Nercamay, Nilen, Morel, Traci, to name a few) are the
key to the kind of magic that Mathers had invested a great deal
of persistent energy in understanding, a magic that was codified
in a number of medieval texts, including *The Sacred Magic of
Abramelin the Mage* and my adolescent companion, *The Key of
Solomon the King.*

Mathers claimed this magic was so powerful that he even
thought to offer a warning regarding some of the spells: "I must
further caution the practical worker against the use of blood;
the prayer, the pentacle, and the perfumes, rightly used, are sufficient and the former verges dangerously on the evil path."

Mathers, along with the two other Golden Dawn founders,
William Robert Woodman and William Wynn Westcott, saw
their new magical order as the perfect synthesis of ancient
wisdom. They believed they would help herald in a new age of
spiritual development. While they borrowed heavily from Jewish

and Christian sources, they ultimately rejected the mainstream views of these traditions, believing that they failed to place the proper emphasis on deeper mysteries and on the power of the human will. The Golden Dawn attracted members from every station, including the Irish poet William Butler Yeats.

While the main tools of these occult societies were the more Western traditions of kabbalah and hermeticism, the East continued to inspire with a romanticized view of Hinduism and Buddhism. Golden Dawn initiates also believed in a group of ascended masters, sometimes called the Secret Chiefs, a group of beings who many believed were originally of Indian descent, who had attained great spiritual power and were waiting for the right moment to expand the consciousness of the rest of the world. Occultists from America and England went to Asia in search of secret mysteries, but they usually found traditional Buddhist and Hindu practices—meditation and yoga, to be precise—that offered little in the way of magical acumen.

One of these men, Allan Bennett, a quiet and respected member of the Golden Dawn, eventually found his own way to Asia in 1900, became a monk for a time, and, like many before him, began to see magic as a corrupted form of spirituality. Bennett worked hard to bring Buddhism to the West, but, sadly, he is known more for his relationship with Aleister Crowley. Crowley was one of the most promising young magicians involved in the Golden Dawn, but always seemed to create controversy wherever he went. Bennett introduced Crowley to Buddhism, which Crowley would reject in favor of his own more magically (and sexually inclined) beliefs. Bennett, rumor has it, also introduced Crowley to drugs, specifically cocaine and heroin, which Bennett, despite his ascetic leanings, had come to rely on for medicinal purposes. As the writer Stephen Skinner explains, many in the later counterculture would look back to Crowley as their patron saint: "More than seventy years before, Crowley had come to the same conclusion, that the doors of perception may be slowly opened by spiritual and magical practice, or rapidly forced open by the application of psychedelic drugs."

The true commingling of magic and mysticism, however, came from H. P. Blavatsky—a Russian immigrant once described as "obese . . . with small pretty hands," and, for a time, the grand dame of spiritualism and spirituality in America. Her Theosophical Society, founded in 1875 and based in New York City, emphasized the true spiritual core underlying all religions. What Blavatsky did so brilliantly in her major works, which include *Isis Unveiled* and *The Secret Doctrine*, was synthesize occultism and Eastern religious philosophy (Buddhism, yoga) into an easily digestible (if not esoterically delivered, for authenticity's sake) idea that would become an essential part of the new mystical and religious thought in America: All religions speak the same internal (or mystical) truth, but their transmission has been corrupted. Blavatsky saw that the ancient mystery traditions, such as hermeticism, were the well from which all the later traditions derived their own vital internal mysteries. Blavatsky wrote, "It is from this wisdom-religion that all the various individual 'Religions' (erroneously so called) have sprung, forming in their turn offshoots and branches, and also all the minor creeds, based upon and always originated through some personal experience in psychology."

The deeper implication is that people from dissimilar religious traditions and backgrounds could all have a mystical experience that would tune their human frequency to their true spiritual identity, an idea that Richard Bucke would eventually call cosmic consciousness and Aldous Huxley would nuance and amplify with his perennial philosophy. Theosophists, however, had a more occult sensibility and believed we all have within us the capability to become "ascended masters," those great people whose teachings can bring about a new world consciousness. (And ad infinitum, the ascended masters are those who came to teach us that we can all be ascended masters to teach others that they can be ascended masters . . .) Blavatsky also reshaped the idea of mysticism by inserting into it a notion of special knowledge: Mystical experiences weren't merely a union with the divine and the creation of a brotherhood of man; they were a tool for learning the secrets of the universe. Mystical knowledge became synonymous with occult knowledge.

This conflation would ultimately lead to a kind of cultural psychic confusion about what spirituality meant. Was talking to spirits "spiritual" in the same way that yoga is? What about making a pentagram in the air with a consecrated dagger? Was that the same as chanting a mantra during meditation?

In Aleister Crowley's book, *Magick in Theory and Practice*, he writes, "Magick enables us to receive sensible impressions of worlds other than the 'physical' universe (as generally understood by profane science)." Receiving sensible impressions from other worlds is a markedly different intention from enlightenment. Magic divorced from a religious tradition was at one time inconceivable. Even *The Key of Solomon the King* situates itself within a Jewish context, and the Renaissance magicians and alchemists were themselves mostly Christian—heterodox, to be sure, but Christian nonetheless.

Even Crowley's peers in the Golden Dawn would find themselves confronted with uncertainty, and some were hard-pressed to do away with their own traditional religious leanings. Waite, who considered himself more mystic than magician, debated constantly with Samuel Mathers over whether or not the Golden Dawn was a magical organization or a mystical one. His overriding belief was that the true magus's intentions should focus on inner union with God, rather than outward magical effects. This tension, and a number of personality clashes, were to split the Golden Dawn. Waite and his followers formed the Fellowship of the Rosy Cross, a decidedly Christian mystical organization.

The intention behind the opening of hidden spiritual doors, be it magical or mystical, would not be easily reconciled—not for the occultists at the turn of the twentieth century, not for the hippies, and not for me in the suburbs of Boston in the twentieth century, where this same tension was being played out in subtle and personal ways. I first glimpsed it with regard to a next-door neighbor who was the leader of the local spiritualist church and a therapist. Years earlier, I had walked his dog and gotten to know him and his wife fairly well. I always felt vaguely self-conscious around them, and with every new phase I went through, I felt as though they were watching me through their window and asking the spirits of the dead how I was going to end up. Their home was filled with shelves displaying giant crystal formations and other rare stones. Everything about them glowed with an inner light, but they were also awfully square. If they had access to some secret knowledge, they didn't do much with it.

One evening the couple invited me to their church to watch a medium perform. I went along, curious and a bit apprehensive. The only other time I had been to any other kind of religious service that wasn't Jewish was with a friend and his mother who had turned out to be evangelical Christians. At that service the minister kept urging everyone who wasn't saved to get up—*get up!*—and come to the front and accept the truth of Jesus. He always seemed to be looking straight at me, and I could feel my friend's mother's eyes on my back, as if she thought staring hard enough would propel me out of my seat. I knew even less about what went on at a spiritualist church; I just hoped I would not be possessed by a spirit.

The medium, a charismatic middle-aged man, started off by guessing the contents in people's pockets, or rather by receiving messages from the dead about what was in people's pockets. Soon he was calling out the names of the deceased and people in the audience were swooning and crying. Uncles, aunts, parents, and even the great-great-grandparent of someone revealed themselves through the medium and offered simple yet insightful advice on their living relatives' lives. I was fidgety, and maybe even a bit bored. It was all so much trickery. There was no real magic here, I thought.

In the 1870s, Madame Blavatsky was having a very public argument with the Boston Spiritualists about the true purpose of mediumship. The spiritualists, then as now, believed that spirits of the dead offered moral instruction and guidance in personal matters. They were there to remind us of God's infinite love and protection. They also believed mediumship was in no way an occult power that only an elect few should or could have access to. Blavatsky, on the other hand, believed magic, not God's love, was the force behind a spiritualist's abilities to contact otherworldly beings and should not be wasted on spirits of the dead, but should be relegated to those higher beings, avatars, who held the keys to profound spiritual secrets.

In an article responding to the Boston Spiritualists, Blavatsky mocked their disbelief in magic: "[F]or a firm Spiritualist, a believer in invisible, mysterious worlds, swarming with beings, the true nature of which is still an unriddled mystery to everyone—to step in and then sarcastically reject that which has been proved to exist and believed in for countless ages by millions of persons, wiser than himself, is too audacious!"

Whether by God or by magic, the purpose was to achieve enlightenment and spiritual insight. So how had all of it amounted to nothing more than superstition and paranoia? It appeared to me that the Buddhists and the Vedantists, Alan Watts and Ram Dass, were all wrong. There wasn't a great unity to which we all belonged. Brahman and Atman were not one. We were, in fact, the very battlefield of a great war being waged between legions of angelic and demonic forces. I myself was not without power, or at least method. So, while I could not control the outcome, I could at least decipher the signs. My tools were tarot cards, *The I Ching*, the magical implements of dagger (air), seal (earth), cup (water), and wand (fire). I kept a small bag filled with bay leaves and cinched with a red string hanging above my door to keep the evil forces at bay. With these magical devices, I could read the narrative of my eventual demise and maybe, just maybe, duck out of the way in the nick of time.

A computer stand I had built in shop class years earlier made a perfect altar. A cast-iron incense holder from Pier 1 Imports could be used to burn herbs to ward off unclean spirits. A small collection of crystals and stones could be laid out in a row to channel occult forces that were, in fact, a pop-collective unconscious that moved from theosophy and magic to yoga and Vedanta to socially conscious altered consciousness, and somehow back to magic and possibly paranoia again.

Despite having surrounded myself with every conceivable expression of the arcane and the paranormal, I had nothing to warn me about how my own thinking would become part of the occult equation that I had no aptitude to solve. It began on the night I perfected a technique of maximizing every toke from every joint. After I took a hit and drew the smoke as deeply into my lungs as it could possibly go, I would hold my breath and swallow. Once I felt the smoke had been fully captured, I would jump up and down, run in place, and do jumping jacks for as long as I could take it. As I exhaled as slowly as possible, the rush of released carbon dioxide and smoke would put me into a two- to three-second trance. By the time I was done with a joint or even a small bowlful of weed, my head would feel like a cathedral of stained glass and choirs. On one occasion when I leapt up from the couch to jump around, the next thing I knew I was lying on the floor, my vision full of flowers, opening and closing.

All this work to achieve hierophany, but something else was settling in for the long haul. First it was a quirk of thinking. Something on the TV or in a song registered in such a way that it reminded me of something else, like déjà vu, but it seemed to stretch beyond my own memories and into the universe. One afternoon I was taking a stoned stroll through the abandoned lot behind my house. Astral beings swirled around, pointing out patterns in rocks and dirt that were really veiled words and symbols. The simple walk became a cosmic drama, and I started noticing dark and infernal ciphers all around me in the pieces of broken concrete and glass. A stick in the shape of a horned animal could only be a sign that I was about to die.

That night, my attempts to calm myself with television only fed the fantasy. A *Cagney & Lacey* episode about a psychic who could channel the dead rang like a siren call. I spent the rest of the evening talking to an ex-girlfriend to let her know it was my last day on Earth. She patiently advised me it was impossible to know such a thing and slowly quieted my stoned, manic ramblings. We hung up the phone and I went to sleep. But no matter the reprieve slumber offered, I was deep in it now. I don't know if technically it was psychosis, but I was not merely a fearful, anxious kid who found both relief and spiritual possibility with drugs and who would eventually grow out of it. My synapses, stoned or straight, were not firing the way they used to.

I found myself trapped between the radio waves of electronic devices and their corresponding frequencies in the numinous. They had to travel through me to arrive at their destination. Unlike tripping, though, when everything happened so fast, it was impossible to follow the waves' entire trajectory, although this phenomenon could happen even when I wasn't stoned at all. Sine and square waves, particles all along the electromagnetic spectrum, were passing through me and leaving little bits of information in the crevices of my mind.

And soon they weren't just passing through. I found there was a difference between being merely high and being stoned enough to tune in to the invisible frequencies emanating from every electronic source. I began to pick up the signals with much greater regularity. Watching David Letterman one night, I suddenly realized that he and his musical sidekick, Paul Shaffer, were sending psychic messages to each other during the course of the show. Sometimes when I caught them, I could channel the message back to the live audience, *right through the TV set*, and cause them to giggle in unison or erupt in laughter.

After a while, the signals were everywhere, no longer separate from me. In fact, everything became a transmission of some kind with information for me alone, and usually, until it was always, it was about my death. My last acid trip chiseled away what was left of my holy dream of the psychedelic release that was supposed to free me from every want, every fear, and every bit of unease that had coiled itself around my young life.

It was raining so hard, the ground became like quicksand. Even the concrete sidewalks buckled and sagged underfoot. The whole world pitched back and forth with the wind. This couldn't be a coincidence. Everything had been like a storm lately; everything was sinking into the mud. Premonitions were crowding out other thoughts, visions of gloom, like a light that could not escape as it fell just past the event horizon. Had it ever been this dark before? Even the glow of the city was washed-out. Nothing could penetrate.

Something was wrong, that much was clear. The thunder became drums from the surrounding mountains that could not be seen, where dark forces were lying in wait. *It's only the acid* became a whisper, then a dull noise on the edge of consciousness, and then it disappeared forever, until there was nothing more real than awful hollow fear and a constant speeding toward the

unknown, which, as it turned out, did not reflect Huxley's beatific scene in which the legs of a simple chair were "St. Michael
and all angels." It was more akin to the vision of Huxley's muse
William Blake, given to him by a fearsome heavenly messenger:

> By degrees we beheld the infinite Abyss, fiery as the smoke of
> a burning city; beneath us at an immense distance was the sun,
> black but shining; round it were fiery tracks on which revolv'd
> vast spiders, crawling after their prey; which flew or rather
> swum in the infinite deep, in the most terrific shapes of animals
> sprung from corruption, and the air was full of them.

This was loneliness. This was madness. How could anyone
understand? Being forsaken, specifically chosen to be exclusively denied. Left alone in the mud and the rain to try to get
back home. Getting back home: the only thing that made sense.

No one talked about how opening the windows of awareness
would also let in all kinds of terrible phantoms, that the wet and
the wind can actually get into the brain, and clinging to each
drop of water is a salamander that the alchemists explain "is
born in the fire / In the fire it has that food and life," and that
confirms the daydreams of Pliny the Elder when he wrote, "The
salamander, an animal like a lizard in shape, and with a body
starred all over, never comes out except during heavy showers,
and disappears the moment it becomes fine."

All the preparation had meant nothing. Chanting, dancing,
comparing one holy text to another, pentagrams drawn in the
air, the tarot consulted, invocations raised on the smoke of
incense and candles. All those angelic beings whose names
shone wildly from the page were in fact these very same beings
of fire. Not the merciful and holy seraphim who sing, "Holy,
holy, holy" before the throne of God, but serpentine things with
mocking and jeering tongues of coal.

Michael was there, the Coast Guard officer with a preach-er's mouth and a pocketful of drugs. Standing in the middle of the street, the mud swirling around his feet like lava, he was drawing down the rain as a great purging of all the sins of the world. The problem was, all those sins were mine. We were no longer friends on the march toward a night of acid illumination. I was the thing to be cleansed. I was the thing to be exorcised.

Worst. Trip. Ever.

In the Park Street subway station, I waited in a slow-burning panic while trains passed by me like serpents. Suddenly I saw Linda and some other people I knew from the Common. I had not seen them in months, but it felt like it had been years, like they were strangers whom I recalled maybe meeting before, but whose names were lost to me. They opened their arms and I wanted to go to them. They spoke to me as if through a tunnel: "Are you okay? Can we help you? Come and be with us." But there was the possibility that they were demons in disguise. How could I trust anyone who glowed that brightly? I waved my hands in front of my face like a ward or charm and turned away from them.

I fled and made my way toward the one place that gave me mild comfort no matter what the trouble: the terminal, to wait for the bus that would take me home. But the bus never came, or if it did, I never knew. At some point there were police cars, ambulances. Then I was sitting in a police car with my legs out the door while the policeman kept telling me to keep calm. His partner peeked over his shoulder and said, "Boy, you sure are holding on to those beads pretty tightly." I looked down and saw a string of Hare Krishna prayer beads in my clenched fists. I opened my hands and all the fear and terror and panic flew out of me like a bolt. The policemen both jumped back and I yelled at them, "You felt that! I know you felt that!"

Later, strapped down to a hospital gurney, I tried to project the same energy at the doctors and the nurses, but they were apparently immune, or all that equipment was acting as a deflector shield.

Coming down, I began to get a sense of what was actually happening. While I had certainly been tripping my ass off, I wasn't completely at the mercy of the fickle fates. I had dialed 911 at the bus terminal. I had told the operator I was losing my shit on acid. I had gone willingly with the police, relieved that finally I had the wherewithal to reach out to a grown-up who might be able to take care of me. Nevertheless, I wasn't sure who could be trusted. There was an IV in my arm; murmuring voices came in and out. The staff psychiatrist came in to talk to me, and every time he spoke I challenged him to be "real," but I was the one strapped to a gurney, so I didn't have much sway. Security guards stood outside my room because part of the reason I was here was that I had been doing something illegal, namely, consuming Schedule I substances.

At one point an old woman in the next room with a two-packs-a-day-for-fifty-years scratch in her voice called out to me, suggesting I take off my glasses because I would "come down faster." A few Valiums took the edge off, but no matter. God still hadn't protected me; the acid had revealed nothing of consequence, except that my friends and I were all delusional and forsaken.

My final assumption that night, before I was released into the trembling care of my devastated parents, was that one of two things, or possibly both, was true. I was cursed, or I had crossed some invisible line into a nervous breakdown. If I was cursed, then it was because I had gone too far in my quest for secret knowledge, to know the mind of God. If I was having a nervous breakdown, then it had to be because of the drugs. I had failed, or they had failed me, but something had not clicked. I was out of sync with whatever angels or chemistry controlled the effects of these drugs. It had all been for nothing. I had not heeded any of the warnings—set and setting and all that.

Before we left the hospital, a nurse whom I couldn't recall ever having seen before but who seemed to know everything about me suggested that drug rehab might be in order. My father waved her proposal away. It was two-thirty in the morning, and he and my mother were still reeling from the initial phone call reporting that their younger son was slowly making his way down from the precipice of drug-induced madness. Who could blame them for just wanting to get the hell out of there and take me home?

We were all quiet in the car. I stared out the window as the final dregs of the acid made rainbow-colored trails on the rain beading on the glass. It must have seemed for them a one-off, what they believed to be my first attempt at taking a hallucinogen, gone terribly wrong. Why punish or scold me, when my horrific trip and subsequent visit to the hospital were enough? None of us ever spoke of it again.

When I got into my room that night, I pulled a pillowcase off a pillow. I tossed into it all my magical and spiritual implements, all my books on magic and Eastern philosophy, my tarot cards, candles, even the three pennies that I rolled the I Ching with. In the abandoned lot behind the townhouse association I got on my knees and dug a hole in the mud until there was room enough for my sack—a sack containing a microcosm of the entire history of the Western quest for spiritual and occult enlightenment—and shoved it in. I covered it back up as well as I could.

For years I had been telling myself that drugs, psychedelics in particular, were grooming me for an ultimate spiritual experience, but in truth I was using drugs to bypass that experience. I was afraid, on some intuitive level, that an encounter with God was also an encounter with the truth of my death, as any good mystical experience should be. I was afraid, had always been afraid, and the closer my LSD trips brought me toward this realization, the more I unconsciously steered myself in another direction, away from the clear light of the void and toward a mystifying, superstitious occultism born of bad movies and New Age reprints of hermetic philosophy. I talked about transformation as a goal, but transformation meant change, and change might mean having to give up the only thing that at one time had quieted the noisome chatter in my skull: drugs.

I went back into my room and smoked the last of the hash I had hidden in my shoe, which the security guards in the hospital had failed to uncover when they searched me. When it was gone, I vowed then and there to stop taking psychedelics and smoking pot, and to rely solely on drink and whatever else might give me the feeling of bliss, without the attendant kaleidoscope of occult ideas, to get me through what I could foresee were bound to be days and nights of turmoil.

chapter six

THE WISDOM OF EXCESS

> [Drugs] do not open the doors of another world nor do they free our fantasy: rather, they open the doors of our world and bring us face to face with our phantoms.
>
> —octavio paz

I was paralyzed. If I moved even my finger in the slightest, a seizure would surely overtake me. My heart was pumping up against my chest like it was knocking to get out. Dread and sweat coated my body like a film. The sickly light of the sun started to rise slowly up the window. I just needed to get to sleep for a few hours and I would be okay. But sleep seemed as far away as hope.

The night had not started off so badly. We had it all planned out: cocaine, managed with three packs of cigarettes and a case of beer, until midnight, when we would stop. We made a deal, shook hands, and began. That was 9:00 PM.

By 3:30 AM we were straightening half-smoked and crushed cigarettes as best we could, with the caveat that as long as there was something to smoke, we could do *one more* line. At 5:00 AM my companion fled, toward some other debauchery or at least away from my panicked and manic chatter: I had come upon the perfect life equation and it settled into my brain like a tick, grabbing hold with its tiny legs and emitting its revelation out of my mouth for what seemed like an hour: "The finite is a drop in the infinite." I kept repeating the phrase over and over, feeling as if I had finally found an answer. It filled my body with wave after wave of vibrations. Finally it turned on itself, and what had appeared as an epiphany turned into a curse. I was nothing in the face of an impersonal *All*, and everything I had done with my life up to that point had been wasted folly. This was not the final enlightenment that would liberate me; I was a drug-addled speck of stardust floating amid an uncaring and indifferent universe.

When I saw that my friend had abandoned me to my madness, I turned off all the lights and crawled under the covers, waiting for the rushing thoughts to slow and for my teeth to stop their incessant grind. As the sun rose, I began to hear a labored breathing from across the room, like a wheeze through a clenched jaw. It started moving toward me, stalking me, like a jungle cat. Closer it came, hungry and fevered, getting louder, until, just as it was about to pounce and rip out my heart, I gasped and realized the breathing was my own. I promised myself over and over if I could just get some sleep, I would never do another line. At least until later the next night.

You really can't get further from the psychedelic experience than by having a daily habit of cocaine and alcohol. Despite overwhelming paranoia and a constant feeling of exposed electrical wires bouncing along my skin, I was still convinced I could dig my way up out of the dirt and mud and eventually, once on solid ground, find my way to the mountain and begin the final ascent toward my own hierophany.

For some time I felt intimately connected to subtle gestures in the natural world: a slight breeze, the chatter of crows on a rooftop. A spiritual language was enfolded into the phenomenal world, but it was a whisper, more texture and rhythm than actual words. There was something hopefully benevolent in its accent, and it always seemed to me like a small gift from the spirits that inhabited all the secret holes in reality. To talk about it, to point it out to friends, was always futile. Even when we tripped together, no one else could detect as I could. So I learned to keep it to myself, whereupon it slowly took root and became less a flowering of ideas and inspirations and more an infestation, growing like weeds in the crevices of my psyche.

But during those days of alcohol and cocaine, the wind and the crows became dark omens, hostile, mercurial in their intent. Just as the tarot and the I Ching more often than not offered divinations of ruin, the portents I gleaned in nature told only one story: Death was inching closer, and any night could be my last. Instead of recognizing how this mounting paranoia was in sync with my growing dependence on alcohol and cocaine, I increased my intake of both.

Giving up pot and psychedelics wasn't as easy as I thought it would be. I was twenty-one, finally able to buy my own alcohol, and almost overnight my drinking intensified. I began the alchemist's task of trying to use chemistry to alter various kinds of moods and illuminations. Valium was good for pulling the wool over my eyes when I needed a respite from the nagging paranoia. When I wanted to feel a little bit of hope and inspiration, a few lines of coke gave me instant awareness that maybe everything in the universe would be okay. As soon as that feeling faded, the oncoming rush of despair could be avoided only by doing another line. Inconceivably, I thought I was holding it together pretty well on the outside. I worked the night shift as a grill cook at a delicatessen and sat in the back of the lecture hall in a philosophy class at the local community college. Otherwise, my world was very small.

I had finally separated myself from having to pretend I was someone else, someone with strong ideals and creative drives. Only a few years earlier, living on the fringe had been part of a great and adventurous spiritual path, but that was no longer viable. All that energy and dope burned up seeking the secret wisdom lodged deep in the mind of God had been a fool's errand. The best thing to do was shave away anything that might require me to keep up that pretense, so that I could just maintain without having to defend any of it any longer.

I was lucid enough to know that at some point my parents would notice that whatever personality quirks of mine they had convinced themselves were just harmless eccentricity were starting to pick up speed and mutate into something else more troubling. I couldn't foresee what was ahead, but the awful irony was that at the very moment I crossed that invisible line into my drug use becoming a mortal liability, I could see it happening but was powerless to stop it.

Because I was now twenty-one, I thought it time to move out of my parents' house. My older siblings had all taken this bold step when they were eighteen, so I was even running a bit behind. By this point, I had constructed an elaborate fiction about college. Unbeknownst to anyone but the school's administration, I had been kicked out for failing all my classes for two consecutive terms but was allowed to register for a single course. I continued to talk to friends and coworkers about my studies, about my dreams to be a poet and a scholar. To move into my own place was the next logical step in building a life for myself. But it was all a sham, a wicker man about to go up in flames.

My friend and I rented a small house on the water, and I made just enough from my job as a grill cook for rent, booze, and peanut butter sandwiches. The day I left, I was carrying boxes up from my basement room; my friend's pickup truck was outside. My father stood at the top of the stairs, waiting to help me. As I placed a box into his hands and was about to turn to go down to get another, our eyes locked. I felt completely exposed, naked, a scared child before this man who had conquered his own fears and doubts even as he had lost everything so many years before. I had moved from a life of earnest seeking (coupled with some vaguely delusional ideas) to an empty existence of daily drug and drink, and I knew I would die like that, with nothing much else, and likely soon. For the briefest moment I wanted to fall into my father's arms and ask him to help me, but I was paralyzed by a greater need: getting the hell out of there so I could score before the day was out. My dad must have also been paralyzed by some fear of his own—that he was powerless, and to reach out without having anything to give would be worse than hoping for the best. Nothing else passed between us, except for a cardboard box, as I thanked him for his help getting stuff out to the truck.

In my own place, I was reduced to figuring out how to get drunk or high, getting drunk or high (or both), and reading the same comic and listening to the same song over and over. The language of comics was a grammar I understood perfectly; I could absorb the narrative like a process of osmosis, even at my most brain-addled. *Batman: The Cult*, written by the great Jim Starlin and drawn by one of the premier horror-comic artists, Bernie Wrightson, was at the top of the small pile I kept near me at all times. Wrightson's artwork was so familiar to me from his work on *Eerie, Creepy*, and *Swamp Thing* that every figure and every background were a comfort to me.

In *The Cult*, Batman is kidnapped, drugged, and brainwashed by the leader of a violent religious cult. The dark-knight detective is given to hallucinations, falling into states of terror and doubt. Batman imagines himself at one moment unraveling like an apple peel and at the other wearing the battle armor of some supernal being. He is beaten, completely, but by sheer force of will he is able to rise above his visions and ultimately defeat his enemy. With every panel, I felt as though Batman's plight were my own, not because I was a superhero, but because I identified at the cellular level with the roller coaster of hopelessness as it turns to hope and back again.

My love of music had been condensed to a single album side and, more specifically, a single song played over and over: "America," by Simon and Garfunkel. While an essential marker of the late sixties, the song is without a single psychedelic vibe. What it has instead are longing and a deep sadness not only for things left behind, but for the inability to foresee even the next day. As with Batman's wavering between dread and rapture, I identified not with the literalness of Simon and Garfunkel's lovers and their bus ride, but the sorrow that uncannily captured the state of affairs in my head and what I thought about the world. I had nothing but regret, had built nothing that I could destroy if only to feel like I was accomplishing something. And the future was nonexistent, just a shadow on the periphery.

If you had asked if it was because of the drugs, I would have flared up and raged. They were the only thing that kept the worst of the demons at bay. Nevertheless, every time I reached for a pill or a snort or a drink, something rose up against it, but it was powerless. While I no longer believed in any transcendental reality beyond the imps that scratched out messages of doom on my brain, I blamed God also.

God had chosen not to descend, neither had I been lifted up. No incarnation had revealed itself to me. I was utterly alone, and so it was up to me to carve my own idols and worship whatever golden calf emerged. But first, one more line. It is true, as writer Octavio Paz says, "Drugs provoke the vision of the universal correspondence of all things, arouse the powers of analogy, set objects in motion, make the world a vast poem shaped by rhymes and rhythms." At this point in my life, however, the correspondence was the mocking copulation of devils, motion was merely the chaotic death of stars, and the poem of the world was best reflected by the words of another drug addict, Baudelaire, in *Les Fleurs du mal (The Flowers of Evil)*: "Always the Demon stirs at my side; he floats about me like an impalpable air."

The most honest account of the warped spiritual awareness that flourishes for the drug addict is in the film *Drugstore Cowboy*, directed by Gus Van Sant. Bob, played by Matt Dillon, is a resourceful and clever drug user who leads his friends through a series of drugstore break-ins in search of the perfect high. His Achilles' heel is his superstitions, centered mainly on the most mundane of details: putting a hat on a bed. When one of his companions commits this most grievous act, their self-fulfilling downfall begins, led in no small part by Bob's maniacal insistence on their very doom.

In the house where I was living, only a few miles away from the home I grew up in, people came in and out at all hours like wraiths. I just watched it all go on: Parties would start, then peak, and then the next morning I would find the place empty except for beer cans and ashtrays filled to overflowing. I interacted with the goings-on only so far as they afforded me a drink or a drug. There had been signposts along the way that this truck of nitroglycerine was heading down a treacherous road, but as long as the next high or drink was in front of me, all I had to do was keep my hand on the wheel and stay on course. Over the year I had been selling my prized possessions for extra money to buy extra drugs: books, an Atari 800 with 32k, and, tragically, unforgivably, my records (which included, among many others, an early demo pressing of Minor Threat's *Out of Step*; first pressings of the Misfits' *Walk Among Us* and *Earth A.D.*;

the *Split LP (Faith/Void)*; Black Flag's "TV Party" single; and the original Dead Kennedys' "Nazi Punks Fuck Off," with the included anti-Nazi armband).

After being out of touch for more than two years, Linda, my dear friend from the days on the Boston Common, somehow found out how to get in touch with me. She called one afternoon when I happened to be anxiously and desperately without anything to drink, or snort. We spoke on the phone for some time, trying to catch up with each other's lives, but I had nothing worth reporting and somehow got around to asking her if she was holding. She said she had some weed. I had promised myself I would never smoke pot again after my harrowing last LSD trip, but an opportunity to get high that day might not come again, so I quickly invited her to drive the thirty miles or so from where she was to my place on the water north of Boston. She had no car, but her roommate agreed to drive. It was going to be a fantastic reunion—two lost, kindred souls finding each other again.

By the time she arrived, I was crawling the walls waiting for her pot. I don't quite know what she saw, but the look on her face when she walked into the house and witnessed how my state of mind was reflected in my surroundings made me feel ill at ease. It was one of the few moments when the observer returned, this time in the form of another person I had once loved and whose idea of me mattered more than anything.

We quickly got to smoking what turned out to be a single and painfully thin joint. Getting only a little high was worse than not getting high at all, but I was stoned enough that I began my inward turn, becoming incomprehensible, pointing out connections and subtle textures in speech and gestures that made no sense to anyone but me. We had nothing to say to each other. I was aware for a few terrible moments how sick I had become, how without humor, self-respect, or lucidity.

Eventually they got up to leave, as if some poisonous gas had suddenly entered the room. I offered to give them directions back to Boston, but I couldn't finish writing them down. I became so immersed in the tiny details that it took me ten minutes to explain how to get out of the driveway. I looked up from my tiny cryptic script and they had fled.

The early experiences of getting high include an aspect of consciousness that objectively observes feeling and thoughts—a witness. This witness also serves as a kind of buffer or conscience between thinking about getting high and actually doing it. One can reflect on the various outcomes: *Is this a good idea? Is the timing okay? Will something about this situation make me freak out if I smoke this joint? Is it worth possibly going to jail for?* But as an addict gets deeper in, the witness grows more and more amorphous, until there is no distinction between the self that is high and the self that has some ability to keep you safe. There is also no distance between the thought of getting high and actually doing it. Consequences are no longer weighed, set and setting be damned.

After Linda left, the witness decided to make an appearance, and what he saw had taken place during his absence was not good. I had gotten mighty sick without that part of myself reminding me to keep on guard against the oncoming madness.

That night the house again filled with people looking for a safe place to party. They were all friends of my roommate, but they appeared as hostile entities. Yet I took everything they had to offer. At about 2:00 AM I was doubled over with sickness, my vision a fractured spinning kaleidoscope. I couldn't stand and finally crawled to the bathroom, where I lay down on the cool tile, again wondering why it always came to this. I was having a spiritual experience, after all, zooming headlong toward a final truth, which is that all things die, but some die sooner than others. If there was a revelation, it was this: My will had collapsed under the weight of forces I could not control nor any longer deny. Searching for God was no good to me now; I needed a way to stay alive so I could continue to drink and get high. But death was coming for me, as it does eventually for all addicts.

Wavy Gravy suggests that a new social and spiritual conscious-ness would have been hard to come by without psychedelics: "I think that maybe we saved one hundred–some years, because we were totally immersed in this Eisenhower, golf-putting men-tality, and along came the psychedelics, which just blasted all this karmic cement away." Would the inverse be true because of the shift from psychedelics to opiates and speed?

There is no doubt that part of the reason why marijuana and LSD gave way to harder drugs was the federal government's intense war on pot and hallucinogens. As the journalist Dan Baum suggests in his 1996 book, *Smoke and Mirrors*, the War on Drugs forced peaceful stoners to have to act like criminals just to get a dime bag. It also framed them as "druggies" in the eyes of mainstream culture and made smoking marijuana look as scary as shooting cocaine. All of this would increase a sense of alienation and paranoia. When you're not even certain if the person selling you drugs can be trusted, there is no one left to trust. This led the once hopeful, determined counterculture to adopt a paranoid and ambiguous sense of their place in the world.

For many who had once held on to the promise of an Aquarian Age, everything had become suspect. Forces beyond our con-trol seemed to be controlling politics. Conspiracy theories were widespread. Actual traumatic events, such as the assassination of President John F. Kennedy and Watergate, were ripe for wild speculation. Images of the Kent State shootings became more ubiquitous than images of Woodstock.

One of the most radical conspiracy theories to come down the pike suggested that Ken Kesey, who was an admitted participant in the early government-sponsored research into the effects of psychedelic drugs, was a kind of Manchurian Candidate. Kesey, the theory goes, was brainwashed into leading a group of radicals on a Day-Glo-painted bus all around the country and dosing thousands of young men and women with LSD in an attempt not only to understand how the drug would affect a large group of people, but also to discredit the hippies by showing them to be nothing more than a group of ineffectual, crazed, dancing loons.

But there was another reason for the aging counterculture to become suspicious: As early as 1968, there were already signs that even the most highly regarded spiritual teachers were suspect, such as when The Beatles discovered that their guru, the yogi Maharishi Mahesh, was happy to provide more profane services along with his sacred ones. During a retreat with The Beatles and other public luminaries, the yogi who introduced the West to Transcendental Meditation was rumored to take some time off from meditation to seek sexual favors from some of the women in attendance.

In interviews on the subject later, John Lennon and Paul McCartney were not that specific as to what really went on when they were traveling in the Maharishi's company, but McCartney was once quoted as saying, "We made a mistake. We thought there was more to him than there was. He's human. We thought at first that he wasn't." In a *Playboy* interview with Lennon, he admits the song "Sexy Sadie" was about the Maharishi: "I was just using the situation to write a song, rather calculatingly but also to express what I felt."

A later *New York Times* article goes far in recovering the reputation of the Maharishi. It appears the rumors were started by Alex Mardis, "a supposed inventor and charlatan who had become a Beatles insider. 'Magic Alex,' as he was known, had agendas of his own, and may have fabricated (or at least exaggerated) the story." Eventually George Harrison and McCartney made amends to the Maharishi. But in the collective unconscious of the seekers of America, the damage had already been done: Gurus were not to be trusted.

Lennon himself had to face this for his fans. Numerous interviews and film clips show him irritated, angry, or just plain exhausted at people's attempts to find deeper meaning or symbols in his lyrics. He in no way wanted to be seen as a spiritual leader or guru. For Lennon, his music was an expression of his human condition, not his higher self.

In a remarkable home-movie artifact, Lennon finds a haggard stranger hanging around his property. The long-haired fellow explains that Lennon's songs had told the truth about him. "It all fits," he says to Lennon. To which Lennon responds, "Anything fits if you're tripping on some trip . . . I was just having fun with words." The poor man is quietly insistent: "You weren't thinking of anyone in particular?" Lennon tries again to explain that his music is about the banality of his own life. Lennon asks the man, "Are you hungry?" and invites him inside to eat. This anonymous character, whose story would have been lost if not for a serendipitous moment with a movie camera, is a stand-in for the end of the sixties and for the underlying secret fear that if all of it didn't mean everything, it meant nothing at all.

I had long ago come to believe that getting high was not a choice, that it was the only true method for achieving contact with the divine will, for perfect liberation from all my fear, doubt, and anxiety. It is said that at some moment in an addicts' sobriety, nothing can keep them from a drug or a drink except a moment of grace.

One night I was outside, in the freezing cold, waiting for a friend who had promised to meet me at the train depot and lend me some money. That night at the train station, waiting—God, why was there always so much waiting, in the cold, so much bloody waiting around?—I was certain my buddy would come through with the real thing. I was waiting in the cold as I had done dozens and dozens of times for whoever was to meet me, not yet stoned—anxious, sure, but grooving in the knowledge I would be high soon. I was getting jumpy. My heart started racing. Time sped up. Then I was scared. Panicked. Nothing was happening. There was absolutely nothing to be afraid of. I had been paranoid before when high, but never when straight and never like this. There was no unseen enemy, no invisible demons or ghosts, familiar spirits that I was used to. This was something else. I was crazy with fear and anxiety. I couldn't wait any longer for my friend. I ran home, ran into my room, got under the covers of my bed, and prayed that this fear would be taken from me.

There is a Hasidic tale of a rabbi who loved God but felt he didn't fear God as he should. So he prayed for the fear of God to be instilled in his heart. One night he was thrown onto his knees, trembling before the divine, and called out, "Please, God, take this fear from me." I did not see God that night. But I felt the coil of Leviathan around my throat, and I knew, I dreaded to know, that it was probably because the drink and the drugs were finally catching up to me.

The next night I got on a rusty ten-speed bike and rode in the pouring rain toward another kind of unknown: the basement of a huge Catholic church where men and women gathered to smoke copious amounts of tobacco and drink thin milky coffee out of Styrofoam cups. When I walked in, I could barely see for the smoke. People sat around long tables. Some brooded. Many more seemed oddly cheerful, despite the dour and explicit discussions of debauchery and degradation. I didn't know if I belonged here, but I didn't have anywhere else to be except home, and all that waited for me there was some kind of shameful bout with drink and drug that would only bring me one step closer to death.

The only thing that kept me there was the nagging idea that these people knew something I didn't about what Baudelaire calls the addict's "frantic craving for any substance—dangerous or not—that could excite his individuality, and set before his eyes, if only for an instant, the second-hand paradise that was the object of his every desire," and that if I didn't at least sit down for this one measly hour, I might never learn.

I found a group of other young people trying to stay clean, and together we formed something like that Boston Common fellowship, only without the drugs and delusions of spiritual grandeur. Some of us had a harder time turning the corner. Jacob, a sensitive, gnomelike man, continued to put aluminum foil on the heating grates of his apartment to keep the snake-headed demons from coming in through the ducts. Juliet, an ex-stripper and opiate addict, had visions of tiny mouths on the tips of her fingers communicating obscene and lurid messages from the dead, and she eventually put herself in front of a train, even after having been clean for several months. Mitch once took twenty-seven Tylenol and codeine to try and stop the voices in his head, only to wake up two days later convinced everyone else was dead and he had emerged into some purgatory. Long after he figured out he was still in the land of the living and started getting sober, he continued to wonder if everyone around him really was dead and part of a conspiracy to keep him tethered to limbo.

I was astonished to meet so many other people who had received hidden transmissions from their TVs and radios. The details of our lives were markedly different, but the thing that connected us was an ache, a deep and abiding spiritual thirst. Carl Jung believed that the "cure" for alcoholism could come about only through a great spiritual transformation. The idea of a spiritual solution to the problem of alcohol addiction would become for Bill Wilson, the co-founder of Alcoholics Anonymous, the foundational idea of his twelve-step program of recovery.

"I was seized with an ecstasy beyond description. Every joy I had known was pale by comparison" is how Wilson described being apprehended by a great white light during a stay in a hospital for alcoholism. He was at the end of his rope, his whole life decimated by drink. A few days earlier Ebby T., an old friend and member of a Christian temperance movement called the Oxford Group, had visited him and explained to Wilson that he had gotten sober through a religious conversion. Wilson was skeptical at best, probably hiding the religious hostility he nurtured. But something about his old friend's changed demeanor made an impression. Wilson agreed to go with Ebby to a meeting of the Oxford Group, but while he seemed moved by the experience, he needed a few more drinks. He ended up back in the hospital, where, as Wilson describes it, "A wind, not of air, but of spirit . . . blew right through me."

There is some thought that this experience was a direct result of the treatment used by William Silkworth, the doctor who treated Wilson. Silkworth used belladonna, a plant that can produce hallucinations, "for reducing stomach acids," but the accounts of belladonna use suggest that while it is capable of producing some pretty top-notch hallucinatory visions, this kind of dramatic mystical experience is not in its chemistry. Belladonna, once used by Victorian women to dilate the pupils to appear sexually aroused, seems to act more as a poison than a hallucinogen. More likely its visions are terrifying and not prone to leading the person toward moral self-inspection.

Soon after Wilson, along with Dr. Bob Smith, founded Alcoholics Anonymous, they were approached by people who wanted to get and stay sober but had not had the benefit of

Wilson's vivid flash of light to keep them on the steady path. Wilson, in an appendix to what is popularly known as the Big Book, the main text of the twelve-step organization, made certain to explain that not all spiritual experiences are sudden and dramatic. His reference for most of what he understood about all this was William James and his *Varieties of Religious Experience*, with which Wilson describes what he calls the "educational variety" of spiritual insight, a spiritual experience that happens on reflection after one realizes that his or her life has slowly, over time, been utterly transformed. Wilson had more in common with James than just agreement on the nature of spiritual experiences: Like James, he would come to understand that chemistry could do very well to provide insight into mystical states of consciousness.

Through a mutual friend, Wilson made the acquaintance of Aldous Huxley, who was very impressed with Alcoholics Anonymous. Huxley told Wilson about some research that Humphrey Osmond (the man who first dosed Huxley) was doing using LSD to treat alcoholics. Osmond's original idea was that if he could induce a state of mind similar to delirium tremens in struggling alcoholics, they might be put off alcohol for good—sort of a "scared straight" approach. But it didn't always turn out that way. Patients in the research program seemed to like acid, and it often produced feelings that were spiritual. Wilson agreed to try it, as he was someone obviously interested in finding the best solution to the alcohol problem. AA was doing a pretty good job as it was, but Wilson was continually interested in ways to expand his alcoholic fellows' religious consciousness: "We are not cured of alcoholism. What we really have is a daily reprieve contingent on the maintenance of our spiritual condition."

In 1956, with Aldous Huxley, Bill Wilson, took LSD. Susan Cheever, in her biography of Bill Wilson, *My Name Is Bill*, writes that he enjoyed his trip and he wanted everyone else to try it,

including his wife, Lois. The official histories of AA put out by
its General Service Committee make no attempt to downplay
this story. Wilson took LSD numerous times, but eventually, for
the sake of the organization he founded, he had to give it up.
Part of Wilson's struggle as a sober man was figuring out how to
continue to help support and guide AA without always having
to be its representative. More than that, he wanted to be just a
regular guy in search of a spiritual life that was sustaining to him
and his sobriety. All the same, he was the very non-anonymous,
de facto "leader" of an organization that claimed no leadership,
no governance, and, most important, no opinion on anything
but alcoholism. But as much as Wilson understood his experiences with LSD to be outside the purview of AA as a whole,
LSD is still a drug. Bill Wilson of Alcoholics Anonymous being
seen tripping on acid was not going to be favorable for the
organization in the long run. So he agreed to stop.

This story, often lost in the annals of twelve-step history,
is important because it continues to illuminate the often precarious relationship between drug and alcohol addiction and
the search for a spiritual experience. If Jung is right that at its
roots alcoholism is a desperate quest for an encounter with
the gods, then it begs the question as to what role psychedelic
drugs specifically play in the nature of addiction. Most phy-
sicians and researchers agree that of themselves, psychedelic
drugs are not addictive, at least not in the same physical way
that opiates like heroin and morphine are, or even psychologically, such as alcohol and cocaine have proven to be. Even
marijuana is believed not to be addictive, and the Drug Policy
Alliance Network, a progressive drug-policy think tank, says
that only a very small percentage of marijuana users smoke on
a daily basis. (Although who hasn't known at least one maintenance smoker?)

But what of experience? Addictions to gambling and sex are

very real dilemmas. It is not a stretch to suggest that any experience that alters normal consciousness could become compulsive. Is there a possibility that this urgent desire for spiritual
nourishment can create a kind of spiritual compulsion? The
transpersonal psychologist Francis Vaughan, who recognizes
the value of psychedelics in therapeutic work, warns of what
she calls their "shadow side." She writes that there is a danger
that people who use these drugs "may become addicted to the
experience and more interested in repeating it than in changing
the quality of their lives."

Bill Wilson again stands out because he tried to use LSD
with a moral intention, as a way to strengthen "one's direct
experience of the cosmos and of God." This God, or higher
power, was essential to Wilson's understanding of how to get
and stay clean. Nevertheless, many people, including me, found
themselves a heap of psychic waste at the door of a twelve-step
meeting because of how badly they wanted that direct experience, and wanted it over and over again.

My first job sober was selling electronics at a local Radio Shack.
It was like coming home. Next to the gaming store the Compleat
Strategist, Radio Shack was always a place to feel secure and
inspired. The salesmen there (we were all men) were another of
the many gatherings of misfits I continued to find myself part of.
Something about this store in particular attracted the marginal.
The store was located in downtown Lynn, where I used to regularly score drugs. To be there newly clean felt vaguely strange and
perilous. But I wasn't the only one with a past that surrounded
me like an aura. Many of the other salesmen also seemed to
be escaping from something. Radio Shack was a perfect place
to start over. At the time not quite mainstream, it was just off
the grid enough that even the customers often were outcasts in
their own right. One regular was a quadriplegic in a motorized

wheelchair rigged with all kinds of scanners and radios. Every week he came in to buy another crystal that opened up a channel in the police- and fire-radio frequency bands. There really were messages that could be heard everywhere.

One morning I walked in to start my shift proudly wearing a new tie and clean shirt (it had been a long time) and saw a large man hunched over one of the electronic keyboards we kept plugged in as a demo for customers to try out. Normally we rarely heard anything from it but the preprogrammed "When the Saints Go Marching In," but this time it was emitting the strained and beautiful chords of a modern classical composition, filled with discordance threaded through melodic melancholy passages. The player was Robert, a misanthrope with thin greasy hair pasted to his head and huge metal-framed glasses with tape holding the bridge together. He was introduced to me as a new salesman. There was something instantly recognizable in his eyes. Robert trembled when we shook hands, his palm wet and cold.

Over time he shared very little, but bits of his secret life emerged like the constant sweat on his brow. I was able to put together that he was or had been a musical genius, but a mix of drink and psychosis had all but crippled him. But here he was, in a downtown Radio Shack, playing exquisite atonal music. He became possessed when he played and even when he talked about music, displaying his range of knowledge of the esoteric and the obscure; he had an unusual confidence. But he could barely make it to work on time. His tie was always stained. A shirttail always managed to crawl out of his pants. He could barely manage to sell a battery to a hard-of-hearing elderly lady. He knew electronic theory and how to take small appliances apart and put them back together, but when he tried to explain to someone how to hook up an AB switch to a VCR, he was palpably confused. Yet he glowed with a fierce kind of knowing. His madness had brought to him a kind of gnosis, and through his compositions he channeled the heavenly source of all things.

It was a Radio Shack that had first brought me to the mall in Swampscott where I met Jacob, and now, amid another Radio Shack, as I negotiated a kind of new adolescence, Robert became a mentor to me in his own unsteady way. I had returned to my pre-stoned phase, again managing magical thinking and anxiety, again beginning a search for spiritual alternatives. I was lucky in that I had not lost external things I was desperately trying to recapture, like a failed marriage, a failed career, lost homes, smashed cars, etc. But I was again a confused and fidgety child and I was looking for someone who held a key to open that rusted lock of my unconscious.

Robert eventually replaced Jacob as a representation of the way pathology could lead to wisdom. He became emblematic of that other side of the mystical quest, which at the time appeared to me to be one part fool's errand, one part self-immolation. Unlike Jacob, though, Robert didn't just offer me a series of coded correspondences; he played the actual incantations on a cheap electronic keyboard and drew down the gods. I'd never felt hope like this. Despite how sick Robert still was at the time, he made me optimistic that what had seemed like a deluded search on my part was not so futile after all. A depth reopened inside me, one that I had previously been shoveling full of alcohol and cocaine in an attempt to stave off the insistent desire for gnosis.

Aside from playing, Robert's other passion was the Estonian composer Arvo Pärt, whose work represents some of the most important examples of what is known as mystic or sacred minimalism. When Robert first played Pärt for me, I was struck by how something so spare could sound so urgent. But it wasn't until I took to listening to it by myself in my own apartment that

I discovered not only a truth about music but something about my own condition as well.

Sometimes we confront within ourselves a peculiar ache—not necessarily born of circumstance—a longing that is being hammered to a fine edge on the very anvil of God. We want so badly for it to mean something; the subjectivity of that feeling can be overwhelming, especially when it seems like a song or a piece of music perfectly contains that ache, or the knowledge of who we are at the moment. With Pärt I realized that my feeling was a reflection of the music. It was the inverse of solipsism. Instead of thinking that I created the reality around me using the force of my emotions, my attention was merely a vehicle by which the music could be realized. It was as if without the listener the composition was incomplete—not because the music had been written for "me," but because hearing it helped write the music.

There was magic here after all, but instead of my hearing some enigmatic message in the music about my own life, something stretched far beyond me. Music, and by extension any expression of consciousness, were a way of taking something particular and crafting it into something universal. What I had long failed to understand was how relative the nature of altered and mystical states of consciousness really is, and that their expression through the filter of culture and language (the very filter drugs are capable of turning off) is what gives rise to meaning, real human meaning. Music, for example, has always been a powerful worldly force that captures these moments, but I had internalized them in such a way as to turn them to psychic mush. As my own nervous system began to unwind, as the nervous tension slowly released, and as my head continued to clear, I had hope that altered states could still be investigated, but it would have to be through their expression in art and music, the transmission of others' experiences. Not mine.

One night I lay in bed and adjusted my speakers so that my head was between them. I listened to The Beatles' "Strawberry Fields Forever." It was like hearing it for the first time, and I was able to tune in to the remarkable use of orchestration and layering. As I drifted in and out, I remembered once seeing the event horizon of my consciousness. I had been in a Friendly's restaurant, of all places, tripping on some decent blotter. I went to the bathroom and while standing at the urinal became mesmerized by a marble pattern on the wall. I stared deeply at it, felt myself being pulled slowly, as if into a drain. I went with it. That familiar tether unhooked and down I went. I was being pulled apart. My consciousness was falling into a black hole. Suddenly, a little red arrow whizzed by my perception. I jerked my head to follow it and was pulled out of the void and back into the flickering fluorescent light of the bathroom. I panicked when I realized how deep I had gone. For a moment I didn't care. As I listened to The Beatles and remembered, I could feel the same kind of release, of letting go, but I was being buoyed by something else, by what I had begun to build and what I was beginning to love.

Staying clean was not simply about keeping off drugs; it was a radical reassessment of how I intuited the world physically, psychologically, and spiritually. For years I had understood my thoughts and feelings as just one level in the infinitely tiered system of correspondences that started in the underworld and moved through the successive layers of hell up through the earth, into the astral planes and onward toward the multiple levels of heaven, until there at the top was the godhead, a perfect unity, unknowable, impenetrable, and totally impersonal. Somewhere near the earthly edge I existed as a kind of transmitter/receiver, and with every signal that passed through me, I felt myself sinking further down toward the infernal, rather than ascending toward the celestial. I had long ago been rewired, so that instead of feeling guilty for having to steal, lie, cheat, and otherwise act the scoundrel in order to stay sufficiently wasted, I abstracted all those deeds into a generalized sense of my own wickedness.

At one point during the last few months of my drug use, I would examine my scalp in the mirror, looking for the three sixes that adorned the boy devil, Damien, in the film *The Omen*, a movie that was part of the ever-growing obsession with devils in the popular culture of the late seventies and that impacted me subconsciously, only to arise as a literal behavioral tic more than a decade later. Could I, merely by staying clean, pull myself out of this cosmic drama?

Interestingly, it took little effort on my part. Once I stopped getting high, I no longer had to behave in questionable ways to stay high. The guilt for specific transgressions was no longer abstracted into a feeling of impending doom. I felt better, stronger, was able to sleep and eat and cut my toenails. But spiritually I was still bereft. My mind had been opened, my consciousness altered. How could I go back to the mundane, the banal, and, more terrible, the suburbs?

One afternoon, some sober compatriots and I drove north toward Gloucester. As we wound our way through the towns, I felt threatened by the homogeneity, the smiling yet foreboding houses. In the yard of one, a man was hammering a piece of wood onto a deck he was building. Nothing seemed more alien to me than the mere convention of a brand-new patio on a manicured lawn. And I knew that even clean, my life ultimately heading toward some form of normalcy, I didn't want that deck or that lawn.

Nevertheless, there was something comforting about the suburbs. I was afraid to go into the city, worried about temptation, knowing I would be drawn immediately back to those places

and people that I was still secretly convinced might be my salvation. I simply could not bear the idea of getting high anymore,
was terrified of that onrush of one second of relief followed by
paranoia and despair. But how could I live? What would my life
be about, if not that perpetual uncovering of symbols and signs?
How could I weed out the obsession from true spiritual insight?
Was there even a difference?

I trusted Bill Wilson when he wrote that it wasn't necessary
to have a conception of God that fit into any category. Following
William James, I understood that while I had experiences on
drugs that could be categorized as touching upon something
mystical, those moments were not authoritative. They did not
necessarily say anything objectively true about God or nature
or the universe. The only thing they revealed, though no less
important, is that there is something beyond our perceptible
limits, but we might not ever know its name. I thought I had
to pretend all my drug trips were just momentary lapses, that
there was no truth to be found, because whatever might have
been real had been twisted beyond all recognition by addiction
and confusion. But I couldn't deny that I would always have this
slight tic in my awareness, that beyond the periphery of everything was another limit, and another beyond that, stretching
toward infinity, and maybe even toward God.

Staying drug free meant arranging my life in such a way as to
keep the phantoms at bay, no longer with incantations, but by
taking care of the simple details that had eluded me for so long:
bathing, doing laundry, showing up to work on time. The spirits
still knocked, and sometimes I could hear the divine static, as if
from an imaginary ghost box. But mostly they bounced off the
surface of objects like dragonflies on a pond.

At first it was all I could do just to go to work, attend twelve-
step meetings, and sleep. But after some time I became inspired
and started seeking out those cultural markers that made me

feel at home. I slowly built up a new record collection—King Crimson, Lou Reed and the Velvet Underground, Brian Eno, David Bowie, all the post-sixties rock that had flecks of psychedelia—but was also inspired by the future, by possibility, by change. I even started buying some comics; I worried at first that I would no longer understand them in the same way, but I found that they had grown and changed as well, adopting an identifiable realism and grittiness. This was during the years following the publication of Alan Moore's *Watchmen*, the comic that showed superheroes as anxious and troubled, heroes possibly, but stymied by public perception and their own fallibility. *Watchmen* paved the way for a new generation of comics that set aside the cosmic and bigger than life for stories that were darker and more earthbound. Art and music taught me, slowly, that drugs, despite the trouble they brought me, have made me sensitive to a particular kind of awareness that would otherwise be lost to me. But is this important? Is the psychedelic vision so essential that I need to maintain a connection to it?

It was a challenge not to read into everything. The truth is, getting and staying clean is often filled with a series of serendipitous events, the least of which is simply not having died. One easily assumes the hand of greater powers at work. Even at my most delusional I wasn't one for the idea of fate, but day after day of keeping sober often suggested I was being led, as my own will was as good to me as a punctured and deflated balloon. If not me, then who? The difference was intuiting that there might just be a higher power attending to some aspect of the universe, but not feeling paranoid as a result. Something had a hold on me, and I could finally be certain it wasn't the Devil.

Staying connected to even an idea of some transcendent reality without devolving into the psychedelic dreamspace was a challenge, and one I was not convinced I had to let go of. How to make it work without being lured back to the drugs themselves? Could I have a psychedelic experience—or even a shadow one—sober from my head to my toes, in my brain and in my blood?

We stood on the shore as the hurricane moved in. It was impossible to see for the rain and the wind. I heard my friends yelling and whooping next to me. All of us had been clean and sober for at least a few months, and we were running wild. We lived like teenagers again, stayed up all night, chased sex and other pleasures with desperation, not unlike the way we chased drugs. We smoked cigarette after cigarette, drank coffee all through the day and night, ate chocolate and pasta to stave off getting high for just one more day.

We had gotten word that a hurricane was coming in, and we had waited until the warning was issued to stay off the beaches to go to the shore. Up on a hill a small fence had been erected above the dunes. We couldn't see the ocean right in front of us. We stood with our arms out and our heads back and it didn't matter if this was our last moment, our last clean moment, our last absolutely free moment—free from fear, from sickness, from hopelessness, from loneliness, and from that awful mangled throat-crushing obsession.

I was in the center of the storm, in the whirlwind that answered Job, and behind the wind and the rain and the crashing of the waves Leviathan was there, waiting for me. I had tried to look God in the face and been scorched almost beyond recognition, but here was the divine again, more terrible than any acid trip, mightier than any angel I had tried to call up from my parents' basement.

In the Syd Barrett song, "Opel," Barrett sings "On a distant shore, miles from land / Stands the ebony totem in ebony sand / The dream in a mist of gray / On a far distant shore." The totem suggests a kind of innocent belief that drugs can induce a spiritual vision. The totem also guards the borderlands, the desolate wastes of addiction and madness. The lyrics also conjure that longing, that most human desire, to experience nonordinary consciousness so that we are utterly transformed by our encounter. God is that "far distant shore" that I ached to know, that I believed drugs could row me toward. My search for a mystical experience was divorced from any religious ritual. I had no set or setting to speak of; neither did any of my peers. We had no real reference by which to understand my desire for a spiritual experience. But inside the storm that day, I had my first glimpse of what I had once craved so maniacally. And yet the siren song still echoed around my head, calling me to that distant shore.

chapter seven

STILL SEARCHING

When I had been sober a few years, I had an opportunity to fly across the country to visit San Francisco. I had been twelve the last time I had been on a plane, and was absolutely terrified of flying. The mere thought of going to the airport weakened my knees, so getting on an airplane, I was sure, would cause them to buckle. I have always been afraid of heights, but that was not the issue. It was about panic.

Here is the scenario that kept me on the ground: I would be on the airplane, and I would start to panic for no reason. Not just generalized anxiety—something I'm pretty accustomed to—but locked-in-a-steel-tube-thousands-of-feet-in-the-air-with-nowhere-to-go anxiety that would become a full-blown panic attack. Of this I was sure. So the truth is, I wasn't afraid of planes as much as I was afraid of my own fear, afraid that my own fear would get the better of me. I wasn't worried the plane would suddenly drop out of the sky. I just couldn't stand the thought of being afraid and having nowhere to go.

I had experienced that kind of fear once before—after being sober for a few months, on a subway in Boston. The train had stopped on the outdoor bridge between Kendall Square and Charles Street. I felt a peculiar rush to my head. A staticky voice probably said something like, "We will be delayed a few moments. Sorry for any inconvenience," but what I heard was, "We will be delayed a few moments. If anyone is having an anxiety attack, please come to the front of the train." My heart tightened. I tried to breathe. I looked around at all the other passengers going about their business, waiting with nary a care in the world, all those people *not* having anxiety. Knowing I must have misheard the conductor's announcement made me feel crazy and more anxious. Then the brakes released and the train lurched, and as it broke free of its delay, my panic subsided. But the idea that I might feel anxiety like this on an airplane, in a tiny pressurized cabin, was too much to bear. Now here I was, sober, trudging through the makings of a real life. I had to find a solution. Valium was out of the question, as was the airline's booze. I asked everyone I knew for advice, but most everyone suggested the same things: drink or take drugs. Until someone mentioned hypnotism.

On my doctor's recommendation, I met the hypnotist Patrick Brady at his office in Quincy, Massachusetts. A solidly built man in his sixties, Brady has worked with law enforcement officials helping victims remember details of crimes, and for a time was director of a hypnosis unit in the Boston Police Department. I had no idea the practice had achieved such legitimacy, but I was certain I could not be hypnotized. My mind races constantly. I'm a classic insomniac kept awake by the chatter and babbling of my restless thoughts. On top of that, I believed I had already stretched my consciousness as far as it could go while on drugs. Hypnotism was a stage trick, at most a form of self-realization. It could never hold a candle to the depths I had sunk to. I told all this to Brady, but while I was spouting off my altered-state credentials, he had already gotten me.

I was in a full trance and able to take suggestions. The first were simple, parlor tricks really. I watched in dazed astonishment as Brady raised and lowered my hand with an invisible string. Soon I was in a state I would liken to lucid dreaming. He had me visualize the entire plane trip, from getting up in the morning, packing, getting in a cab, and arriving at the gate to stepping over the threshold into the plane, taking off, and landing. The whole thing couldn't have lasted more than ten minutes, but I was aware of every moment as if it were the full eight hours from my house to California. Even the smells, from my deodorant to the stale air of the airplane, were tangible and real. When he awakened me from the trance, I was in a stupor, relaxed and hazy, as if roused from a deep and restful sleep.

It didn't last. When I left Brady's office I began to feel sick, toxic, as if some dormant poison had been released throughout my body. I felt tense and anxious, worse than when I had gone in. Eventually it subsided. Once home, I began the breathing exercise Brady had taught me. Going under hypnosis had released me to a greater degree than I had ever achieved without drugs or drink, and all the old, calcified shit was churning and coming to the surface. All the dark and secret places I had thought were the depths of my psyche were just the ripples on the surface. But I was not ready for what this really meant: that merely being sober didn't mean I had gotten any closer to the underlying cause of why my desire for a spiritual experience ended in addiction and full-on craziness. At the time I was still afraid of anything that felt like an altered state. I focused on the fact that I was relaxed and no longer afraid to fly. That was what I had gone to see Brady for in the first place, not to bring about some confrontation with my subconscious. That didn't happen until a few years later, after a confrontation with a true ultimate reality.

In 1999 my mother died after a brief battle with cancer, and I struggled to make meaning of her life and the life she had shared with my father, and the fact that it could be gone in a flash. The paranoia and anxiousness that characterized my later drug and alcohol use came back to haunt me. Everything I had begun to learn about seeking God in a way that was no longer dependent on magic and superstition vanished down the trapdoor of my mother's death, and feeling securely sober dropped down into the abyss, where God followed. Desperately looking to make sense of it all, I retreated toward a familiar worldview in which everything was again charged with hidden and occult meanings. My relationship with God became a vaguely hostile interaction; I never fully understood the cosmic demands on me, yet I knew that I had to do everything in my power to meet them. I grew deeply anxious as ethical dilemmas took on precise cause and effect significance— a spiritual life hardly more sophisticated than avoiding cracks in the sidewalk. If I watched scrambled porn on late-night cable, would I not get that essay published that I had sent out a few weeks ago? Sure, maybe black cats weren't bad luck, but there was no good reason not to toss salt over your shoulder after you spilled it. Just in case. It was looking like my fear of flying was a symptom of some other, more profound anxiety.

The hypnotherapist's office was decorated tastefully with a Mediterranean motif. She sat across from me in a classic Eames recliner and ottoman, cradling a cup of tea, her notes on her lap. Myra is mild, with a vaguely distracted affect. She started

to ask me why I wanted to see her, and I had to admit, out loud
to another person, that I had anxiety. This had been my secret
since I was a young boy. People knew me as sometimes exhib-
iting a certain high-strung nervous tendency, but I never let on
to anyone that I had been plagued by anxiety my whole life, that
it wreaked havoc on my digestion and my ability to concentrate,
that I could be suddenly caught unaware, full of fear. In the
middle of the night, on my way to the bathroom, I would be
inundated with a nameless, all-consuming dread. The anxiety
was like a heated wire under the surface of my skin, a vague
buzzing of impending doom that was a constant companion.

During our first session I was able to go into a pretty good
hypnotic state, and on subsequent visits I felt I was becoming
more and more proficient. I could go down fairly quickly.
Whatever image was suggested to me or that I called up came
to me quite easily. I was able to control and explore whatever
I wanted: open fields, beaches, riverbanks, caverns, crumbling
mansions, wherever I chose to go. Once, Myra suggested my
anxiety was controllable by a device I held in my hand, like a
control box that regulates the speed of a toy train. I was able,
under hypnosis, to play with the degree to which I felt anxious
and was even able to turn it up to such an extent that I nearly
sent myself into a full-on panic—all merely by the suggestion of
turning an imaginary dial.

Then, during one session, I went into a trance by the usual
methods, but I sensed myself going deeper than I thought possible. I found myself somewhere familiar that I couldn't quite
name. It was more like an olfactory memory, a consuming
feeling that I had been there before. I was floating in a perfect
emptiness, tethered like a balloon to the world below. From my
vantage point I could see the curvature of the planet, which was
like a hill of grass. The sun was setting slowly or rising, the sky
an orange and blue wash, as if on canvas. I began to let go of

something I had been holding on to, but the more I let go, the more I could feel a part of me was dying, and I became afraid.

The psychologist James Hillman wrote a controversial book called *Suicide and the Soul* in which he argues that those who want to commit suicide have mistaken a physical death for a spiritual one. They do need to die in a real way, but our ideas of death are so tied in to our bodies that we have lost the ancient, mythical sense that death is really a transformation of sorts. A journey to the underworld is always a part of the hero's quest, but we have come to associate death only with literal loss of life. Hillman believes that for those who are suicidal, it is the responsibility of their clinician to help them *die*, to turn their attention away from their wrists and their necks and direct it toward their soul, to their spiritual self that is in need of transformation.

While not suicidal, I could feel myself in need of this transformation. Yet I was afraid that it meant more than the spiritual death Hillman speaks of. I had been here before, it was true, in the dream of perfect spiritual understanding, born from the depths of psychedelic experiences that had blown open a door I could never fully close. But it had meant death before—not the mythological death of my soul as I handed Cerberus a honey cake and stepped into Hades like Heracles had done, but the end of my life. How could I fully embrace this when it had all gone so terribly wrong? Nevertheless, I kept floating, the tension of the line tugging at me, reminding me of the ground below, and although I was afraid, it seemed I could have stayed in that trance forever.

I had been captured by this moment, and it made me admit that over the years there had been others, each of them a kind of manifestation of something I had lost, some missed chance, a closed door, something I had buried long ago. I wanted to understand how hypnosis fits within the often muddled definition of an altered state. I wondered if maybe all mystical experiences have at their root a hypnotic state.

Charles Tart, a psychologist and teacher at the Institute of Transpersonal Psychology, is considered one of the foremost authorities on altered states. He believes hypnosis and mystical states likely have interesting shared qualities: "Everyone has expectations as to what is supposed to happen. Those expectations have a determining factor as to what people experience, especially when people are seeking them," Tart explains.

When assessing the validity of a mystical experience, it's not enough to know the method used (psilocybin, fasting, hypnosis) to achieve the altered state; one must know what the expectations are. One exercise Tart uses with students is to have them draw a circle over and over. They often stop after a while, bored and confused about why they were asked to do it. Tart then explains that for Eskimo shamans, this is the classical technique for entering the spirit world. "The expectation is everything," he says.

Dr. Tart was raised a devout Lutheran and got involved in science when he became a teenager. He then noticed the many contradictions between science and religion and became proud of his facility at spotting church members' hypocrisy. But a sense of the spiritual always stirred within him. Eventually Tart came across the writings of English intellectuals who took spiritual and psychical research seriously, such as William James. He had a revelation of sorts: If science is a method for refining knowledge, it is a method that can be applied to religion and spirituality. Tart turned from engineering to psychology.

As for what is meant by "altered consciousness," Tart's work has led him to define it as "a qualitative shift in the pattern of the overall organization of consciousness." As with all human experience, an altered state will differ depending on the individual. "With hypnosis," Tart explains, "some people won't respond, a few will become deeply hypnotized, and others will experience deep responses to suggestion beyond ordinary capability. The experience of hypnosis, like all altered states, is multidimensional and can't be overgeneralized." When you question people to whom a hypnotherapist has given the same suggestions about what their mind felt like after hypnosis, their responses are always different. Nevertheless, as James discovered in regard to mystical states, some phenomena are common among most individuals.

As I related my own hypnosis experience to Tart, I was grasping at something, vaguely pleading for him to tell me that hypnotic states are somehow mystical states boiled down to their essence. I wanted to believe I was well on my way, and that what I had always believed was a true mystical experience was possible for me through hypnosis, without drugs. Tart wouldn't say, except to tell me that no matter what its place in the spectrum of altered states of consciousness, hypnosis has its own simple value: "If you experience a deep hypnotic state, you have a bit of perspective that here are other ways your mind can function." When I explained that all my previous attempts at seeing the "other ways" had ended in disaster, he offered this: "Sometimes the value of psychedelics is [that] what manifests later on is more important than the actual experience."

The country's relationship with both drugs and spirituality has changed since the sixties and seventies in ways that are no less than extraordinary. At the time of this writing, fourteen states have legalized medical marijuana and Massachusetts has decriminalized holding small amounts of pot for personal purposes. The Native American Church has full protection to use peyote in its religious practices, and the Santo Daime Church, a synthesis of Christianity and shamanism that uses ayahuasca, the brew of vines and leaves utilized in South American shamanic practices, is close to having full legal permission to employ the hallucinogenic brew containing the Schedule I substance DMT. Although mostly devoid of its religious roots, yoga is taught in cities and suburbs all over the country, and meditation is a normal part of American spiritual life. Zen and kabbalah are taught at adult-education centers.

The normalization of what were once considered alternative religious practices, as well as some historical distance from Timothy Leary and the Harvard scandal, has made it possible for scientists to once again broach the subject of psychedelics as a legitimate topic for research—though, despite this kind of tacit and tentative public tolerance, the DEA has not slowed down its arrests and prosecutions related to psychedelics: In November 2000, Leonard Pickard and Clyde Apperson were arrested for the manufacture and distribution of LSD. Pickard was sentenced to two concurrent life sentences. They were believed responsible for more than 70 percent of the LSD manufactured in the United States at that time, which put a damper on many a rave.

In 1990, the clinical psychiatrist Dr. Rick Strassman was given approval to conduct psychedelic research on human patients, the first in twenty years. Strassman wanted to understand if naturally occurring DMT in the pineal gland could explain occurrences like recorded mystical and near-death experiences. His research excited those who were hoping to enlarge the conversation about psychedelics and whether they had any health benefits. His work also made the underground ecstatic. They hoped Strassman would provide the proof they needed that drugs like DMT should be made legally available.

In a strange turn, Strassman would later give up this research when many of his test subjects reported encounters with powerful alien entities. Strassman worried that using DMT might have opened a gateway to an otherwise closed-off dimension, be it within or without human consciousness. But still, there was no controlled, scientifically sound research on the long-term effects these plants and compounds have on the spiritual lives of those who have such experiences.

Then, in 2006, after almost two years of overcoming hurdles with the U.S. Food and Drug Administration and Johns Hopkins, Dr. Roland Griffiths and Robert Jesse of the Council on Spiritual Practices (CSP)—an organization that takes the spiritual dimensions of human experience seriously as a subject worthy of scientific investigation—along with Dr. William Richards, a psychiatrist in private practice (now at the Bayview Medical Center) and a respected figure in the world of psychedelic research and therapy, put together a rigorous research project to investigate the effects of psilocybin (the active ingredient in the more common variety of hallucinogenic mushrooms) and its relationship to what are defined as mystical experiences. Long after William James, Richard Bucke, and even Madame Blavatsky, the question continues to bubble up to the surface: Is there a universal, core mystical experience that is unmediated by tradition and culture? The research at Johns Hopkins might not offer a definitive answer, but it has helped frame the question in a way that is impossible to ignore.

Griffiths, professor of behavioral biology and neuroscience at Hopkins, has a long history of tracing the effects of drugs on human beings. Griffiths has published hundreds of papers on drug dependence and the behavioral effects of psychoactive substances, including caffeine. When he was introduced to Jesse, founder of the CSP, Griffiths had been meditating seriously for fifteen years, a practice that revealed to him the importance of having a psychological understanding of mystical states of consciousness.

Jesse was just out of college and working in the software industry when he became intrigued with the literature on altered states of consciousness, the ability of psychoactives to bring them about, and how they relate to spiritual practices and religion. He began to seek out others, people he refers to as "elders in related fields." Toward the end of 1993, he found himself invited to be a bystander at a small conference at Esalen, which Jesse describes as about twenty experts—scientists, psychiatrists, psychologists, policy analysts—comfortably arranged in a circle on the meeting room floor, sharing ideas about what they hoped the future for psychedelics might look like. But this was not a shadow of Millbrook. These folks wanted to figure out a way to bring rigorous science to bear on the subject.

But for all the talk about serotonin neurochemistry and possible psychiatric treatments using these drugs, the one thing that stood out for Jesse was a side conversation about how these substances can occasion, as Jesse explains, "states of consciousness that appear indistinguishable from what the mystics and the saints of the ages have described."

This was not, at least overtly, what had brought these people together originally, but it was what would bring many of them back together later, what a few of them conceived as an idea to form a network of people from every interested discipline—behavioral sciences, medicine, public policy, religious studies—who would brainstorm and ultimately set out courses of action. This was the genesis of what would become the CSP.

Near its inception, the CSP drafted a *Code of Ethics for Spiritual Guides*. The members wanted to outline, for guides and practitioners that may lack the support of traditions or institutions, a set of concerns and conventions that they felt would lay important groundwork. Jesse explained that the *Code* was not specific about the methods a guide may offer to bring about a strong experience, as "there was no need to privilege one means over another, except insofar as there exists, or there may later exist, empirical evidence favoring one or another."

The CSP aimed to get beyond an emphasis on the experience itself and focus more on the consequences of the experience. Was a person's life changed or enriched as a result? While Jesse says that CSP does not necessarily favor one trigger over another, at present what he calls entheogens appear to work more quickly and with greater likelihood than, say, lengthy meditation practice.

The term "entheogens" (roughly, psychoactive plants or chemicals with sacramental potential) is itself a little loaded because it stresses the spiritual component of substances like psilocybin and DMT. But the folks at CSP felt that the word "psychedelic" carries too much cultural baggage and that the medical word "hallucinogen" may be misleading in other ways.

Jesse is convinced that for some people, under some circumstances, entheogens can offer a more direct route to a primary religious experience, more than the age-old, tradition-tested practice of meditation: "Let's imagine a hundred people at a thirty-day meditation retreat, people who were willing and able to give up four weeks of vacation time. Over the course of that month, it would not be uncommon for a few people to drop out because the experience is disturbing to them." Of those who stay, Jesse explains, maybe one or two will have a revelatory experience that they believe will change their lives. "For a daylong psilocybin session in the 2006 John Hopkins study, the comparable fraction at Hopkins seems to about two-thirds," Jesse says. He repeats the caution of his elders, however: Altered states do not necessarily lead to altered traits. "To espouse the experience alone is to miss the mark," says Jesse, "and may actually be a disservice."

The necessary question to ask, then, is which experience has more staying power, meditation or psilocybin? Who is more likely to continue a spiritual practice? Those few at the meditation retreat might yield a 100 percent return on continuing meditation and spiritual practice, whereas the psilocybin users might find the experience transformative but not walk away with any tools by which to deepen their understanding nor change the way they live. In the words of Brother David Steindl-Rast, a Benedictine monk who has spent considerable time in dialogue with Buddhist teachers and those interested in the psychedelic experience as it relates to mysticism, "A primary religious experience is no more (though also no less) than a seed for a spiritual life."

But what is peculiar to psilocybin that makes it the preferred psychoactive agent for such research?

Jesse explains the choice was a no-brainer. The Johns Hopkins scientists needed something the research participants could take as a pill. Smoking and needles have too many druggie connotations; in addition, needles seem too clinical and smoking would have made it impossible for the researchers to deliver the exact dose. Psilocybin is a naturally occurring substance with a long track record of sacramental use. It can be taken orally and, as a refined chemical, in calibrated amounts. It is shorter-acting than, say, mescaline, and so better suited to the routines of the research setting. "It's a beautiful substance," Jesse says.

At Johns Hopkins in a double-blind study, thirty-six participants, all of whom had no prior experiences with hallucinogenic drugs, were given either psilocybin or an active placebo that contained methylphenidate hydrochloride (Ritalin), which produced a subtle stimulant effect. For the purposes of this experiment, and to counterbalance the expected effects of psilocybin when taken in its more usual settings—one's parents' basement, for example, or a kegger in the woods—Griffiths paid particular attention to the atmosphere. His research took place in a comfortable, living room–like environment where the blindfolded participants listened to classical music—Bach masses—while an assistant helped provide support.

After seven hours, the participants filled out a series of questionnaires. A two-month checkup followed, as did a questionnaire given to the friends and family of those involved. Fourteen months later, research subjects answered another series of questions. For Griffiths and his colleagues, the results were nothing less than astonishing. As they wrote in the journal *Psychopharmacology*, "When administered to volunteers under supportive conditions, psilocybin occasioned experiences similar to spontaneously occurring mystical experiences and which were evaluated by volunteers as having substantial and sustained personal meaning and spiritual significance."

Twenty-two of the thirty-six participants described what would be called complete mystical experiences after psilocybin. In the follow-up, 67 percent rated their experience with psilocybin the single most meaningful event in their lives, or at least in the top five.

In 1984, when Rick Doblin, the founder and president of the Multidisciplinary Association for Psychedelic Studies, was looking for a legitimate psychedelic-research project, a follow-up to the Good Friday Experiment Timothy Leary and Walter Pahnke conducted at Harvard made perfect sense. "The Good Friday Experiment was a major inspiration to me and many others," he says, "about the potential of psychedelic research to use the scientific method to investigate religion, spirituality, the mystical experience, and the social-justice implications of the mystical experience."

Doblin saw the potential of such a study in what he calls the "fruit test." What results did it bear? Did the experience actually change the life of the person who had it? The Good Friday Experiment offered Doblin two unique opportunities. The first was the ability to do some psychedelic research without having to win government approval. More important, enough years had passed that a follow-up study would provide a real-world test of whether or not the dramatic mystical experiences reported by the students in Marsh Chapel actually changed their lives.

After interviewing sixteen of the original participants,

Doblin found that among those who had received psilocybin, there was a general consensus that they had shared a genuine mystical experience. They believed after all these years that they enjoyed "persisting" positive effects as a result.

Nonetheless, because all the participants were drawn from the same religious tradition, this research couldn't really speak to the question of a core mystical experience. As Doblin explains, "We would need to conduct research with people from lots of different religions using the same questionnaire and compare responses."

Talking to researchers and scientists and reading scholarly journals still didn't get me closer to an answer about why. Only a story, a telling by one of the participants, would give me something to match up against not only the research, but also my own past debacles with these substances. I needed to hear about an experience with psychedelics that had worked.

Until 2006, John Hayes, a psychologist and self-described Zen Catholic, had never taken a hallucinogenic drug. In the 1960s, Hayes was a Franciscan friar watching with curiosity while the counterculture used psychedelics with impunity. Through his own meditation and religious practice, Hayes believes he has had sensations that he would label mystical. But these mystical states—which he described to me as "moments of unitive experience"—were significant enough that when he heard about a surprising research project at Johns Hopkins, he was more than intrigued. After some considerable thought, he signed up. For three sessions, Hayes is certain, he received a placebo. Then, in the fourth session, something happened that had never occurred before in all his years of prayer and meditation.

"It was like, 'All right, what's the big deal?' Then, *ba-boom!*" he says. "There was a sense of moving in some sort of astral space with stars whizzing by me. It was like getting the big picture."

Hayes accepts that his faith and background helped to shape

his experience at Johns Hopkins. However, he believes that religious images are best described as "circuit breakers to carry and figure the overwhelming presence of the numinous." For Hayes, all of his life is mediated in some degree by his culture and his religion, particularly as someone who attends mass regularly and has a disciplined meditation practice. But Hayes claims his psilocybin trip was less mediated than any other experience. It has provided, he says, a framework for being more open and sensitive not only to nature, but also to his work as a psychologist. For someone who has a religious life predicated on certain kinds of mystical experiences, this one was simply different by degree, not kind.

"I had no real question that what I was experiencing was something that I often experience," he says, "but just in a much less mediated, diluted way."

At first, Hayes had a difficult time describing what psilocybin had made him feel. He used words like "dream" and "elusive," and explained that it was like trying to reference something from a different dimension of space and time. Slowly he began to use some concrete terms, religious terms, to describe the indescribable:

I could find myself going back to things in my very early childhood and walking through rooms and spaces. It felt very connected and real. I had this overwhelmingly sublime, ecstatic feeling of the presence of the divine. I had images of Jesus, Mary, Buddha, my partner Karen. It was just very radiant and beautiful and very joyful and very ecstatic. I had this experience of being loved and being in ultimate reality in a very profound, sublimely beautiful way.

Was Hayes anticipating, on some unconscious level, that this was the experience he would have, given what he already knew, as a religious person, about how a classical mystical illumination would arise?

According to the published studies, a great effort was made to prevent what is called expectancy. Researchers videotaped the study to make sure their test monitors didn't say or do things that might be suggestive or leading, and they chose only participants who had no history with hallucinogens. While this approach guarded against studying those with firsthand experience of the effects of drugs, little could be done about the deep pop-cultural language or preconception that most of us share. It is easy to imagine someone signing up to be a participant in the research and immediately going home and googling all the associated terms, reading about Marsh Chapel and the studies of the past, even watching movies on YouTube of Timothy Leary describing his psychedelic breakthroughs.

The problem of expectancy is heightened by the nature of the questionnaires administered to the participants after the experience. The first questionnaire was made up of one hundred items, fifty-seven of which were actually irrelevant and meant to distract from the genuine questions. The remaining forty-three items had been used in previous psychological tests, but this was the first time they had been incorporated into a study involving psychedelics. These relevant questions dealt with the following characteristics: internal unity (union with an ultimate reality or God); external unity (generally understood as pantheism, in which all of nature is one); transcendence of time and space; ineffability and paradoxicality (the experience is beyond words or difficult to describe); sense of sacredness (what has been called awe or a sense of *mysterium tremendum*); noetic quality (the appearance of some insight or revelation); and deeply felt positive mood.

One problem with these categories is elucidated by Professor Robert Sharf, of the department of East Asian languages and cultures at Berkeley. As Sharf explains, religion and religious experiences cannot be reduced to what he calls a "supposedly value-neutral, empirical, scientific kind of domain." Sharf contends that even while most rabbis, Evangelical ministers, Catholic priests, and Buddhist monks would agree there are some common elements, the very way in which religion is presented would not be considered valid, since none of them believe that all religions are ultimately the same. There have always been records of these kinds of experiences from Christian saints, Hindu yogis, Jewish kabbalists, and Sufi mystics. These traditions all have very different ideas about the creation of the universe, how to pray, what you can eat, what caste you can marry into, if God is one, three, or thousands, or if even those numbers are simply an illusion. Witnessing Christ as your beloved and seeing angels self-immolate before God's heavenly throne would seem to be unique visions. The late, great scholar of Jewish mysticism Gershom Scholem remarked that there is no such thing as generic "mysticism"; there is only Jewish mysticism or Christian mysticism or Hindu mysticism.

Because the questions are so general, and correspond to well-established cultural ideas about mystical experiences, there's a danger the questions themselves will lead the participant to recall the psilocybin trip based on what is offered in the questionnaire. There is also a certain generality that precludes the participants' describing specific religious imagery. Hayes himself admits a level of frustration with the initial questionnaires, which included such queries as whether his experience felt more "real" than ordinary experiences, or if there was a sense of unity of space and time. "Those types of questions fail to capture the elusiveness of the experience," Hayes explains. "They are not poetic questions that would link you back to the experience in some way." He was happier with the follow-up questions, which allowed participants to relate attitudes about their own lives, their sense of self, and altruistic feelings. For Hayes there was a pronounced change, but, he confessed, a subtle one: "I think what it has done is deepen and open up a sense of conviction of the sacred dimension of experience. I think it has amplified a sort of heartfelt trust in that experience . . . I'm in a sense living and moving in a greater reality that's friendly."

One metaphor that has been offered about primary religious experience that Jesse finds valuable, he credits to Brother David Steindl-Rast: "The primary religious experience can be likened to a lava flow. It's glowing, it's fiery, it's elemental, it's dynamic. When it flows out of the ground and begins spreading, it cools and solidifies and becomes the stuff of structure," Jesse says. The structure includes the "secondary religious phenomena" of doctrine, ethics, and ritual. Many religious institutions tend to emphasize the secondary religious phenomena and have lost sight of, or de-emphasize, the primary experience. Moses had it, Jesus had it, and we may feel that our job is to simply continue to celebrate and be grateful for their revelations and teachings. "Given the relative rarity of returning to a direct, primary experience," Jesse explains, "it's understandable that most people who go into religion as a profession will not necessarily have had a profound primary religious experience themselves. How many of us in our lifetimes have an opportunity to go on a monthlong retreat? Maybe only a few people in such a retreat may taste nondual consciousness."

Rick Doblin believes this desire for transcendence is in some ways misguided, and is part of what brought the idealism of the sixties crashing down: "For me the goal was to recognize that the other side of this 'Me Decade,' which was in many ways characterized by people as selfishness, was the recognition that we are our own instruments and that part of the reason that this collapse has come is because of our own flaws and limitations." Any inner work was not ultimately for some kind of spiritual enlightenment, but rather to learn how to be more politically effective in the outer world. For Doblin, an effective spiritual life must include social justice. Psychedelics inspired Doblin not to "drop out," but to work within the system to try and change people's minds.

If at the end the emphasis is on the spiritual, then it doesn't take into account that consciousness is, as Doblin muses, a prism that can reflect various colors in the spectrum. "We tend to think that the spiritual is more important than everything," Doblin suggests, and this can undervalue what it means to be merely human and how being merely human is a way to effect change that can actually have ripples in the world.

Psychedelics grant us an opportunity to visit the irrational aspects of the mind, the same part that urges us to make art and pursue spiritual disciplines, and maybe even the part that can love. Do they have a future that is not bound up in the question of mystical realities or their effectiveness in medicine for Western dilemmas, such as post-traumatic stress syndrome?

Dennis McKenna is often name-checked as merely the brother of the late Terence McKenna, known in psychedelic circles as one of the most radical and original thinkers, and who replaced Timothy Leary as the spokesperson for the psychedelic underground. Dennis has made his own mark, however, as one of the most important contemporary researchers in the area of ethnopharmacology, a branch of science that studies the relationship between ethnicity and medicinal plants.

During the seventies, the brothers trekked around South America looking for magic mushrooms, detailed in their wildly popular counterculture book, *True Hallucinations*. Through their experience, Terence came to see the model for a deeper

and more subtle understanding of consciousness as resting
within shamanic teachings, but he believed their value went far
beyond any particular religious or spiritual tradition. Terence
believed the evolution of human consciousness was intimately
tied to hallucinogenic plants as both agents of that evolution
and the best method for continuing our awareness, and that it
was possible that psilocybin was originally an intelligent alien
spore floating through the cosmos and seeking out human DNA
that would bring it to its own next evolutionary stage.

Dennis offers much less speculative ideas about the role of
psychedelics and the nature of consciousness. Most important,
he believes these plants offer far more than religious or spiritual introspection. Dennis describes them as "tools to explain
consciousness" and says that for many people without spiritual
inclinations, they can be used to solve problems, gain insight
into natural phenomena, or simply explore what human consciousness is capable of. "[Psychedelic experiences] do not have
to be specifically spiritual or religious, although I do think they
catalyze what we call mystical experiences," Dennis explains.
He thinks that what is often described as spiritual is merely an
interpretation. People need to put these very alien encounters
into some container, and religious language is the most effective
at describing the irrational and the mysterious.

Dennis even believes that too much authority is given to shamans and other spiritual guides: "Ultimately, the experience is
yours." For him, the best guides are merely there to make sure
you are safe, that you don't get into trouble, and that if you do,
they can help you get back to a stable place. "The bottom line
is, you're there to confront the experience on your own terms."

Trying to make sense of any experience that "ruptures the
plain of ordinary reality or normality" inspires a tendency to
try to create a context around it and then get other people to
buy into that context. McKenna sees religion as being both the

vessel and the stopgap for giving people access to the mysterious. Ritual and myth develop out of the primary experience but then suppress it, make it so the hierarchies own it and decide who is fit to have access. This is where Dennis differs from someone like Robert Jesse, who continues to see religious practice as a valuable way to integrate the psychedelic experience.

Dennis sees religious practice as having some importance, but not nearly as much as the immediate and specific context of the actual experience. "People often think you have to go through the priest or go to this shaman," Dennis says. "To a certain degree, I think that is important and necessary, but it also removes the individual's responsibility and ability to have experiences and have their own conclusion." For Dennis, the actual psychedelic experience often undermines religion and religious language anyway. Psychedelics' true value for Dennis is that they have the potential to shatter categories. "What I learned [from psychedelics] is how little I know, that all my assumptions are open to question, all I thought I knew, I have to make it provisional."

While Dennis supports the transpersonal and psychological use of psychedelics to treat people spiritually and possibly help people with terminal cancer come to terms with dying, he worries that the only reason researchers are emphasizing the drugs' potential psychological and medical benefits is that that is what the FDA allows. A suggestion of spiritual or transpersonal benefits would be categorized as a cover for recreational use. Dennis believes psychedelics to be capable of much more than that—of shaping our very evolutionary consciousness and bringing us into more direct contact with our mind's true creative potential.

The final assessment of the Johns Hopkins study was the proposal that these kinds of experiences had a deep impact on those who had them, and that serious consideration should be given to the use of psilocybin, or other such drugs, in certain therapeutic environments. There is nothing to suggest, however, that the authors were trying to say definitively whether there is a universal mystical core to human consciousness. "We didn't come at it with a theological agenda," Jesse explains. "This is not about proving the existence of God by any definition."

Nevertheless, the use of those particular scales to assess a mystical state is drawn from a well-established school of thought that created the governing principles for the questions. It's impossible to deny that the study relates to what is understood of classical mystical states and, by extension, the perennial philosophy made popular by Aldous Huxley that, while steering clear of the question of God's existence, still suggests that some transpersonal divine reality exists that underlies all the religious traditions.

Griffiths insists he did not go into the study with any preconceived notion about how a mystical reality or mystical state would arise in his research participants. "I was skeptical that hallucinogens would model [traditional mystical states] in any meaningful way. I would have been perfectly happy if the results had suggested there was no overlap, or a little overlap," Griffiths says. "After having talked to all these people, I've been turned in terms of believing there is something here that is cohering and making it look like [these are] biologically normal kind[s] of phenomena. We are wired for these experiences, in some sense."

While Griffiths is optimistic that one day science will understand the neuro-networks that activate mystical experiences, there is still a mystery that gives him pause and fills him with awe. His research has in no way convinced him about the existence of God, but his curiosity about the nature of the mystical experience has increased. His meditation practice had already planted that seed, but the psilocybin study has given him the ability to observe, as a third party, the phenomenon itself as it takes place in others.

"It's the phenomenon of the mystical experience that remains

intensely interesting to me," he says. "Whether or not it's occasioned by psilocybin is of secondary interest." Griffiths believes
that psilocybin is merely a tool for occasioning these kinds of
experiences, in the same way as meditation and prayer. "It's just
absolutely clear to me that [the mystical experience] is part of
the biology of the human organism," Griffiths says.

At the time of this writing, Griffiths has not yet been able to
secure any federal funding to do his research. While the FDA
will give him permission to do the research, there is still too
much potential for political fallout to actually fund such a study.
What this means is that the funding that he does have comes
from the private sector and that instead of writing federal grants,
he is writing proposals to audiences that may have all kinds of
agendas. "I'm concerned that our research will not be perceived
as having a strong agenda attached to it, because I don't think
the agendas are very useful." Yet because the funding for the
projects is coming from the private sector, Griffiths finds himself participating and giving papers at conferences he would
otherwise be reluctant to attend.

Part of this has to do with the way these conferences continue
to keep one leg in the speculative. Unlike any other science,
psychedelic research is still completely wedded to the interests
that first spawned it—namely, the role of spirituality in human
life. As someone with his own meditation practice, Griffiths is
in no way opposed to thinking about spiritual matters, but he
worries that spiritual matters are often too caught up in conjecture, emotion, and dogma to be useful when one tries to
apply the tools of science to understand something essential
about these drugs. While something like the American Astro-
nomical Society conference would never even consider a panel
on astrology, psychedelic conferences offer symposia and talks
on subjects such as plant deities and alchemical divination. The
issue of both scientific rigor and public perception often has

Griffiths feeling at odds with the psychedelic culture at large, a culture that employs everything from astrology to shamanism, UFOs, and conspiracy theories in its internal mythos.

Just as legitimate science is again turning its attention to psychedelic drugs, the popular culture is reintegrating these drugs and their mystique into strange configurations of nostalgia, apocalyptic prophecy, and futurism. The writer Daniel Pinchbeck has introduced a new generation of seekers to the outrageously powerful hallucinogenic brew ayahuasca, which he took under the guidance of shamans as he trekked around South America. His experiences have played no small part in inspiring an entire industry of ayahuasca tourism, whereby for about two grand or more you can take a weeklong shamanic workshop in Peru that includes nightly ingestion of ayahuasca within the context of indigenous ceremonial and ritual practice.

Pinchbeck grew up with an interest in the arts and literature and in 1990 founded the highly regarded *Open City* literary journal. But he always felt a sense of dissatisfaction and longing for something beyond what had become a claustrophobic New York literary scene. He eventually had what he calls a spiritual crisis and, leaving his quickly rising literary career behind, went off to meet with shamans and other spiritual teachers. It was during an *iboga* (a hallucinogen extracted from rain forest shrubs) ritual in West Africa that he had an experience that made him aware of the deeper possibilities of psychedelics: "For a few hours I was granted a powerful lens through which I could see my life—that complex assemblage of habit, moods, past events, and relationships—like a constellation viewed through a telescope."

After Pinchbeck continued exploring various shamanic practices that involved psychedelics, he eventually came to an understanding that shamanic culture had something valuable to teach people not only about consciousness, but about our place in the natural world. He became fascinated with the Mayan cal-endar, which some believe predicts an either literal or psychic transformation for the world in 2012, and began writing and lecturing on a kind of psychedelic eschatology. While Pinch-beck has worked tirelessly to reconnect psychedelic drugs with religious tradition and myth, his message still contains an under-lying evangelism that privileges shamanism and indigenous cul-tures, and regards psychedelics as the best tool to prepare us for whatever planetary or psychic transformation might be coming.

Inherent in this idea is a kind of proselytizing and fundamen-talism that doesn't look much different from any religious tradi-tion that gives itself primacy over all others. This has made it difficult for Griffiths to feel like a conference that includes any discussion of 2012 or the like is not in opposition to the spirit of science he wants to privilege. The conference attendees haven't always made it easy. In a 2008 *AlterNet* article on the Horizons Perspectives on Psychedelics conference in September of that year, it was reported that a number of what might be considered speculative ideas were presented: "In the conference's closing session, [Daniel] Pinchbeck suggested that the current renais-sance in psychedelic culture came about because Saturn was at right angles to Pluto. And when one audience member asked who doubted the 'official 9/11 story,' more than half the crowd raised their hands."

Robert Forte, a faculty member at the California Institute of Integral Studies, later claimed that it was Albert Hofmann, the LSD inventor himself, who suggested a Jewish involvement in the September 11, 2001, attacks on the World Trade Center towers in New York and the Pentagon, but admitted he was convinced that the U.S. government's record of what happened that morning is woefully, and deliberately, wrong. For Forte, a discussion about 9/11 belongs at a conference on psychedelics as much as the hard-science papers being delivered. In a comment on a blog post I had written about the *AlterNet* article, Forte explained how he and many others view psychedelics as a tool by which to "question authority, enliven your inner resources, and think for yourself." But for Griffiths, any such ideas create, rightly or not, other scientists' impression of an agenda on the part of the conference overall and, by extension, skepticism around Griffiths's work.

There is also the problem of how to talk about psychedelics and psychedelic research with a skeptical and drug-wary public always looking at such things with scorn. People will always perceive this kind of research, a legacy Timothy Leary left, as just a bunch of people getting stoned. However it's framed, whether as science by people like Griffiths, or as ideas about consciousness expansion and personal transformation by the psychedelic counterculture, it still can look a lot like people just getting wasted.

For Jesse, this is why he has cleansed his vocabulary of the word "psychedelic," except when he wants to evoke the flavors of the "psychedelic sixties." The instant Day-Glo associations work against what Jesse and the CSP have worked toward: an understanding of how these substances, these entheogens, can be remarkably powerful tools for personal insight, transformation, and growth. Though he admits the vocabulary shift is "swimming upstream," Jesse believes that to most ears, "psychedelic" miscommunicates what the research volunteers at Hopkins experienced at best. People receiving the substance "did not emerge from the session room saying, 'Wow, that was entertaining'; what a majority reflected over a year later, in one way or another, was, 'Goodness, that was important; that was one of the most meaningful events of my life,'" Jesse says.

Whether or not there is such a thing as an unmediated religious experience, the one element that seems to be unquestionably universal is that narrative is what shapes its transmission.

Before and after the Hopkins study, Hayes considered himself a believing Christian. Still, he does not believe it was his Christianity that ultimately furnished whatever truths he gleaned. "I'm certainly aware that I'm going to be inclined to use archetypal images. Yes, I'll see it in Christian terms, because that's my tradition, but do I think there was something exclusively Christian about the experience? No."

While it makes sense to understand these experiences as being particular to the individual, is there something about a certain kind of mystical consciousness, including ones that psychedelic drugs can occasion, that can transcend those cultural and personal filters? James Fadiman explains it as putting water through a hose: "The water is pure water, but it tastes a little bit of hose," no matter how much we claim the hose is just a vehicle for delivering water.

There can be no pure experience.

Even if, for example, as the Johns Hopkins research shows, psilocybin actually acts on the brain in such a way as to occasion "experiences similar to spontaneously occurring mystical experiences," then it must follow that the drug actually opens up a particular kind of awareness that goes beyond even what one might expect the experience would be like. I would contend that the drug also opens up deep layers of the unconscious mind: dreams, ideas, memories, even the images from an old Ray Bradbury story read in junior high school but long forgotten.

Being an addict means that I am forced to accept the limitations of my consciousness, be they spiritual or otherwise. What merely bends for others is liable to break for me, as it did once before. And yet I cannot extract that desire for a direct spiritual encounter, like a splinter. While Evelyn Underhill was a believer in "the Reality behind the veil," it was only because of a peculiar tendency among nonordinary people that this reality could be apprehended. These visionaries are, she writes, "tormented by the Unknowable, ache for first principles, demand some background to the shadow of things." But Underhill saw the kind of mysticism espoused by someone like Madame Blavatsky as a corrupted form of this endeavor. Because for Underhill true mysticism is governed by a love of God, anything that seeks to elevate the human person is mere pantheism, which is defined as that spiritual belief that sees God in all things and leads to, as Underhill warns, the "deification" of human beings. Yes, Underhill, agrees, the mystical consciousness is latent in all of us, but without the grounding and discipline of traditional religion we will be too easily swayed by something that is dangerously only an "extension of sensual experience."

Hermes, the title given to the supposed author of the *Corpus Hermeticum* who first inspired those Renaissance magicians to crack the secret code inside the mind of God, is the deity that haunts my own history, as well as the story of psychedelics. One would do well to remember that Hermes is a trickster god. While he served as a messenger and aided communication, he is also the god who brings us the ability to interpret, as in "hermeneutics." This process of interpretation can become something of an obsession, where every encounter, every gust of wind, every placement of stone, the buzz of every insect, and all the unspoken glances between two people are a code to be cracked, a text to be read over and over again. More than that, Hermes is god of transitions, helping travelers and vagabonds on their journeys. As part of this role, he escorted souls into Hades. Death was often the final consequence for many on that path—lest I forget.

The difference between ecstasy and illumination is the same as that difference between magic and mysticism. Magic is often about instant results. Mysticism, while often characterized by dramatic singular moments, is about the long haul. In the same way I mistook magic for mysticism, I mistook ecstasy for illumination.

The very first time I ever altered my consciousness with psychedelics, I was changed in an essential way. The doors of perception had shifted, just enough so that even with only the smallest opening, an unimaginable bright light poured in. For years I tried every conceivable method available to me to push that door open, sometimes even to break it down. All I was left with were the proverbial sore shoulder and bloody knuckles. It budged, but it would never give enough to let me through completely. But the light still came through. Evelyn Underhill described this as "a little hole in the wall of appearances," in which one catches "a glimpse of that seething pot of spiritual forces whence, now and then, a bubble rises to the surface of things." Thankfully, there are other methods by which to continue to peek through that crack in the door.

chapter eight

THE FRAGILE ART OF PSYCHEDELIC SOBRIETY

On a Wednesday night in an Allston, Massachusetts, night-club, four fellows—mostly hirsute, the drummer oddly clean-cut—are setting up onstage for a gig. I practically used to live in clubs like this, and the only thing missing from the familiar smell of sweat and alcohol is the waft of tobacco, now that Boston law prohibits smoking in bars. The sickly-sweet smell of marijuana I caught outside irritated me; pot no longer makes my heart race in anticipation. And honestly, I just don't go to shows anymore. It's 10:00 PM midweek, and normally I would be in bed. I also always feel a little guilty leaving my wife home alone with our son.

Once everything is plugged in and tuned, the four band members sit on stools arranged in a kind of semicircle, evoking the communal sensibility of a prayer group. The set begins with what sounds vaguely like Americana, acoustic guitar under a kind of gospel-laden vocal. Then, as the drummer slowly comes alive and the other musicians begin to add their own elements, you suddenly realize that while the music is urging you near, drawing you in, the band members themselves appear to be transforming. They close their eyes and rock back and forth. They hoot and yell out. While they each play one of the key quartet instruments, they also contribute in a variety of other ways: glockenspiel, banjo, melodica. Their technique seems largely improvisational, but at its core the music is crafted. They recognize each other's signatures, and this gives them freedom and courage. In a moment, I sense that their performance offers the promise that music can somehow change you, knock out the cotton in your brain, and give you a new kind of hope.

A dozen musical references begin to take hold—Syd Barrett, the Grateful Dead, Tyrannosaurus Rex, The Incredible String Band, the progenitors of the music we call psychedelic. Then their contemporary counterparts—a host of others that have been dubbed psych-folk. Yet, as much as they depend on what came before, or on what their friends are doing, this band is building something new. After the first song climaxes and then reaches its denouement, the next song takes hold in a different way. No longer a movement toward some new musical syncretism, this song seems more about the band's trying to groove in what they have just created. They begin a long jam. There is a palpable tension, as if they are trying to work it all out as they go along, not sure where the song (or the evening, for that matter) will take them, but more than willing to go for the ride.

Standing there at my first late-night show in a year, with a child sleeping at home, work in the morning . . . well, it becomes a little bit personal. I begin to experience that old ache, that desire for a mystical communion with a transcendent reality. Contained in this desire is necessarily a world-weariness. Call it melancholia, the disease under my disease of addiction. The music on the stage sounds like it is trying to invoke a spirit, and it seems possible that the musicians—their eyes rolled back, their feet pounding the stage—are merely the vessels through which whatever is coming will make itself known. I know there is transcendence here, or rather, I hope there is. But my sense of the transcendental and transformative potential of this kind of music has shifted from where it once sat.

What am I looking for in this music? It's something quite different today from what it was before I got clean. Sometimes it seems that psychedelia is not about the actual reality of other worlds, but merely the desire to imagine them. What is this desire for another kind of reality? It's a longing not for another world beyond death, but for a journey that skirts death's edges.

As I continued to stay clean, I found that efforts to fulfill this desire often involved a lot of effort with very little reward, fasting that only led to more hunger, prayer that revealed the emptiness, meditation that quieted everything but the longing. Over the years my early sobriety was characterized as a struggle between what seemed to be a spiritual experience that helped me stay clean and a fear of anything vaguely mystical, lest it bring me back to drugs, or at least the same kind of religious paranoia. But staying sober seemed to be something I simply couldn't do without "God's help," so I tentatively started to explore religion—without the magic mushrooms. For a time, I made a feeble attempt at becoming more "Jewish" and for a few weeks even prayed with a prayer shawl. I took on too much too soon, though, and the part of me that still secretly wanted a mystical experience grew bored. I settled on keeping mildly kosher and fasting on Yom Kippur and continued to search.

After college, I went to divinity school, hoping that my longing for religious experience, still intimately connected with my past drug addiction, might be fulfilled by turning toward a more academic approach wherein I was less likely to get into trouble. Finally living in the city, as I had always longed to, and not just a stoned teenager from the suburbs anymore, I embraced urban life, learning the buses and subways like a sacred text. A psychedelic sensibility still continued to permeate, however subtly, the most common of occurrences. Standing in Porter Square station, I was waiting like everyone else, shuffling back and forth against the yellow line, every so often peering down into the tunnel. Then it happened, as if by magic. First, a light along the wall illuminated the whole tunnel. It brightened as it got closer, a slow wash of yellow against the filthy bricks. There was a sudden pause, a kind of potential in the air, and the squeal of the wheels against the track. I still couldn't see the train, and then the light and noise went from being the idea of a train to being a charging behemoth rattling into the station at full speed. The wind of it filled the entire station as it slowly began its stop. It was glorious. It wasn't Ezekiel's heavenly chariot, sure. But it was some kind of ancient serpent that swam below the city, if it was anything.

While in divinity school, I was seduced by the new wave of postmodern thought that has overtaken even theological studies. I took to smoking cigars and reading Michel Foucault, all the while hiding my inner spiritual struggles from my divinity school peers. I started smoking even more, moving to rolled tobacco, and spent my free time in art-house movie theaters. Still obligated to my family in the suburbs, I returned for Passover dinners. I sensed in my parents a kind of kindred sensibility, that we could have been closer than we were but that my life as an addict had made that all but impossible. Sober, I could get to know them again in a new way.

I began to see that on some level my father shared my spiritual longing, but his had been made quiet and practical over the course of his own life. I now understood that my mother was also sympathetic to how much I had needed to pursue a nonordinary existence as a teenager, and why getting a little wild was one way to feel alive and close to the heart of some greater divine truth. In her own youth, she had been certain that sneaking out at night to jazz clubs, staying up listening to music in the late hours, could save her from the dreariness and slog of a working-class life.

My mother also had artistic aspirations of her own, though she never spoke of how they had been subsumed under the weight of parenthood. After she died, I inherited some books on the history of art and between some of the pages discovered scraps of her sketches of nudes, all of them unfinished. Was this why she had allowed me so much freedom, a chance for her youngest child to break out of what must have sometimes felt like self-imposed mediocrity?

Ultimately, my years at divinity school were less spiritual than I might have hoped. Chasing girls and academic rigor left little time for prayer. After a string of failed relationships, I found myself alone and more confused. I hit another bottom of sorts and discovered that part of what had made relationships so difficult was that I treated sex and women in the same way I sought mystical release through drugs. That search for the mystical was in some ways a search for instant gratification. Once the initial glow began to fade, I found myself moving on to the next experience, again hoping to recapture that initial magic. But I discovered that love, like the kind of spiritual experience I was after, is often something that requires patience, and, more than that, it requires work and not a little bit of sacrifice.

In August 1998, I married after a short engagement, normalizing more of my life. But the calling toward a directly mystical experience never fully left me, and I began to wonder if there might be a worldly kind of mysticism to be had. Where to look was really no mystery: in the things that had first opened my mind to the possibilities of new ways of thinking, how beautiful the fringe of culture can be, how exciting to look beyond prime time, beyond the Top 40, beyond the conventional.

In a most baffling section of *The Doors of Perception*, Huxley dismisses art as having any true visionary potential: "Art, I suppose, is only for beginners, or else for those resolute dead-enders, who have made up their minds to be content with the *ersatz* of Suchness, with symbols rather than with what they signify, with the elegantly composed recipe list in lieu of the actual dinner." This is easy to say after ingesting 0.4 gram of pure mescaline.

What Huxley fails to recognize is that art might be the only possibility of universalizing a mescaline trip and other experiences that refuse to be contained in any other way. The great surrealist Salvador Dalí explained how with art, drugs might even be unnecessary: "I have never taken drugs, since I am a drug. I don't talk about my hallucinations, I evoke them. Take me, I am the drug; take me, I am hallucinogenic." The Spanish surrealist Joan Miró used to keep himself from sleeping for days, until he started to hallucinate. His visions eventually made it onto canvas, and you can see, in vivid abstract detail, the shapes and colors of a mind pushed up against the precipice. Art also recognizes its own limitations in the way that religions often don't or can't. Even Vedanta, which (somewhat arrogantly) claims to be the only tradition willing to suggest that all religions are at their roots the same, is still bound by its contexts, language, geography.

Michael Murphy rightly explains that most religions are merely syntheses of other traditions and practices, but that synthesis is completely bound up in all the historic and cultural forces that delineate which parts belong and which don't.

Modern-day occultists and hermeticists still claim that the *Corpus Hermeticum* is the outline to the true mystery religion from which all others derive. They often cannot acknowledge the vast evidence that shows much of the *Corpus* borrows from Christianity and gnosticism. Spiritual traditions, no matter how evolved, still need to turn a certain blind eye to the light that pours through the cracks in their structures.

Art has no such illusions. Rock 'n' roll, for example, at its height, embraces what is really just glamour, a spell woven out of creative energy, technology, and artifice. When rock draws down the ineffable, it's not trying to go direct but clothes itself in its cultural moment, as well as its inspirations and its roots. Those who are interested in nontraditional, nonordinary states of consciousness are often already on the fringe or identify with some kind of counterculture or underground movement. That's something that has always driven artists, musicians, and writers who see themselves standing outside the mainstream and who have no interest in a Johns Hopkins research project, who see something like that as contrary to an understanding of the world that requires a certain eschewing of authority, homogeneity, and anything government sanctioned to lose its special, inherently spiritual quality.

If, as I learned, the psychedelic experience is intimately tied to the history of America's love affair with mysticism (and, by extension, the occult), then understanding all the cultural manifestations of this phenomenon is of great value. Psychedelic music and art are particularly tied to their many associations because, simply put, they are made out of language and language is nothing if not a construction of cultural markers and colloquialisms. More personally, I am hardwired to seek out those expressions that key right into my spiritual receptors. When I got clean, I emerged just as psychedelic culture was having its own rebirth.

Psychedelic music in the 1980s was influenced by Grateful Dead acid rock and/or British pop. Progressive rock had gone the way of arena rock, and its forebear krautrock all but disappeared, until it reemerged as New Age music. But the fanzine *Ptolemaic Terrascope*, founded and published by Phil McMullen, went out of its way to see if there was something else that could be classified as psychedelic. McMullen explains that his magazine was launched, in 1988, as a way to give some notice to bands that were experimental but still working within a kind of playing field that included heavy nods to the sixties. *Terrascope* found itself swimming in an ocean of music that simply hadn't been categorized before. "It wasn't all traditional psychedelic rock by any means. Apart from the more interesting pop, electronic, and avant garde artists, we covered an awful lot of folk music, too, back when it was extremely unfashionable to do so," McMullen recalls.

At the leading edge of the psychedelic revival is a subgenre often called psychedelic folk, as it usually involves some fusion of traditional American and British folk elements alongside experimental forms, usually containing, but certainly not limited to, psychedelic tropes. Sometimes the folk sound takes precedence, and what is psychedelic is more subtle. In other cases, the folk elements are woven into noisy rock structures, often giving a kind of melancholia to discordant and aggressive frameworks. It's not easy to do successfully. Veer too far to the folk spectrum, and the songs are the soundtrack to a gathering of the Society for Creative Anachronism. Excessive heaviness and pagan death metal are not too far away. Nevertheless, when done well, it's music that can be both transcendent and deeply grounded.

The band Blithe Sons is made up of two highly regarded psychedelic/folk musicians—Loren Chasse and Glenn Donaldson—and demonstrates the most human elements of the

underground folk movement, as well as offering the least contrived and most authentic strains of psychedelic tropes. Blithe
Sons reaches out beyond their own inner world and tells a story.
At times it feels extremely subjective, just two guys nodding
back and forth at each other, but more often it reminds you of
something that feels familiar, even if the actual event or feeling
eludes you. Other bands and musicians are similarly capable of
manifesting something intensely personal and universal: Woods,
Akron/Family, Richard Youngs, Steven Smith, and Sore Eros, to
name a few current, consummate examples.

In this music was something that made sense to me. It wasn't
music to take drugs to; it was music that mirrored a kind of
mood and psychic velum in which to illuminate and inscribe
that unspoken quality of the drug experience, or at least the
romanticized notion of that experience. It was exactly that
transmission of something deeply human, but neither akin to
our normal waking consciousness nor simply the telling of a
dream. Nevertheless, there was something undeniably psychedelic going on here. Not only was something being revealed,
but it was possible the music itself could evoke, or instill, some
measure of altered consciousness in the listener. Yet, unlike the
Eastern-informed music of the 1960s, today's psychedelic artists are moving more and more deeply into Western religious
imagery and sensibility.

Gregory Weeks, a solo musician and member of the lush
pastoral psych band Espers, explains this transition from East
to West: "Eastern mysticism seems much more like an escape,
whereas the natural world is there to be seen and felt. When
something threatens the natural world, that threat is tangible,
as are the rewards and examples of nature and environment."

This focus on the corporeal is evident where the space-out
of the jam has given way to a more physical musical effect: the
drone. Strictly speaking, a drone is any repetitive or sustained,

usually dissonant chord that creates a musical theme grounding the rest of a song or movement. Wagner's *Rheingold* contains a classical version, but for the most part, the drone is usually found in indigenous music, such as that of the bagpipe; in spiritual music, such as the chants of Tibetan monks; in Indian ragas; or, more recently, in experimental and underground music, such as doom metal.

There is no more disconcerting and unsettling music than doom metal when it incorporates the drone, and yet it is somehow frighteningly gripping. Almost completely in opposition to any notion of transcendence, drone metal gets its energy from a subterranean volcanic core. It can make you feel as if the very plates of the earth are shifting in your belly. Beyond the apocalyptic, which at its heart includes an idea of hope and final redemption, doom metal sounds the alarm that something is on its way slowly dragging its behemoth body across the scorched earth. Nevertheless, the two most influential doom metal bands, Earth and Sunn 0))), have both spoken in interviews about how theirs is a music intent on a kind of spiritual transport. The use of drone is key.

Weeks describes the drone's relationship to psychedelia and spirituality as the quickest route to a state not unlike a drug experience for both the musician and the audience. He compares a well-crafted drone to watching a fire: "Invisible frequencies manifest in the ear much like an elusive green flame appears amidst the oranges and yellows. A fire never gets old, there's something primal and primordial about its engagement."

Music has long played an important role in religion, but the particular phenomenon of the chant or other intonations has often been believed to be attuned to actual physical vibrations that have an effect on the body. The mystical experience is about not just the mind, but the whole self as it exists in space. In this way, the tension inside the psych-folk sensibility, particularly with the drone, seems to be a primary tension within any mystical experience: How close can you get to God before you are shattered?

The psychedelic experience often wavers between bliss and terror, between touching the fire of the holy and in turn being burned up by it. Contemporary psychedelic music, when done well, can gracefully inhabit this space. This also means the music is often not what might be called joyful, but rather is filled with sounds of dread, of melancholy, of the noise in the soul as you realize your incantation actually worked and God is staring at you from the inside of the grove.

Glenn Donaldson, member of Blithe Sons and cofounder of the Jeweled Antler Collective (a group of musicians producing homemade tapes and CDRs incorporating drone, noise, and field recordings), makes a careful distinction between psychedelia as a genre and psychedelic as a state of mind. Psychedelia is born of a whole cultural consciousness and aesthetic that include art, history, and, of course, music. As for a state of mind, Donaldson believes many different forms of music can create an altered state: "A psychedelic song puts you in a waking dream, the sound and the sentiment overtake you and the rest of the world is erased momentarily." This erasure of the world, so close to the notion of ecstasy that religious mystics have described, would seem to suggest that there is something inherently "spiritual" about certain kinds of psychedelic music.

Donaldson is skeptical about these kinds of associations: "Only snake-oil salesmen will tell you their music is spiritual or an esoteric practice. It's marketing and myth. I love that aspect of music. Maybe I am one of these charlatans. I know a few." Nevertheless, Donaldson agrees that music does have the potential to alter consciousness, or at least transmit the experience of altered states. It has to do with the physicality of music, the way it affects the brain as an organ: "It's corporeal, in the form of sound waves entering the body through the ears and the skin, strong stuff, but I'm not sure if those resulting 'altered states' are intrinsic to certain kinds of music or just something the listener is creating."

Yet the whole look and feel of the Jeweled Antler Collective captures the mystery and strangeness of so many aspects of psychedelic culture, particularly the synthesis of occultism and mysticism. Donaldson admits some of that is done with a wink and a nod, and that there was something playful about what he calls "quasi-mystical images." His band Skygreen Leopards is easily heard as a meditation on gods of earth and sky, but Donaldson insists much of it is tongue-in-cheek: "Some of the things we put in our records that we thought were funny, people took them at face value, thinking we were trying to be pagan mystics or something. We are not anything like that." The Jeweled Antler music and art were not about paganism, but about the natural spirituality of the outdoors. And it was certainly not meant to be visionary. It is nature as itself, not pointing to anything more than the actual: "Musically it was not ecstatic, but ponderous and minimal, sometimes harrowing, sometimes tedious, playing as few notes as possible so the landscape would seep in."

I am skeptical, however, that one can evoke a mood and an idea so readily without some intention. There is a certain disingenuousness that musicians are often capable of, not wanting to admit how much they are influenced by what came before, or too modest about how original and insightful their music really is. There is something palpable in psychedelic music that can't just be a product of artifice. The aspect of contemporary psychedelia that is perhaps artificial—the looping, electronic bleeps and blurps, static—means that the genre will sustain itself for a new generation. It belongs to the twenty-first century. McMullen explains, "There's an impression that drone music is music by drugged people for people to do drugs to, but it's also a sound which is eminently suited to the modern world. Drone music can be created by solitary individuals collaborating via the Internet. It doesn't necessarily require practice space, drums, or vocals, traditionally the trickiest areas for young bands to embrace." So maybe holiness is hidden in the world, after all, and the right tool, maybe the drone of a computerized loop, can be the incantation that sets it free.

Arik Roper is an artist who is helping to shape a new idea about psychedelic art, one that is also rooted in the earth, rather than in a transcendent, impersonal, rarely witnessed reality. His vision is more akin to psych-folk and stoner rock that prefer the knotted branch of a tree to a vision of Krishna in his chariot. His work evokes both William Blake and comic books, ancient behemoths standing against a backdrop of castle ruins and giant mushrooms.

Roper was very young when he first came across the world of underground art and comics. His father collected pulp science fiction and fantasy art, so Roper was exposed to this aesthetic early on. But it was the magazine *Heavy Metal* and the 1981 movie based on it that turned Roper—as well as a lot of kids growing up in the late seventies and early eighties—onto the world of horror and science fiction comics, with a good dose of sex, violence, and drug references. Cable television made films that had before been inaccessible or just plain rare available for the first time to a new generation. Roper was one of many who saw the film *Wizards* for the first time on HBO. Made in 1977 by the animator Ralph Bakshi (also responsible for animating Robert Crumb's comic *Fritz the Cat*), the movie featured fairies, elves, and other stock fantasy characters battling evil technology across a nuclear-devastated landscape, gleefully fucking and fighting.

Creepy and *Eerie* magazines introduced Roper to the work

of artist Bernie Wrightson, whose emphasis on anatomy made his vision of monsters all the more grotesque. Unlike many who shared his passion for the weird, Roper didn't actually play Dungeons & Dragons—because, as he says, "I didn't have the patience to learn the rules"—but he still collected lead miniatures and pored over the illustrations in the manuals. His truer inspirations, as with many more of his peers, were music and album cover art, including Jethro Tull, Black Sabbath, Pink Floyd, and Roger Dean, best known for his work with the band Yes. Dean's work, whose vision can be gleaned in Roper's paintings, is the landscape of psychedelic dreams: cities carved out of stone, floating islands, bone-white roads stretching over gaseous seas.

When he was around nineteen, Roper started taking mushrooms and noticed that they brought out the natural patterns that are easily overlooked. "There's this kind of fabric or web you can see as part of your visual field. I started drawing this stuff that I was seeing, this texture, this kind of organic root pattern that I was getting from the mushrooms." For a time he purposely avoided characters and other concrete ideas in his art, in favor of exploring abstraction. Eventually these patterns made their way into the backgrounds of his more representational art.

Mushrooms appealed to him more than LSD because there was something familiar about psilocybin; it spoke more readily to how he already understood art and where art originated. Roper is often classed as a visionary artist, but his work is markedly different from that of most other artists working with the drug experience as the primary manifesting inspiration. Roper's art is earth-centered, rather than a vision of cosmic, exploding consciousness. "It sort of makes sense when you think about mushrooms. Anything that's out of the earth can get you back to the source, which is kind of the ultimate place to be because it's the same as the outside. Looking inward is just as infinite as looking outward."

Another aspect of Roper's artistic vision that exists in opposition to what we traditionally think of as psychedelic is that
it is replete with monsters and other grotesques. There are
things lurking, and they are not always hopeful cosmic entities.
Sometimes the unknown can be a little bit scary and creepy
and burrow up from under the ground. Roper doesn't want to
make distinctions between good and evil but admits, "Evil and
scary things are all part of the psyche, and I find that kind of
stuff really fascinating because it's all part of us." Roper believes
other forms of visionary expression are a little cowardly when it
comes to looking at the shadow side. "It's all about exploding
fractals and a billion shimmering points of glass. Technically,
it's impressive sometimes, but it's a little bland." Expressions of
cosmic consciousness can often begin to look the same. On the
inner journey you're much more likely to meet the personality
of self than you are in the external, where everybody's "one."

When it comes to the topic of drugs, Roper isn't shy. He
is well aware of the stigma but is bemused by all the extreme
stances that people have. There is no reason to deny their influence, but it can be just as irresponsible to suggest drugs are easy
to manage. Nevertheless, his days of regular mushroom eating
are past, mostly because he eventually came to understand their
power and that they require a more serious sensibility. "I really
take it as a ritual and I try to get a lot out of it and integrate it
into my life, if possible, and my art, which is my life as well. It's
not for everybody, of course, and I don't blame people if they
can't or don't want to pursue that or they aren't interested. It's
like a lot of other spiritual practices, where it's scary, too." For
Roper, mushrooms have become a kind of sixth sense that continues to operate even when he's not using them. It only takes
checking in once in a while to sharpen the edge.

For Roper, inwardness and, by extension, earthiness are
something we immediately have access to. "You can't always

look outside, you can't always go out to the stars and look, but you can always look inside. It's all inside, and all this stuff exists in a microcosm."

Using the language of comics as a method to capture a visionary perspective might seem counterintuitive, but the underground comix of the sixties showed that the medium is particularly suited to wild psychedelic imaginings. While someone like Roper is influenced by more understandable sources, such as *Heavy Metal* magazine and Ralph Bakshi, others seek to subvert more traditional cartoon tropes as vehicles for unlocking their altered visions.

Picture, if you will: Frank, an anthropomorphic catlike creature with buckteeth and a stout tail, is walking down a path with a small, four-legged, house-shaped companion. The two come across a pipe sticking out of the ground and leaking a curious viscous substance that on further inspection becomes a small creature with an arrow-shaped tail. Suddenly there appears a giant toad in the midst of digesting some other animal, whose lower torso and legs are sticking out of the toad's mouth. Frank pulls on the legs and extracts a grotesque pig-man. The pig-man, noticing the tiny organism Frank has rescued from the pipe, jumps back into the toad's mouth.

The creator of this curious strip, Jim Woodring, experienced spontaneous spells of paranoia, accompanied by vivid hallucinations, when he was a young child, which he describes as "silently jabbering heads at the foot of my bed, distorted animals and objects hanging in the air over me." Some of these images were so terrifying, they induced nausea, and some took on an almost mystical quality: "Often I saw a huge staring eye that made me vomit with fear. I also saw radially symmetrical shapes made of beautiful flame-like colors hovering over me. They made pretty, harmonica-like droning noises."

As Woodring got older, the hallucinations came much less

frequently, until, in his twenties, he had them only two or three times a year. But as a child, he experienced them every day. Because he was distrustful of the only religion he was really aware of at the time—Christianity—he didn't attach any spiritual significance to these images, though he did think them meaningful, if only as internal messages to himself.

It wasn't until junior high, when he saw the work of the Russian illustrator Boris Artzybasheff, that he realized not only that he was not alone, but that there was a medium through which to express his inscrutable mental phantasms. Artzybasheff was a mid-twentieth-century Ukrainian artist who worked in the United States, drawing book and magazine covers, and was known for his bizarre illustrations that merged men with machines. Woodring's epiphany, however, wouldn't be complete until 1968, when he saw an exhibit of surrealism and Dada at the Los Angeles County Museum of Art that completely transformed him. Woodring recalls, "That experience goddamn near put me in a coma for days, discovering that there were adult men and women who devoted their lives to portraying through oblique yet incisive symbolic language the most elusive and dangerous and appalling truths about reality." From there, Woodring's childhood interest in drawing turned into a calling and a hope that was truly a vehicle for the expression of his bizarre inner world.

Other underground comix artists made it seem more doable. Surprisingly, though, while Woodring eventually had his share of experiences with psychedelic drugs, he doesn't credit them with formalizing his artistic style. While he admits that drugs influenced his work, Woodring's themes and ideas remained essentially the same after he experienced LSD: "Like surrealism, those experiences confirmed and expanded my ideas, rather than providing them."

Woodring would go on to become one of the most formidable

and influential artists working in underground comix. Ironically, while there is no other comic strip that comes as close to portraying the precarious mental landscape one encounters on LSD, Woodring does not consider himself a psychedelic artist. However, he does attribute to the drug a certain teaching point: "If a few molecules of LSD can wipe away the world like a wet sponge demolishing a watercolor painting, then that world as we know it must not be very durable . . . I was already looking for what lay beneath the surface when I first took the stuff. I just didn't know how easily the surface could be demolished."

For Woodring, psychedelics proved more of an amplification of his work than a direct influence. The inspiration gained from drugs, in fact, wound up going in the other direction: Woodring's vision was enfolded into the cultural psychedelic imagination. Woodring and other comic-book artists created a new language for tripping—such as organic arrows and strange hovering objects that begged to be grasped and pulled on—a world that organized the most nonfigurative impressions and gave them form and narrative. Remembering a trip might as well have been remembering a Woodring strip. Who could say which was which?

These contemporary musicians and artists look back to original ideas about what is psychedelic to hit on something essential, but they also glimpse the future. To make music, to paint, suggests that the transmission is more valuable than the experience, because the experience is only contained and articulated by its expression. What art is also able to capture is the dark side, that peculiar melancholy, that special kind of madness, that characterizes certain drug experiences.

Samuel Taylor Coleridge, another addict and kindred spirit to drug users everywhere, deeply understood how the telling of an encounter with a divine or inexpressible force becomes something of a terrible burden. In Coleridge's poem "Rime of the Ancient Mariner," the mariner, who is a guest at a wedding, tells how he watched as one of the spirits of the sea killed the entire crew of his ship after the mariner killed an albatross. Eventually the spirits of his dead comrades guided him home, but he is forced to tell the story over and over again as his penance. What good is language, the poem suggests, when it only guesses at something that consumes one's entire being? After he first killed the bird, the crew, fearing bad luck, forced the mariner to wear it around his neck. Once home, free of the literal bird, he is still forced to wear its spirit. No one telling of the story will ever be sufficient to lift the burden from him forever. At the same time, his story binds him to the listener, and so what was his alone becomes communal and then cultural. Even if it feels as if words can never fully capture the experience, they still offer a simple kind of bonding. It is why, some argue, twelve-step programs seem particularly suited to alcoholics and drug addicts: They offer a language with which to share those experiences that are without equal in the normal day-to-day.

Addiction is an albatross, for sure, but, as in Coleridge's poem, it is also a force of the divine as reflected in nature and demands a certain amount of respect. My addiction to drugs is an addiction to that promise all those other travelers along the difficult road gave me. I heard it echo in Kerouac's firecracker prose, in Shunryu Suzuki on Zen, and in the strains of Syd Barrett's madness rotating infinitely on my turntable; I saw it just as far as I could see as I dove off a stage into the sea of bald and spiked heads at a hardcore show. Then again, clean, I heard it in the torn and fragile speech of my newly sober compatriots who had also gone down the rabbit hole in a tangle of thorns and thicket, and who always, like me, saw the rabbit just as he turned the corner, always just out of reach. What to call it? Has it a name after all? It has been called illumination, enlightenment, nirvana, *moksha*, gnosis, cosmic consciousness. But sometimes it was nothing more than getting perpetually wasted, head-rattlingly stoned, until all the cotton had disintegrated and there was, for a brief moment, clarity—perfect, would-do-anything-to-have-it-again clarity.

In a remarkable little essay written in 1958 for the *Grapevine*, a magazine published by Alcoholics Anonymous, Gerald Heard (the man who introduced Bill Wilson to Aldous Huxley) wrote about the special kind of sickness that besets the alcoholic. Echoing Carl Jung's letter to Wilson, Heard writes, "Though alcohol is a narcotic, alcoholism (like all addictions) is not at base a search for utter sedation. It is a desire for that *ecstasis*, that 'standing out' from the land-locked lagoons of conformity, out onto the uncharted high seas where the only map is the star-set heavens." A bit flowery, perhaps, but Heard honestly accounts for that part of addiction that has characterized all the various ways in which everything from punk rock to magic has spoken to that craving in me.

And so only through the communion that develops among addicts, clean or using, have I found the manner in which I can remain clean. While many of my sober companions tend to look upon their overall drug use with regret and some measure of disappointment, there tends to be a general agreement that our particular experiences with psychedelics will always have their own special value. Friends who aren't drug addicts but experimented with LSD and magic mushrooms also treasure those trips. They were, for all of us, a glimpse into a way of thinking and perceiving outside of time. One person described it as being a poem for a brief moment, something eternal, rather than following a schedule or being a citizen. Years later, even after choosing family life and steady jobs, we will always have the knowledge that this world is not all there is, that normal waking and dreaming consciousness are not everything the mind is capable of.

So every once in a while, despite all I know to be true, I still sometimes ask, *Damn, so why can't I?*

It's not an easy question to answer, partially because the questions come at me like storm clouds charged with rain and electricity. You want to head right into them for the thrill, just as a part of you knows to turn back. But for an addict, even entertaining questions like this can prove disastrous. There is often enough justification to drink or get high again, as the saying goes, over a broken shoelace. When just about all the evidence shows that psychedelic drugs are not addicting, why should I be afraid? Maybe it really was just a matter of the set and setting being totally off. Over twenty years later, I'm clean, healthy, not prone to sitting on the floor and rolling the I Ching for hours on end. If everything is as it should have been, why not try to have the experience I always longed for?

But then I remember the essential thing that can never be different: As much as I have longed for it, a spiritual life without a direct encounter with the divine heart of the cosmic egg seems better suited to me. (Even as I write that, something in my heart breaks.)

Could it be that God, or the gods, or the universe has denied me this experience for a reason? Maybe my wiring is no good for transmitting the ancient alien knowledge of the spores. It is hard to admit spiritual defeat, especially when the message is often "Ask, and it will be given to you; seek, and you will find; knock, and it will be opened to you" (Matthew 7:7).

What I have learned, though, is twofold. First is the sticky nature of addiction itself. I can never again trust my motivation, and I can never be sure there is not some neurobiological component to addiction that could be activated by a psychoactive agent. Second, and more important, is that I am nothing if not a whirlwind of cultural and religious debris, spun around until those things are a blur and what is left is simply the force of the spinning. At every moment I was fed by culture and then I brought to each experience not only the language of all the music, art, comics, and literature, but the expectations that those things held for me.

Halfway into the set, the crowd at the bar, having talked almost all the way through to that point, slowly begins to make their way toward the stage. Something is beckoning them. The music is probably not what they were expecting in a typical Boston rock club. I become acutely attentive to the audience, watching who stays, who is drawn, and who runs away. Some huddle at the front of the stage from start to finish, not moving, taking it all in. Others move in and out of the crowd, lost, it seems, not sure if they want to give over to this experience, sometimes uncomfortable, the way the band members yelp and sway. Still others don't want to know about any of it—whatever this is, it is not just a "show." There is mystery here, and danger.

I stay until the end. But once home, I creep into my son's room and kiss his forehead. The best kind of transcendence is the kind that can be seen sleeping its own dreams, and the best kind of psychedelic is the kind with its feet on the ground and its eyes toward heaven, feet firmly tapping the guitar pedal, fingers getting blistered from so much strumming.

notes

20   "hippie paganism . . ." Davis, **Led Zeppelin IV**, 61.

20   "Who do Zeppelin swear fealty to . . ." Ibid.

28   "this divine and infinite life . . ." Underhill, 28.

CHAPTER **2**

Page(s)

36   "You should not be a smoky fire . . ." Suzuki, 63.

36   "his wound blossomed . . ." Hesse, 119.

36   "I see a man who is terribly wounded . . ." Vonnegut, 240.

36   "He realized miserably that . . ." Heinlein, 83.

40   "Meanwhile . . . do you have any of the stuff on hand . . ."
      Huxley, **Moksha**, 31.

40   "excessive, too obvious glory" Huxley, **Doors of
      Perception**, 59.

41   "At present there is a lamentable tendency . . ."
      Huxley, "The Magical and the Spiritual," 115.

41   "a direct apprehension of Reality and Eternity . . ."
      Ibid., 114.

41   "Swami Prabhavananda was virulently opposed . . ."
      This and related details drawn from Vrajaprana.

42   "Drugs may induce psychic . . ." Swami Prabha-
      vananda, "Vital Questions on Religion."

42   "According to the scholar Laura Quinney . . ." This
      and related details drawn from Quinney.

43   "a somewhat fuller account of exactly . . ." Roueché.

43   "1/2 tablet of Dramamine . . ." Zaehner, **Mysticism,
      Sacred and Profane**, 212.

44   "Eastern mysticism, drugs . . ." Zaehner, **Zen, Drugs,
      and Mysticism**, 40.

44   "pinch of psychedelic . . ." Quoted in Martin.

45   "seemed to be standing . . ." Huxley, **Doors of Per-
      ception**, 59.

45   "Seeing is not so simple . . ." Castaneda, **Separate Reality**, 111.

45   "nonordinary reality" . . . Ibid., **Teachings of Don Juan**, 38.

CHAPTER 3

Page(s)

58   "The trip, in fact, the whole deal . . ." Wolfe, **Electric Kool-Aid Acid Test**, 87.

58   "[Being on the bus] probably had spiritual ramifications . . ." Babbs.

59   "America needs indians . . ." Trips Festival Flyer.

59   "A new concept of human relations . . ." Quoted in Perry, 32.

60   "Nor do I think anything . . ." Duncan.

60   "We're all the same person . . ." Wavy Gravy.

60   "Between March and September 1967 . . ." Perry, 33.

61   "wearing guru suits and hair . . ." Baker.

61   "Hashbury . . ." This and related drawn from Thompson.

62   "You can get high on a mantra . . ." Didion, **We Tell Ourselves Stories**, 91.

75   "For the bass player, Mark Tulin . . ." This and related details drawn from Tulin.

76   "In a short documentary . . ." **California Rock**.

77   "name-checked planets . . ." Cavanagh, 2.

CHAPTER 4

Page(s)

87   "reducing-valve . . ." Huxley, **Doors of Perception**, 23.

87   "The intensity with which . . ." Dass, 94.

87   "concentration of interest on the Transcendent . . ." Underhill, 358.

88   "Ecstasy! . . . Your very soul is seized . . ." Wasson, 37.

88   "Individual Freedom . . ." Leary, **Politics of Ecstasy**, 5.

90   "an uninterrupted stream of fantastic . . ." "Conversa-
      tion with Albert Hofmann," 13.

90   "Kaleidoscopic, fantastic images . . ." Ibid., 16.

90   "In four hours . . ." Leary, **Flashbacks**, 33.

92   "All of a sudden . . ." Quoted in Doblin, "Pahnke's
      'Good Friday Experiment.'"

93   "We receive this mystical knowledge . . ." Quoted in
      James, **Varieties of Religious Experience**, 398.

93   "There was one universal man . . ." Quoted in Doblin,
      "Pahnke's 'Good Friday Experiment.'"

94   "We hoped that by living . . ." Quoted in Leary, **Flash-
      backs**, 193.

96   "[A]s long as people fail . . ." "Conversation with
      Albert Hoffman."

97   "When Michael Murphy was a boy . . ." This and related
      details drawn from Murphy.

98   "The work at Esalen was too important . . ." Kripal,
      132–33.

98   "the contemporary debasement of Gnosticism . . ."
      Bloom, 17.

98   "there was energy and there was healing . . ." Albanese,
      505.

99   "James Fadiman, a psychedelic psychotherapist . . ."
      This and related details drawn from Fadiman.

102   "The old alchemical dream . . ." Wolfe, "'Me' Decade."

103   "Manson was insane . . ." Bromell, 124.

104   "a horror that comes and goes . . ." Ibid.

104   "I remember . . ." Didion, **White Album**, 208.

104   "space colony" . . . "attempting to create . . ." Leary,
      Flashbacks, 190.

108   "The nature of the experience . . ." Leary, **Psychedelic
      Experience**, 11.

108   "Because a 15-year-old . . ." "**Playboy** Interview:
       Timothy Leary."
109   "Do what thou wilt shall be the whole of the law . . ."
       Crowley, **Book of the Law**, 13.

CHAPTER 5
Page(s)
114   "All movements are accomplished in six stages . . ." **I
       Ching**, 98.
115   "Those who persevere . . ." Ibid., 95.
115   "Perseverance furthers . . ." Ibid., 101.
116   "What we do know is . . ." This and related details on
       tarot drawn from Davis, "Pop Arcana (1)."
117   "In 1947, an American . . ." This and related details on
       Case drawn from Horowitz, 250ff.
119   "one who both knows . . ." Yates, 199.
120   "In Heaven am I . . ." Mead.
120   "The Hermetica pictures . . ." Davis, **Techgnosis**, 35.
122   "I must further caution . . ." **Key of Solomon the King**, viii.
123   "One of these men, Alan Bennett . . ." This and related
       details drawn from Owen, 191ff., and related.
123   "More than seventy years before . . ." Crowley, **Magical
       Diaries**, x.
124   "obese . . . with small pretty hands . . ." "Mme. Bla-
       vatsky Dead."
124   "It is from this wisdom-religion . . ." Blavatsky, "Is
       Theosophy a Religion, 10.
125   "Magick enables us . . ." Crowley, **Magick**, 400.
127   "[F]or a firm Spiritualist . . ." Blavatsky, "Science of
       Magic."
131   "By degrees we beheld the infinite Abyss . . ." Blake, 41.
131   "is born in the fire . . ." **Book of Lambspring**.
131   "The salamander . . ." Pliny the Elder, 147.

CHAPTER 6

Page(s)

136   "[Drugs] do not open the doors . . ." Paz, 77.

141   "Drugs provoke the vision . . ." Ibid., 76.

142   "Always the Demon stirs . . ." Baudelaire, **Flowers of Evil**, 149.

145   "I think that maybe we saved . . ." Wavy Gravy.

146   "We made a mistake . . ." The Beatles, 286.

146   "I was just using the situation . . ." Quoted in Sheff, 191.

146   "a supposed inventor and charlatan . . ." Kozinn.

147   "In a remarkable home-movie artifact . . ." This and related details drawn from **Imagine**.

149   "frantic craving for any substance . . ." Baudelaire, **Artificial Paradise**, 81.

150   "I was seized . . ." **Pass It On**, 121.

150   "A wind, not of air, but of spirit . . ." Ibid.

150   "for reducing stomach acids . . ." Ibid., 120.

150   "Belladonna, once used by Victorian women . . ." Stewart, 33.

151   "educational variety . . ." **Alcoholics Anonymous**, 567.

151   "We are not cured of alcoholism . . ." Ibid., 85.

153   "shadow side . . ." Vaughan, 193.

153   "may become addicted . . ." Ibid., 194.

153   "one's direct experience . . ." **Pass It On**, 371.

CHAPTER 7

Page(s)

169   "Charles Tart, a psychologist and teacher . . ." This and related details drawn from Tart.

172   "Griffiths, professor of behavioral biology . . ." This and related details drawn from Griffiths.

172   "Jesse was just out of college . . ." This and related details drawn from Jesse.

176 "In 1984, when Rick Doblin . . ." This and related details drawn from Doblin.

177 "Until 2006, John Hayes, a psychologist . . ." This and related details drawn from Hayes.

180 "One problem with these categories . . ." This and related details drawn from Sharf.

180 "there is no such thing as generic 'mysticism' . . ." Scholem, 5–6.

182 "Denis McKenna is often name-checked . . ." This and related details drawn from McKenna.

187 "For a few hours . . ." Pinchbeck, 42.

188 "official 9/11 story . . ." Wishnia.

190 "The water is pure water . . ." Fadiman.

190 "the Reality behind the veil . . ." Underhill, **Mysticism**, 4.

191 "tormented by the Unknowable . . ." Ibid., 8.

191 "deification . . ." Ibid., 99.

191 "extension of sensual experience . . ." Ibid., 72.

192 "a little hole in the wall of appearances . . ." Underhill, **Column of Dust**, 32.

CHAPTER 8

Page(s)

198 "Art, I suppose . . ." Huxley, **Doors of Perception**, 29.

198 "I have never taken drugs . . ." Dalí, 97.

200 "McMullen explains that his magazine . . ." This and related details drawn from McMullen.

201 "Eastern mysticism seems . . ." This and related details drawn from Weeks.

203 "A psychedelic song . . ." This and related details drawn from Donaldson.

205   "Arik Roper is an artist . . ." This and related details
      drawn from Roper.
208   "The creator of this curious strip . . ." This and related
      details drawn from Woodring.
212   "Though alcohol is a narcotic . . ." Heard.

bibliography

Albanese, Catherine. *Republic of the Mind*. New Haven: Yale University Press, 2007.

Alcoholics Anonymous: The Story of How Many Thousands of Men and Women Have Recovered from Alcoholism. 4th ed. New York: Alcoholics Anonymous World Services, 2001.

Babbs, Ken. Email interview with author. December 5, 2009.

Baker, Russell. "Observer: Dr. Leary Endangers the 'Cop-Out.'" *New York Times*, May 11, 1967.

Baudelaire, Charles. *Artificial Paradise*. Translated by Ellen Fox. New York: Herder and Herder, 1971.

———. *The Flowers of Evil*. Translated by Keith Waldrop. Middletown, CT: Wesleyan University Press, 2006.

Baum, Dan. *Smoke and Mirrors: The War on Drugs and the Politics of Failure*. 1st ed. Boston: Little, Brown, 1996.

Blavatsky, H.P. "Is Theosophy a Religion." *The Theosophical Path*. Vol. 15, No. 1, July 1918. http://www.theosociety.org/pasadena/ttp/ttp_no.htm (accessed December 15, 2010).

Beatles, The. *The Beatles Anthology*. San Francisco: Chronicle Books, 2000.

Boehme, Jacob. *The Confessions of Jacob Boehme. Sacred Texts.* http://www.sacred-texts.com/eso/cjb/cjb16.htm (accessed January 10, 2011).

The Book of Lambspring. Alchemy. http://www.levity.com/alchemy/lambtext.html (accessed May 15, 2010).

Blake, William. "The Marriage of Heaven and Hell." Chap. 1 in *The Complete Poetry and Prose of William Blake.* Edited by David V. Erdman. New York: Anchor Books, 1988.

Blavatsy, H. P. "The Science of Magic." *Spiritual Scientist* 3 (1875): 64–65. *Theosophical Society.* http://www.theosociety.org/pasadena/bcw/b75-10-14.htm (accessed July 1, 2010).

Bloom, Harold. *Omens of the Millennium.* New York: Riverhead, 1997.

Braude, Ann. *Radical Spirits: Spiritualism and Women's Rights in Nineteenth-Century America.* Boston: Beacon Press, 1989.

Bromell, Nicholas Knowles. *Tomorrow Never Knows: Rock and Psychedelics in the 1960s.* Chicago: University of Chicago Press, 2000.

Bucke, Richard Maurice. *Cosmic Consciousness.* New York: E. P. Dutton & Company, 1901.

California Rock: Under the Covers. Directed by Bill Day and Terry Schwartz. Los Angeles: Lightyear Entertainment/Triptych Pictures, 2000.

Case, Paul Foster. *The Tarot: A Key to the Wisdom of the Ages.* Richmond, VA: Macoy Publishing Company, 1947.

Castaneda, Carlos. *A Separate Reality: Further Conversations with Don Juan.* New York: Simon & Schuster, 1971.

———. *The Teachings of Don Juan: A Yaqui Way of Knowledge.* Berkeley: University of California Press, 1969.

Cavanagh, John Eric. *The Piper at the Gates of Dawn.* New York: Continuum, 2003.

Cheever, Susan. *My Name Is Bill.* New York: Washington Square Press, 2004.

"A Conversation with Albert Hofmann." *Newsletter of the*

Multidisciplinary Association for Psychedelic Studies 8, no. 3 (1998): 30–33. *MAPS*. http://www.maps.org/news-letters/v08n3/08330hof.html (accessed April 3, 2010).

Corpus Hermeticum. Sacred Texts. http://www.sacred-texts.com/chr/herm/index.htm (accessed February 2, 2010).

Crowley, Aleister. *The Book of the Law*. Boston: Red Wheel/Weiser Books, 2004.

——. *The Magical Diaries of Aleister Crowley*. Edited by Stephen Skinner. Boston: Weiser Books, 1996.

——. *Magick: Book 4, Liber Aba*. York Beach, ME: Samuel Weiser, 2000.

Dalí, Salvador. *Dalí by Dalí*. New York: Abrams, 1970.

Dass, Ram. *Remember, Be Here Now*. San Cristobal, NM: Lama Foundation, 1971.

Davis, Erik, and Led Zeppelin. *Led Zeppelin's Led Zeppelin IV*. New York: Continuum, 2005.

——. "Pop Arcana (1)." *HiLobrow*, January 30, 2010. http://hilobrow.com/2010/01/30/the-comic-book-of-thoth/ (accessed February 10, 2010).

——. *Techgnosis*. New York: Three Rivers Press, 1998.

Dick, Philip K. *A Scanner Darkly*. 1st ed. New York: Pantheon Books, 2006.

——. *Valis*. 1st ed. New York: Vintage Books, 1991.

Didion, Joan. *We Tell Ourselves Stories in Order to Live: Collected Nonfiction*. New York: Alfred A. Knopf, 2006.

——. *The White Album*. New York: Simon & Schuster, 1979.

Doblin, Rick. "Pahnke's 'Good Friday Experiment': A Long-Term Follow-Up and Methodological Critique." *Journal of Transpersonal Psychology* 23, no. 1 (1991): 1–28. http://www.druglibrary.org/Schaffer/lsd/doblin.htm (accessed April 5, 2011).

——. Interview with author. December 15, 2009.

Donaldson, Glenn. Email interview with author. November 16, 2009.

Duncan, Gary. Email interview with author. March 20, 2010.

Eco, Umberto. *Foucault's Pendulum*. Translated by William Weaver. Orlando, FL: Harcourt, 1989.

Fadiman, James. Telephone interview with author. November 17, 2009.

Ginsberg, Allen. *Collected Poems, 1947–1980*. 1st ed. New York: Harper & Row, 1984.

Griffiths, Roland. Telephone interview with author. February 26, 2010.

Gruen, John. *The New Bohemia: The Combine Generation*. New York: Shorecrest, 1966.

Hayes, Charles. *Tripping: An Anthology of True-Life Psychedelic Adventures*. New York: Penguin Compass, 2000.

Hayes, John. Telephone interview with author. November 22, 2008.

Heard, Gerald. "The Search for Ecstacy," *Grapevine*, May 1958.

Heinlein, Robert A. *Stranger in a Strange Land*. New York: G. P. Putnam's Sons, 1961.

Hesse, Hermann, and Joachim Neugroschel. *Siddhartha: An Indian Tale*. New York: Penguin Books, 1999.

Hillman, James. *Suicide and the Soul*. Woodstock, CT: Spring Publications, 1997.

Imagine: John Lennon. Directed by Andrew Solt. Burbank, CA: Warner Brothers Pictures, 1988.

Huxley, Aldous. *The Doors of Perception/Heaven and Hell*. New York: Harper & Row, 1990. Print.

———. "The Magical and the Spiritual." Chap. 16 in *Vedanta for the Western World*. Edited by Christopher Isherwood. Los Angeles: Marcel Rodd Company, 1945.

———. *Moksha*. Edited by Michael Horowitz and Cynthia Palmer. Rochester, Vermont: Park Street Press, 1999.

James, William. *Varieties of Religious Experience*. New York: The Modern Library, 1936.

Jesse, Robert. Telephone interview with author. February 26, 2010.

Kitchen, Denis. Telephone interview with author. January 20, 2010.

Kerouac, Jack. *On the Road.* New York: Penguin, 1985.

Key of Solomon the King: Clavicula Solominis. Edited by Samuel Liddell MacGregor Mathers. Boston: Weiser Books, 2000.

Kozinn, Allan. "Meditation on the Man Who Saved The Beatles." *New York Times,* February 7, 2008. http://www.nytimes.com/2008/02/07/arts/07iht-07yogi.9826732.html (accessed March 9, 2010).

Kripal, Jeffrey. *John Esalen: American and the Religion of No Religion.* Chicago: University of Chicago Press, 2007.

Lattin, Don. *The Harvard Psychedelic Club: How Timothy Leary, Ram Dass, Huston Smith, and Andrew Weil Killed the Fifties and Ushered in a New Age for America.* 1st ed. New York: HarperOne, 2010.

Leary, Timothy. *Flashbacks: An Autobiography.* 1st ed. Los Angeles and Boston: J.P. Tarcher; distributed by Houghton Mifflin, 1983.

———. *The Politics of Ecstasy.* Berkeley: Ronin Publishing, 1998.

Leary, Timothy. *High Priest.* Berkeley: Ronin Publishing, 1995.

Leary, Timothy, Ralph Metzner, and Richard Alpert. *The Psychedelic Experience.* New York: Citadel Press, 1992.

Markoff, John. *What the Dormouse Said: How the 60s Counterculture Shaped the Personal Computer Industry.* New York: Viking Penguin, 2005.

Martin, Douglas. "Humphry Osmond, 86, Who Sought Medicinal Value in Psychedelic Drugs, Dies." *New York Times,* February 22, 2004. http://www.nytimes.com/2004/02/22/us/humphry-osmond-86-who-sought-medicinal-value-in-psychedelic-drugs-dies.html (accessed December 11, 2009).

Mead, G.R.S. *Thrice Greatest Hermes: Studies in Hellenistic Theosophy and Gnosis,* Volume 2. London: Theosophical Publishing Society, 1906. *Gnosis.* http://www.gnosis.org/library/hermet.htm (accessed 12 January 2010).

McKenna, Dennis. Telephone interview with author. November 24, 2009.

McMullen, Phil. Email interview with author. December 8, 2009.

"Mme. Blavatsky Dead," *New York Times,* May 8, 1891. Murphy, Michael. Telephone interview with author. December 8, 2009.

Mystic Arts Book Society advertisement. *New York Times*, July 16, 1967.

"The Occult Revival: A Substitute Faith." *Time*, June 19, 1972. http://www.time.com/time/magazine/article/0,9171,877779,00. html (accessed October 30, 2009).

Owen, Alexander. *The Place of Enchantment*. Chicago: University of Chicago Press, 2004.

Pass It On. New York City: Alcoholics Anonymous World Services, 1984.

Paz, Octavio. *Alternating Current*. Translated by Helen R. Lane. New York: Viking, 1973.

Perry, Charles. "From Eternity to Here." In *20 Years of Rolling Stone*. New York: Friendly Press, 1987.

Pinchbeck, Daniel. *Breaking Open the Head*. New York: Broadway Books, 2003.

"Playboy Interview: Timothy Leary." *Playboy*, September 1966. http://www.archive.org/details/playboylearyinte00playrich (accessed January 3, 2011).

Pliny the Elder. *The Natural History*. Edited by John Bostock and H. T. Riley. London: Taylor and Francis, 1855. *Perseus Digital Library*. http://perseus.mpiwg-berlin.mpg.de/cgi-bin/ptext?doc =Perseus%3Atext%3A1999.02.0137 (accessed May 6, 2010).

Prabhavananda, Swami. "Vital Questions on Religion Answered." *Vedanta Press and Catalog*. http://www.vedanta.com/store/vital_ questions_prabhavananda.php (accessed October 25, 2009).

Quinney, Laura. Email interview with author. December 2, 2009.

Ram Dass. *Remember, Be Here Now*. Albuquerque: Modern Press, 1978.

Roper, Arik. Telephone interview with author. December 19, 2009.

Roueché, Berton. "Shimmering Hours." *New York Times*, February 7, 1954.

Scholem, Gershom Gerhard. *Major Trends in Jewish Mysticism*. 3d ed. New York: Schocken Books, 1954.

Sharf, Robert. Telephone interview with author. November 10, 2008.

Sheff, David. *All We Are Saying: The Last Major Interview with John Lennon and Yoko Ono*. New York: St. Martin's Press, 2000.

Smith, Huston. *Cleansing the Doors of Perception*. New York: Jeremy P. Tarcher, 2000.

Stewart, Amy. *Wicked Plants: The Weed That Killed Lincoln's Mother and Other Botanical Atrocities*. Chapel Hill, NC: Algonquin Books of Chapel Hill, 2009.

Shunryu, Suzuki. *Zen Mind, Beginner's Mind*. New York: Weatherhill, 1998.

Tart, Charles. Telephone interview with author. November 11, 2009.

Thompson, Hunter S. "The 'Hashbury' Is the Capital of the Hippies." *New York Times*, May 14, 1967. "Trips Festival Flier." *Prankster History Project*. http://www.pranksterweb.org/tripsflier.htm (accessed January 25, 2010).

Tulin, Mark. Telephone interview with author. February 17, 2010.

Underhill, Evelyn. *The Column of Dust*. London: Methuen & Co., 1909.

———. *Mysticism*. New York: Image Books, 1990.

Vaughan, Frances. "Transpersonal Counseling: Some Observations Regarding Entheogens." In *Psychoactive Sacramentals: Essays on Entheogens and Religion*. Edited by Thomas B. Roberts. San Francisco: Council on Spiritual Practices, 2001.

Vonnegut, Kurt. *Breakfast of Champions, or Goodbye Blue Monday!*. New York: Dell Publishing, 1973.

Vrajaprana, Pravrajika. Email interview with author. January 25, 2010.

Wasson, Gordon R. "The Hallucinogenic Fungi of Mexico: An Inquiry Into the Origins of the Religious Idea Among Primitive Peoples." In *The Psychedelic Reader*. Edited by Gunther M. Weil, Ralph Metzner, and Timothy Leary. Secaucus, NJ: Citadel Press, 1973.

Watts, Alan. *This Is It*. New York: Vintage Books, 1973.

Wavy Gravy. Telephone interview with author. March 1, 2010.

Weeks, Gregory. Email interview with author. April 27, 2006.

Wishnia, Steven. "What Happens When You Put 300 Experts on Psychedelics in the Same Room?" *AlterNet*, September 25, 2008. http://www.alternet.org/drugs/100381/what_happens_when_you_put_300_experts_on_psychedelics_in_the_same_room_/ (accessed May 20, 2010).

Wolfe, Tom. *The Electric Kool-Aid Acid Test*. New York: Bantam Books, 1997.

———. "The 'Me' Decade and the Third Great Awakening." *New York* magazine, August 23, 1976. http://nymag.com/news/features/45938/ (accessed March 15, 2010).

Woodring, Jim. Email interview with author. November 15, 2009.

"Worship: Instant Mysticism." *Time*, October 25, 1963. http://www.time.com/time/magazine/article/0,9171,830527,00.html (accessed November 1, 2009).

Yates, Francis A. *Giordano Bruno and the Hermetic Tradition*. Chicago: University of Chicago Press, 1991.

Zaehner, R. C. *Mysticism, Sacred and Profane: An Inquiry into Some Varieties of Praeter-natural Experience*. Oxford: Clarendon Press, 1957.

———. *Zen, Drugs, and Mysticism*. New York: Pantheon, 1972.

acknowledgments

Numerous people made this book possible, but it was the instincts and advice of my agent, Matthew Elblonk, that brought it all together. Denise Oswald saw something in the idea, and her smart and tough edits shaped it into a book. Her continued support has been a guiding light. Laura Mazer at Counterpoint quickly became a friend and has made this one of the finest experiences an author could have. And all the rest of the folks at Soft Skull and Counterpoint put so much time into getting all the details just right. Thanks to Rob Spillman at *Tin House* for a dream come true. Very special thanks also to Peter Coyote.

I also want to thank the inspiring folks who bravely tread the realms of the unconscious, the artistic, and the fantastic and kindly shared their time and ideas—in particular, Dr. Roland Griffiths, Robert Jesse, Rick Doblin, Denis Kitchen, Arik Roper, Wavy Gravy, Dennis McKenna, Jim Fadiman, Glenn Donaldson, and Jim Woodring. Much of this book is also dedicated to the memory of Mark Tulin.

My family and wonderful friends have been a stable foundation on which to undertake this project. Ezra and Melissa Glenn Haber; Richard and Tobe Stomberg; Jason Patch and Marianne Lefas-Tetenes; Joe Gallo; Ruth and Stefan Economou;

Seth Riskin and Donna Marcantonio; Nancy and Tony Tauber; Moungi Bawendi; Amy Ross; Emily Neill; Sarah Neill; Carrie Armsby; Bob Neill; Jim Neill, Judy Ashworth; my father, Byron; my sisters, Karen and Lisa; and most especially Scott Korb, who continues to be the best writing partner I could have.

All my love and gratitude to my wife, Amy, and my son, Sam, whose humor and warmth kept it all fueled.